Fast & Fabulous Parties

MICHELE BRADEN

Explore & Enjoy!

Michele Braden

PENMARIN BOOKS

Dedication

*In memory of my Uncle Willie, who
partied until his passing at the age of 93.
With love and thanks to my husband, Alan,
and daughter, Nicole, along with my entire family,
who inspired, taught, and, most importantly, believed in me.
In particular, my grandmother, who passed her gift on to me.*

Editorial Offices:	*Sales and Customer Service Offices:*
Penmarin Books	National Book Network
P.O. Box 286	4720 A Boston Way
58 Oak Grove Avenue	Lanham, MD 20706
Woodacre, CA 94973	(800) 462-6420

Penmarin Books are available at special discounts for bulk purchases for premiums, sales promotions, or education. For details, contact the Publisher. On your letterhead, include information concerning the intended use of the books and how many you wish to purchase.

ISBN 1-883955-01-7

Layout and typography by Rick Gordon and Myrna Vladic.
Black-and-white photographs of the seasons by Wolfgang Kaehler.
Cover photograph and interior color photographs by Patrick Tregenza.
Some photo props supplied by Bill and Ginny Cooperrider and by Pier 1 Imports.

Printed in the United States of America

94 95 96 97 98 QP 9 8 7 6 5 4 3 2 1

Contents

Fall 160

Winter 232

Introduction

*I*t is amazing how one word can have such a diverse effect on people. The word is "party." People either experience panic or, on the other hand, great anticipation of fun. After all, parties present us with the ultimate opportunity for adult play, business and social intercourse, and a vehicle to create fantasy. Parties are plain and simple celebrations, affirmations of life. I can't think of any time in history when the necessity for parties has been greater. Parties are just as essential when life is good as when life is difficult. My most dramatic example of the latter is when I was recovering at home from major back surgery. We had many parties while I was laid up in a hospital bed in my family room, and they really raised my spirits. The challenge lies in how to create celebrations for ourselves when our lives are already hectic, without causing more stress or anxiety. This is precisely what Fast & Fabulous is about.

Fast & Fabulous Parties covers the full gamut of parties from brunches to cocktail parties. Brunches and lunches mark an extreme departure from our everyday schedules, which make them particularly enjoyable. You will find that everyone feels as if they have been given a license to lounge—or loaf—for the day and simply concentrate on pleasure.

Since brunches and lunches are something out of the ordinary, the menu should reflect this. Eggs and bacon or a tuna on white do not fit the bill. Here's where many of us hit the wall and draw a culinary blank. We are not accustomed to thinking of these meals with a creative spirit. This book will show you the sky's the limit and help you to understand your creative ability.

Hors d'oeuvre parties (otherwise known as cocktail parties whether there is a cocktail in sight or not) offer all of us food freaks and flavor junkies (of which I am a member in good standing) the glorious opportunity to "graze," indulging in a wide variety of tastes. For the host, this type of party is just as glorious. They are easy to give, since the food can just be put out and does not require that the hostess jump up to serve courses.

As for dinner parties, they are viewed by many as the ultimate in home entertaining. Many people fear them, feeling that they require too much time and effort. Hopefully, *Fast & Fabulous Parties* will put an end to this myth.

Most of the dinners are casual by nature, inviting us to break rules and create our own guidelines. This means formal is out, but elegance can and does live on. Gone are the days when casual was simply used as an excuse not to bother. What an insult it is to be invited to someone's home when it is obvious that the host did not make a serious effort to create a treat for their guests. It clearly shows that they didn't care.

With a casual party, the focus of the event is transferred from pretense to pleasure. Casual should not be confused with something lackluster, uninspired, unimportant, frumpy, or unsophisticated. Casual is first and foremost friendly, allowing the guests to act and dress how they choose. The host creates an atmosphere that encourages guests to enjoy themselves and have fun. Comfort becomes the operative word and helps to remove inhibitions and allows the fun to flow. Casual is all about good food and friends in a relaxed, nurturing environment. What could be better?

Casual parties are also easier on the host. The menu, while every bit as delicious as formal menus, is usually simplified, and the menu planner has free reign. If caviar pasta is what you want, feel free to serve it as the entrée with a salad, rather than as the appetizer course. You do not need to serve all the obligatory courses. Be bold and free-spirited. Break rules, create a menu according to your own mood and style, and enjoy!

The food in this book is daring, exuberant, and brazen. It has absolutely no intention of being refined but rather strives to capture the gusto of peasant food. It's hearty, not delicate! Most of us are fed up with the school of nouvelle cuisine where the plate is designed primarily for visual appeal. In this book, you find attractive food that is also satisfying.

Fast & Fabulous Parties is for people who love to cook, entertain, dine, and just plain party! *Fast & Fabulous Parties* is concerned with excellence and style in both food and ambiance. Cooking and entertaining are valuable forms of personal expression, a living, three-dimensional art form, and an essential ingredient for a full lifestyle. It is designed to charge your batteries and get your creative juices flowing. The intent is for these recipes and menus to build your confidence and inspire you to create variations of your own. That, after all, is what cooking is all about. Never again will you be stumped for a creative menu, an imaginative tablescape, or a garnish. It is especially for busy people who must be time-efficient. You will see how you can have and do it all, with flair!

Many of you will be amazed to realize how easy this process becomes when you give yourself the necessary advance time. It is often surprising to discover that the entire process can be pleasurable. If, for instance, you decide to have a party in three weeks, each weekend several dishes can be partially prepared and frozen. By the time the party arrives, the menu has come together comfortably, allowing you the necessary time and energy to devote to all areas, including the ambiance and look of the table.

After all, when tackling any major project, you would not begin to think you should be able to finish it in one day. Why then do we feel that we should be able to awaken on Saturday morning, shop, cook, clean, and be prepared to entertain guests? What an overwhelming task! No wonder "party pressure panic" exists. By the time your guests arrive, you're ready to faint, not party! This results in a negative statement rather than a positive one in which you distinguish yourself. What a waste of time and money!

I'm convinced that the fear factor associated with entertaining stems from something as simple as not having the necessary organizational skills. Once you put those skills into practice, you'll find that staging a party no longer seems like the impossible dream. Automatically, your confidence level is raised, and no matter how busy you are, you see that there is still time for celebrating.

Fast & Fabulous Parties is organized by spring, summer, fall, and winter menus. Food, cooking, and entertaining styles should reflect the season. To fully understand this point, visualize a rich, hearty stew served on a hot summer night. Or worse yet, an icy cold slice of watermelon, eaten in the freezing rain, or a saucy pot roast at a picnic. It simply does not work.

Not to worry. If you fall in love with a menu from the "wrong" season, don't despair; adapt it. I call this process "seasonizing." The possibilities are endless. For example, if you wanted to "seasonize" Apple Walnut Egg Rolls with Caramel Sauce for a summer menu, substitute any seasonal fruit for the apples. Apricots, peaches, nectarines, or plums would make excellent choices.

All of the menus are designed for parties of eight. I have found this number to be a good middle ground. It is not too large a group for the average home to accommodate but is small enough to maintain intimacy. When you need to entertain a larger group, simply adjust the recipes as needed. Of course, for smaller parties the recipes can be reduced.

It is important to consider your home and its role in a successful party. First of all, your menu has to take into consideration any limitations that your kitchen may pose. For instance, if you have one oven, your menu should not be made up of all oven-cooked dishes.

Comfort is also a prime consideration for having fun. Seating and lighting are essential to comfort. If you have ever been packed around a table with the elbows of those on either side jabbing you, you know what I am talking about. Good seating also facilitates the free-flow of conversation.

Lighting is every bit as important. Bad lighting, whether it is too dim or bright, destroys the ambiance you have worked so hard to create. You can transform a cold, stark space into a warm, dramatic, or romantic room. Candles are an inexpensive but effective way to create lighting magic. It is amazing to see how personalities change and how social interaction is sparked by good lighting.

Flowers and arrangements of fresh greens are invaluable props for creating ambiance. They symbolize the celebration of nature and provide a festive aura. If budget is a concern, relax; flowers need not be costly. Most of us have greens or flowers in the garden or on the patio that we can pick. In the fall and winter it's fun to take walks in the country and collect interesting dried plants, weeds, and greenery for arrangements. As for flowers, if your garden is not in bloom, or if you do not have one, ask a friend. Sharing flowers is something most gardeners take delight in. Purchasing exotic flowers and using them individually to create stark and dramatic arrangements is another approach. One of my favorite ways to create a centerpiece is to fill a basket or container with pots of flowers from the nursery. I intersperse them with herb cuttings or greenery. This is an effective and economical approach. After the party you can plant the potted flowers.

Be sure to include the entrance to your home when decorating for a party. This instantly welcomes your guests and establishes a festive mood. When decorating, I also pay attention to my kitchen and bathrooms. Bowls of fruit, pitchers of flowers, and jars of pasta are just a few ways to dress up the kitchen. Bathrooms can be adorned with bouquets and even a scented candle.

Keep in mind that the rooms in which you stage a party play an important role in establishing the desired mood. For example, the family room has a relaxed warmth, whereas a living room projects more formality and elegance. If you need to use a certain room, but don't want the party to take on the feeling of that particular room, work with your props to create the mood you want. Dress up family rooms with candles and flowers, and try using tinted bulbs in the lights. Living rooms can be given a more casual feel by using pillows on the floor and arranging the furniture in a more intimate manner. Formal pieces can also be removed. Don't forget your yard—outdoor parties offer the opportunity to turn an open space into a wonderful party setting, and the outdoors is the ideal place to throw a lunch or brunch.

Now that you know what *Fast & Fabulous Parties* is, I want you to know what it is not. First of all, it is not "fast & tacky." It does not rely on gimmicks or on packaged or prepared convenience items. It stresses high-quality, fresh ingredients. Although the Faster & Flashier menu variations are intended to show how each menu can be further streamlined when time is a problem and call for the use of some prepared items, I naturally assume that when shopping for these items you will be discriminating enough to select only the highest quality products. For example, when buying butter cookies, look for ones that are prepared with real butter without colorings, preservatives, or artificial flavorings. This standard should be applied to any prepared item.

Fast & Fabulous Parties does not for a minute mean to insinuate that you will be able to throw a fabulous party without investing any effort. The old adage that anything worthwhile requires work is true. At the same time, the complete party process should be a pleasure, from planning, to preparing, to the actual party. What this book is about is how to approach a party intelligently and with confidence, without wasting time or leaving tasks for the last minute, thereby sabotaging your efforts, forcing you to become a "kitchen recluse."

You will notice that I rely heavily on the food processor and utilize it whenever possible. It is one of the best ways to reduce the time you spend preparing food. I also view freezers as a real necessity. They cut chilling time in half, and there is no greater convenience than to be able to pull out a scrumptious hors d'oeuvre, soup, sauce, entrée, or dessert from the freezer, warm it up, and serve it.

Fast & Fabulous refers to my method of fearless cooking and entertaining. Viewed as a blueprint, it liberates Culinary Clones and Kitchen Martyrs. Culinary Clones follow recipes as if they were heaven-sent. They forget to use their own judgment or to follow the all-important rule that there are no absolutes in cooking. After all, we are dealing with an art form involving organic ingredients that are impossible to standardize. Have you ever seen two identical cloves of garlic or smelled onions of the exact same strength? Kitchen Martyrs may also be Culinary Clones. They are the people who leave their organizational skills outside of the kitchen. Consequently, they end up being servants rather than star performers at their parties. Both the clones and martyrs are ungracious entertainers.

Fast & Fabulous cooks involve every one of their senses. The look, smell, texture, sound, and taste of food are all essential in the cooking process. Often

I'm confronted with resistance when I suggest that it is absolutely necessary for the cook to taste as they prepare recipes. This does not mean consuming huge amounts of food and ruining appetites and waistlines. I am talking about developing and sensitizing your palate. Only a tiny taste—¼ to ½ teaspoon—is required.

My Fast & Fabulous methodology is based on two simple principles: organization and advanced preparation. Intelligent and successful people rely on these two basic principles in every area of their lives, but for some unknown reason they discard them when it comes to cooking and entertaining. Why would you take time away from your guests to slice bread, unwrap a stick of butter, or make a sauce? Most of these tasks can be taken care of in advance.

Let's look at a simple detail such as preparing bread. Slice it earlier in the day or even the day before, wrap it in foil to keep it fresh, and put it in the freezer. Then warm it before serving. If this is done while guests are there, not only have you taken time away from your primary role, but you've also created a needless mess in your kitchen.

Setting the table and selecting serving pieces and wine glasses are vital to a fabulous party and should be given great consideration. Take care of these items when there isn't much cooking to be done. For example, if there is time two days in advance, do it then, leaving only the flowers for the day of the party. This is where you must think of every possible detail. Anticipate what serving pieces and plates you will need, and set them out. We have all been in the position of frantically scrounging for dessert plates or a serving spoon, trying to remain outwardly calm in front of guests while the food is getting cold.

Fast & Fabulous Parties is carefully designed to reinforce this methodology. The party plan, a Fast & Fabulous timetable, gives a breakdown of all the major menu tasks and when they can be done, without sacrificing quality. In addition, every recipe is followed by invaluable tips that may include:

FAST: How far in advance the dish can be prepared and refrigerated or frozen without sacrificing taste or quality.

FLASHY: What to serve with a particular dish and ideas for garnishing and presentation.

FABULOUS: Alternatives and variations that will stimulate your own creations, as well as how else to use a dish.

FURTHER: Innovative ways for handling leftovers.

Now it is time to create a battle plan. *Fast & Fabulous Parties* to the rescue. Too many of us just do not know how early things can be done. Most recipes leave you guessing by saying that the dish can be prepared in advance. How far in advance is critical. Following the introduction to each menu, you will find the timetable for preparation, which breaks the menu down into manageable steps. It provides you with a bird's-eye view of the party.

The timetable is set up so you leave very little to do on the day of the party. It is amazing how much time last-minute details take, and it is best to avoid that trap. On the day of the party, schedule time for rest and relaxation. A tired and haggard Kitchen Martyr cannot be a vivacious host or hostess. The Fast & Fabulous entertainer makes everything appear easy and ensures that everyone has fun!

Table Talk

Dressing a table offers the host a multitude of options for creating the desired mood for a party. Most of us can remember when a table was considered party-perfect when covered with a white cloth and with a symmetrical arrangement of two candlesticks flanking a small pincushion flower arrangement. Thank goodness today's standards are radically different. We are encouraged to stretch artistically, to use our imaginations, and to have fun. Approach the tablescape as a three-dimensional still-life. Think past the usual. Fresh and dried flowers and herbs, fresh raw produce, dried beans, nuts in their shells, potted plants, candles, interesting objects, and even rocks or bricks can become part of an exciting look. Centerpieces instantly bring to mind floral images, but they need not involve flowers. A composition of fresh fruits and/or vegetables arranged directly on the table in a basket or a bowl is a great change of pace.

Rather than a standard tablecloth, use solid or patterned bedsheets or cotton bedspreads from import stores. Interesting cotton throw rugs, quilts, scarves, swatches of fabric, and/or shawls also work well. If paper makes more sense for your table covering, be sure to stay away from the run-of-the-mill tacky variety. Instead, buy a roll of white butcher paper from a restaurant supply or discount warehouse grocery store. Brown mailing paper from an office supply store is another possibility. Use this paper as is, or go off on a visual tangent and decorate it with magic markers, paint, and/or stickers.

Working with multiples of a decoration creates a bold and dramatic look. Try using several pots, vases, or baskets on the table. Either place them down the center of the table or scatter them. Candles in proper candlesticks are fine, but remember that you have options. Using three or more is much more visually exciting. They need not be in matching holders or all be the same size. It's fun to work with a variety. Try a combination of candles in different colors, sizes, and shapes, or even try using brass and silver candlesticks together. Be brave and dare to mix and match to create your own look. Candle pillars or votives are fabulous placed on a platter in flat baskets, in terra-cotta or china saucers, in terra-cotta flowerpots, in old skillets, on planks of wood, or on glass or masonry bricks.

Garnishing

Garnishing is a real passion of mine. It is almost as important as the flavor of the food. Neither one can stand alone. We are a fast-paced, visually oriented society. This makes first impressions extremely important. An ungarnished dish sends out the same message an unset table does. It says to your guests that they are not important enough to warrant any extra effort on your part to make them happy or comfortable.

Here is where you call upon your artistic talents as well as your sense of the whimsical. Relax, we all have this talent; some of us have simply suppressed it. I'm sure you have noticed that there are several schools of thought when it comes to garnishing. Some people prefer an austere, minimal presentation. This school abides by strict laws limiting the garnishes to the ingredients used in the dish. That is to say, if parsley does not appear in the recipe, there is no possible way it should be used in the garnishing. The other school of thought, to which I belong, embraces abundance and generosity. I want everything to appear lush and lavish. Visual appeal and excitement are what I focus on, rather than strict rules.

For me, garnishing is an abstract art form. I do not strive to make cream puffs into swans, cucumbers into snakes, apples into birds, watermelons into whales, or chocolate into ballerinas. There is nothing more uninspired than the obligatory lone piece of parsley or, worse yet, a white doily. Instead, I gravitate toward nontoxic flowers and leaves, fresh herbs, and fruits and vegetables, all appreciated for and used to project their own beauty and appeal. It's just not my style to want to make foodstuffs into lifelike zoo forms.

The following list includes some of my favorite garnishes. It is not possible to mention every one of them, but hopefully this will start your creative juices flowing.

Parsley   The most commonly used and widely available garnish. It has gotten something of a tarnished reputation simply because it is often used without any imagination or thought. It can be used sparingly or with wild abandon, either in clumps or minced. It works with almost everything except brownies!

Baby greens, alfalfa sprouts, or other varieties of sprouts   These can be used as a bed to place hors d'oeuvres on, or in clumps to create borders as you would parsley.

Green onions   Use these minced and scattered on the platter, or make them into green onion flowers by cutting off the root and making many thin cuts through about ¾ the length of the white part. To get these to fan out, place them in a bowl of iced water for about 20 minutes. This can be done up to two days in advance and refrigerated. The green part of the onion can also be handled in the same manner by making very thin cuts lengthwise down the green portion.

Leek flowers   Cut the root end off the leek and make very thin cuts, just as done with the green onion flowers.

Fresh herbs   Herbs look nice minced, or use the leaves scattered, or use cuttings. Herb blossoms are also wonderful for garnishing. Some of my favorites are basil, oregano, chives, mint, thyme, sage, rosemary, cilantro, dill, and watercress.

Whole raw vegetables and fruits

Red, green, purple, and/or
  yellow bell peppers
Brussels sprouts
Chiles (all varieties)
Heads of lettuce
Heads of garlic
Eggplants (all varieties)
Zucchini
Winter squash
Baby bok choy
Tomatoes (all varieties)
Grapes
Apples

Oranges and tangerines
Persimmons
Pomegranates
Peaches
Plums
Kumquats
Apricots
Kiwi
Pears
Nectarines
Berries
Cherries

Tomato roses   Use a sharp carving knife and cut a wide, thin strip of skin, starting at the bottom of the tomato and continuing in a circular fashion to the top. Cut using a back-and-forth sawing motion. To form the rose, start with the end where you finished cutting and wrap the peel around itself. For greater impact, use several tomato roses grouped together. Place the rose in a plastic bag and refrigerate until you are ready to use it. This can be done up to two days in advance.

Carrots, parsnips, and cucumber curls   Peel the vegetable thoroughly. Then, placing the vegetable down flat on your work surface, press down firmly with the peeler. Wrap the strips around your finger to form a circular shape. Secure them with a toothpick, and place them in a bowl of ice water to firm the curls up for at least 30 minutes. Remove the toothpicks and place the vegetables carefully or scatter them to garnish platters. Curls can be prepared up to two days in advance if left in the bowl of water to prevent them from drying out.

Twisted slices   This can be done with turnips, cucumbers, zucchini, yellow squash, oranges, lemons, and limes. Trim the fruit or vegetable at both ends to prevent it from rolling, then slice it into very thin slices by hand, using an electric slicer or food processor. Stack several slices on your work surface and cut halfway across the fruit or vegetable. Twist and use as desired. This can be done up to two days in advance if the slices are refrigerated in a bowl of water to prevent them from drying out.

Some nontoxic flowers for garnishing

Baby's breath *(Gypsophila paniculata)*
Bougainvillea
Cornflower *(Centaurea Cyanus)*
Chrysanthemums
Hibiscus *(Hibiscus moscheutas)*
Johnny jump-ups *(Viola tricolor)*

Lilac *(Syringa vulgaris)*
Marigold *(Tagetes)*
Nasturtium
Pansy *(Viola cornuta)*
Poppy *(Papaver rhoeas)*
Rose *(Rosa hybrids)*

Some nontoxic leaves for garnishing

Japanese aralia *(Futsia japonica)*
Grape leaves
Loquat leaves

Fruit tree leaves
Herb leaves

The Chef's Palate and Prejudices

Before you proceed to the kitchen to prepare my recipes, it is important for you to understand some of my flavor prejudices. This is just as important as knowing the personal bias of a movie critic or a restaurant reviewer.

Okay, let's begin with the hors d'oeuvres. Their role is awesome! This is when you make first impressions on your guests. Hors d'oeuvres are also great party starters. Most of us are all too aware of those first few awkward minutes when the party momentum needs to be jump-started. Interesting and impressive hors d'oeuvres are called for. Those adorable little cubes of cheese speared with colored, frilled toothpicks do not exactly fit the bill. Delicate miniature pastry tartlets, pâtés, magnificently marinated seafood, warm cheese concoctions, and exotically flavored dipping sauces with crisp, garlicky melbas or pita chips (not generic chips) do rise to the occasion. I always lean toward offering my guests choices, as I have found this to be an instant ice breaker. This means that instead of preparing one hors d'oeuvre, often I will do three. Remember, the perfect hors d'oeuvre teases the palate but never satisfies, always arousing the appetite. I am definitely of the opinion that this can be a party maker or breaker. Be flamboyant; set the tone for the party with these "palate pleasers and teasers."

As for the rest of the meal, all of the dishes should make strong and exciting statements. Unusual, luxurious, and enticing flavor is the goal. As for the pacing, it should be leisurely, allowing everyone the opportunity to truly enjoy the food and the company. Speaking of food, I only have one rule. Any discussion of calories, fat, or diets is forbidden. End of subject . . . case closed. There is an appropriate time and place for everything. Guilt has no place at a party. However, if a low-fat diet is essential, I have included low-fat options.

Another prejudice of mine is against hosts and hostesses who are unable to be at the table. You know the type. They are locked away in the kitchen madly trying to keep up with the dishes. The remedy is simple—hire help. This is a necessity and need not be out of reach for anyone's budget. If yours happens to be limited, use your kids and their friends, and/or neighborhood teenagers. However, you must let anyone who you employ know what is expected. I have been to many parties where the hostess has plenty of professional help but still is busy doing God only knows what! Don't fall into this trap; it simply projects insecurities.

I also like desserts that are not very sweet. If you enjoy yours sweeter, simply adjust the sugar.

You will rapidly notice that I gravitate toward big flavors. I would be the first to categorize myself as a flavor junkie. Please adjust the seasoning to your own palate.

Texture is vital to good food. I balance the textures in each dish I prepare, as well as in the entire menu. The perfect example of poor textural composition is the standard Thanksgiving dinner. Almost everything is mashed or puréed. How boring!

Now, in regard to portion size, my culinary style values abundance. That does not mean that I am waging a one-woman war on anorexia. I want my food to look gracious and generous. I do not want it to appear as if each lettuce leaf has been counted. It is a terrible feeling to be at a party and be afraid to take a decent serving. "It is always better to have too much than not enough," most of us have heard from our mothers and grandmothers. What wisdom!

The Cook's Shelf

Just as a painter needs a full palette, the home cook and entertainer needs a well-stocked pantry. These are the items that will help create gastronomical ecstasy for your family and friends, whether preparing for a fabulous party or a mid-week dinner.

Don't panic over cost; it's not necessary to purchase everything at once. Collect these items gradually and be a smart shopper. Don't go to the priciest food boutique. Hunt around at discount and import stores and take advantage of sales.

Assorted Dried Herbs and Spices

Apple pie spice (ground)
Bay leaves
Basil
Cardamom
Caraway seeds
Celery seeds
Chili powder
Chiles (whole, red)
Cinnamon
Cumin (ground and seeds)
Curry powder
Dillweed
Fennel seeds
Fines herbes
Hungarian sweet paprika
Italian herbs
Mace
Marjoram
Mint leaves
Mustard (prepared and seeds)
Nutmeg (whole or ground)
Oregano

Assorted Dried Herbs and Spices (continued)

Poultry seasoning
Peppercorns (Szechuan, white,
    pink, green, and black)
Pumpkin pie spice (ground)

Rosemary
Tarragon
Thyme (leaves and ground)

Assorted Nuts and Seeds
(Toasted and stored in the freezer to prevent them from becoming rancid)

Almonds
Pecans
Pine nuts
Pistachios
Poppy seeds

Pumpkin seeds
Sesame seeds
Sunflower seeds
Walnuts

Assorted Oils

Avocado oil
Canola oil
Grapeseed oil
Olive oil (extra virgin and pure)

Peanut oil
Sesame oil
Walnut oil

Assorted Olives

Black olives
Greek (calamata) or Italian olives
Spanish olives

Assorted Marinated or Pickled Items

Capers
Greek pepperoncini
Marinated or water-packed
    artichoke hearts

Pickled ginger
Pickled mango

Assorted Rices, Grains, and Beans

Arborio rice
Basmati rice
Black beans (dried)
Bulgar
Couscous
Garbanzo beans (canned or
    dried)

Great northern beans (dried)
Long-grain white rice
Pastas (assorted, dried)
Polenta (regular and/or instant)
Short-grain white rice
Wild rice

Assorted Sauces

Barbecue, Chinese-style
(canned or in jars)
Hoisin sauce, Chinese-style
(canned or in jars)
Mango chutney
Mayonnaise

Plum sauce, Chinese-style
(canned or in jars)
Soy sauce
Tonqatsu sauce (Japanese-style
Worcestershire sauce)
Worcestershire sauce

Assorted Staples

Baking powder
Baking soda
Brown sugar
Cake flour
Cornmeal
Cornstarch

Flour
Granulated sugar
Instant polenta
Powdered sugar
Unflavored gelatin

Assorted Vinegars

Balsamic*
Cider
Rice
Raspberry

Sherry wine
Tarragon wine
White and red wine

Wines for Cooking

Dry vermouth
Madeira
Merlot and dry red wine

Port
Sherry (dry and regular)

Cheeses
(Stored in freezer)

Bleu
Feta
Mizithera*

Parmesan (Parmigiano-
Reggiano)*
Pecorino Romano*

Miscellaneous

Anchovies (tinned and paste)
Black fungus (dried)
Garlic (fresh)
Green chiles (whole, canned)

Mustard (Dijon)
Mustard (coarse ground)
Onions (fresh)
Pancetta (stored in freezer)*

*Refer to Terms & Techniques.

Miscellaneous (continued)

Pasilla chiles (dried)*	Shiitake mushrooms (dried)*
Porcini mushrooms (dried)*	Sun-dried tomatoes
Potatoes (fresh)	Tomatoes (canned or boxed)
Prosciutto (stored in freezer)*	Tuna (canned)

The Cook's Herb Garden

Fresh herbs add a lovely dimension to cooking and food presentation. Herbs provide an excellent way to keep in touch with the seasons and to celebrate them. I can't imagine not having an herb garden. Trust me, you don't need a green thumb. Herbs grow like weeds. If you're still not convinced you can do it alone, visit a library or bookstore. They're loaded with good books on growing and preserving herbs. As for the required space, it can be a sunny window, an apartment patio, or an entire garden. Once your herbs start to thrive, the fun begins. It's time for you to start experimenting.

You'll be thrilled by the limitless possibilities for matching herbs with different foods. In terms of garnishing, the results are just as exciting. Fresh herbs can be used in three different ways for garnishing: minced, sprigs, and blossoms.

You can also preserve your surpluses. The most common method is to dry them by hanging a bunch, tied with string, upside-down at room temperature. When placed in olive oil, wines, and vinegars, they infuse the liquid with their essence, and the liquid becomes a delicious way to season food. When bottled attractively, they make lovely gifts and are decorative displayed in the kitchen. Fresh herbs can also be frozen, either chopped or straight from the garden.

The following is a list of some of my favorites. By all means, feel free to go beyond these recommendations.

Anise   A dill-like plant with a licorice scent. The leaves are lovely for garnishing or flavoring. The seeds are more potent. Both the seeds and leaves are suitable for seasoning soups, sauces, baked goods (both savory and sweet), sausages, fish, poultry, meats, seafood, vegetables, pastas, and/or rice dishes. Anise grows in the full sun and is perennial, returning every summer. Use caution; it is a rapid self-sower.

*Refer to Terms & Techniques.

Basil   One of the most popular herbs. It is a compact, bushy plant with white blossoms. There are many varieties, ranging from purple basil to lemon basil. The leaves are used fresh or dried and impart a very pronounced flavor. It is an annual and thrives in full sun. Use it to enhance anything but sweets. Soups, sauces, salads, pastas, vegetables, meats, fish, poultry, and seafood all adore basil.

Bay laurel   Commonly referred to as bay leaves. An evergreen tree with small yellowish flowers. Dried leaves are used to flavor soups, sauces, rice dishes, pastas, and so on. Bay leaves are an excellent garnish because they hold up well under all sorts of difficult conditions. Cut branches are lovely in floral arrangements.

Calendula   Also called pot marigold. Has beautiful flowers with no flavor, but they provide color. This hardy annual has a flat, daisylike flower that closes at night and in cloudy conditions. It blooms from spring through fall and comes in yellow, gold, apricot, orange, and cream. Use the whole flower or petals to garnish anything from salads to ice cream.

Chervil   Has not become a superstar herb yet. Is part of the herb combo that we purchase dried called "Fine Herbs." It looks like parsley but is more delicate. It has an anise-like flavor and fragrance, but with a hint of pepper. Chervil is a hardy annual and a self-sower, meaning that the seeds replant themselves. It requires climates where the nights drop below 55°F. Chervil is delicious in soups, salads, vinaigrettes, compound butter, fresh veal, and seafood.

Chive   Chives have a cluster of narrow, green, hollow leaves, about 8 inches high, with pink to purplish flowers that resemble balls. The taste and smell is a combination of onions and leeks. Use the blossoms for garnishing and in bouquets. Minced leaves may be used fresh or dried to season and garnish anything from potatoes to eggs. Chives are a rapid-spreading perennial that will thrive in conditions ranging from full sun to light shade.

Fennel   An exquisite fernlike plant, the bulb is used raw or cooked, and is similar to celery, except that it has a slight anise flavor. Use it fresh as a seasoning or garnish.

Garlic   A member of the lily family, garlic has dark green foliage and pink flowers. When the leaves are dry, the garlic is ready to be harvested. Use leaves as you would use sorrel or spinach. Blossoms are lovely as a garnish, and the cloves can be used fresh or dried as a seasoning. We now also revere garlic for its healthful properties in combatting high blood pressure.

Lavender   A beautiful shrub used in landscaping. It has spikelike flowers that are long, narrow, and lavender colored. Lavender is used in floral arrangements and in fragrance and beauty products. Flowers can be used sparingly in soups, sorbets, jellies, ice cream, or with fowl.

Leeks   A member of the lily family with a mild, oniony flavor. Once they were known as "the poor man's asparagus," but they have since become expensive. The leaves grow about two feet tall and are flat and solid, not hollow, like an onion. Both the leaves and the bulb are used in cooked dishes. The leek has a very ornamental bloom in white or lavender.

Lemon verbena   Grows up to ten feet tall and is deciduous. The leaves have a lemony scent and are used in teas, fruit drinks, perfumes, soups, sauces, marinades, or with fish, seafood, meats, and poultry. It has the only leaves that retain a lemon flavor when dried. This plant loves the heat but is not tolerant of cold climates.

Lovage   This perennial looks like large, dense celery leaves and has an intense celery flavor. Both the stalks and leaves are used to season soups, sauces, and stews. The leaves can be used fresh or dried and in salads or as an all-purpose flavoring. It thrives in cold weather.

Marjoram   It is usually grown as an annual due to its fragility, even though it is a perennial. It thrives in the summer. The oval leaves are long, with a bit of a velvety texture. Use it fresh or dried in tomato dishes, and for vegetables, salads, meats, chicken, soups, and sauces.

Mint   A lush, low, spreading plant in orange, apple, lemon, spearmint, and black peppermint varieties. The leaves, fresh or dried, are used to flavor teas and both sweet and savory dishes, and to garnish. Watch out; this is a fearless spreader.

Nasturtiums   Often thought of as simply a flowering plant, this plant has a joyful look, with smooth round leaves and brilliant flowers ranging in color from yellow to orange to dark red. They grow like a weed and are self-sowing. Every part except the root may be used fresh for flavoring. The leaves, stems, and flowers may be tossed into salads. Chopped leaves and stems can be substituted for watercress. Their peppery flavor is also reminiscent of a radish. The flowers are beautiful for garnishing.

Oregano   A small shrub about two feet tall that has tiny oblong leaves and purple blossoms. The leaves can be used fresh or dried as an all-purpose seasoning. Fresh cuttings are nice in floral arrangements. There are countless varieties, ranging from decorative to pungently flavorful. The best way to purchase a full-flavored variety is by rubbing a leaf. The more fragrant the leaf, the more flavorful the herb.

Parsley   One of the most common herbs, it has a fresh, clean flavor. There are two varieties, one with curly leaves and one with flat leaves, often referred to as "Italian parsley." The latter has more flavor and vitamins. This herb is best grown as an annual, even though it is a biennial. It has a bitter flavor the second season. Parsley is an all-purpose savory flavoring.

Rosemary   A woody shrub with tiny spikey leaves and purple to pink flowers. It works well in landscaping and comes in varieties ranging from a creeping ground covering to tall shrubs. The leaves are used fresh or dried as an all-purpose savory seasoning. The cuttings are nice in floral arrangements and as a garnish. It has a sweet smell and a pleasantly bitter flavor.

Sage   An aromatic and hardy perennial with a woody stem and thick leaves that are soft and velvety. It usually blooms after the second year, in June, with blue to pink spikey flowers. Sage attains a height of about two feet, and the leaves change color with the season. Use the leaves, fresh or dried, to season poultry, veal, pasta, and cheese dishes. It is a must in poultry stuffings and for garnishing.

Scented Geranium   Native to South Africa, geraniums have more varieties of fragrant leaves than any other plants. They range in aroma from chocolate to lime. Geraniums are usually grown as annuals, even though they are perennials. They thrive in the heat and grow to four feet in height. The flowers range in color from white to purple but are secondary to the fragrant foliage. Rub the leaves to release the scent. Use the fresh leaves for garnishing or to flavor baked goods, desserts, fruits, jellies, syrups, sauces, drinks, or teas.

Shallot   A member of the lily family, it has a mild, oniony flavor. The bulb can be used fresh or dried, as with garlic. It has green foliage similar to chives or green onions. It rarely flowers, but it grows to a height of about eight inches.

Sorrel, French   A very hardy plant, its bittersweet leaves have a lemonlike flavor. Use the leaves fresh, either raw or cooked, in soups, salads, pasta, or vegetable dishes.

Tarragon   It is available in two varieties: French and Russian. Only the French variety is used in cooking. When purchasing, it is essential to taste a leaf to be certain of the variety. French tarragon has a licorice flavor. It is used to season soups, sauces, vinaigrettes, salads, fish, veal, poultry, and seafood dishes. Tarragon is a perennial that can handle heat, but it requires cold winters.

Thyme   A hearty perennial with a slender, woody stem, it is about eight inches tall. It makes a good ground cover or border in landscaping. The leaves range in color from green to grayish and bloom in early summer. The leaves are very small and can be used fresh or dried. They have a pleasant, earthy flavor. Use the cuttings and the lavender-blue flowers to garnish. Lemon thyme is a variety with a marvelous lemony flavor. All varieties can be used in egg, meat, vegetable, fish, poultry, rice, and pasta dishes, as well as in soups and sauces.

The Cook's Flowers

Flowers for Arrangements

Amaryllis *(Amaryllis belladonna)*
Season: Late summer through fall
Available in many colors, it has six to twelve blossoms at the head of a leafless stalk. The amaryllis arranges nicely with poppies and irises.

Anthurium *(Anthurium andreanum)*
Season: All year
It is a deep red, waxy, heart-shaped flower with a whitish tail coming from its center on a leafless stalk. It is an exotic flower that is long-lasting.

Aster *(Aster novi-belgii)*
Season: Summer and fall
Available in vibrant pink, purple, and lavender, their petals surround a bright yellow center. This is a long-lasting flower and arranges well with zinnias, lilies, and irises. A wire may be needed to hold the stem.

Baby's Breath *(Gypsophila paniculata)*
Season: Summer
It is a twiggy-looking plant that is covered with tiny white blossoms. It is an excellent filler plant and is good for drying. In addition, it is nontoxic and can come in direct contact with food.

Bird of Paradise *(Strelitzia reginae)*
Season: All year (best in cool season)
An exotic, long-lasting flower, it has a tall, straight stalk with a bloom that is purple and orange and resembles a bird's head.

Camellia *(Camellia japonica)*
Season: Fall to winter
Its nontoxic flowers and leaves can be used with food. The flowers are available in a wide range of colors, while its leaves are a dark, glossy green.

Carnation *(Dianthus caryophyllus hybride)*
Season: All year
They come in miniature and standard sizes in a range of colors. They are long-lasting, accessible, and inexpensive.

Celosia *(Celosia argentea)*
Season: Summer through fall
Available in red, yellow, and orange, this long-lasting flower is feathery and oval in shape.

Chrysanthemum *(Chrysanthemum morifolium)*
Season: All year
Like the carnation, chrysanthemums are available in many, many colors at inexpensive prices. Their sizes range from 1 inch across to the large pom-poms, which are 5 inches to 6 inches across.

Cornflower *(Centaures cyanus)*
Season: Spring through fall
Available in pink, white, and blue, with a thin, delicate stem, the cornflower has leaves that are gray-green in color. They are not a long-lasting flower, but, being nontoxic, you can use them in direct contact with food.

Cosmos *(Cosmos bipinnatus)*
Season: Summer through fall
Available in red, yellow, orange, white, and rose, cosmos has large petals surrounding a yellow center. It is not a long-lasting flower.

Cymbidium Orchids *(Cymbidium orchis)*
Season: Late winter to late spring
Available in a variety of colors, it will have many blossoms on a long stem.

Daffodil *(Narcissus poeticus)*
Season: Late winter through spring
These are fragrant flowers that come in yellow and white. The trumpet-shaped flower sits on a firm stem with long, upright, slender leaves.

Dahlia *(Dahlia hybriden)*
Season: Summer through fall
Dahlias are available in a variety of colors except for blue. They are long-lasting; they look lovely alone or mixed with gladiolus, asters, and chrysanthemums.

Feverfew *(Chrysanthemum parthenium)*
Season: All year
They come in white and are very fragrant.

Forsythia *(Forsythia X intermedia)*
Season: Late winter through spring
Forsythia is a cluster of little yellow flowers on a stem. It mixes well with spring-blooming flowers.

Freesia *(Freesia hybriden)*
Season: Spring
They have a beautiful scent and are available in many colors.

Gerbera Daisy *(Gerbera jamesonii hybriden)*
Season: All year
Available in a variety of colors except for blue, they are, as their name suggests, a daisy-like flower that lasts four to five days.

Gladiolus *(Gladiolus hybriden)*
Season: Spring through fall
Available in a variety of colors, they are a long-lasting flower. The flowers open up one at a time on a strong extending spike.

Hibiscus *(Hibiscus moscheutos)*
Season: Spring to summer
Hibiscus is a shrub with deep green leaves and large single or double tropical flowers in pink, red, and white. It is also nontoxic.

Iris *(Iris reticulata)*
Season: All year
Available in shades of white, lavender, and blue, their lifespan is short.

Johnny Jump-Up *(Viola tricolor)*
Season: Spring
These look like mini-pansies and come in blue or in a mix of colors, including lavender, yellow, mauve, apricot, and red. It re-sows itself profusely.

Lilac *(Syringa vulgaris)*
Season: All year
Available in blue, lavender, purple, and white, they are masses of tiny blossoms on a woody stem with heart-shaped leaves. They are nontoxic, so they can be in direct contact with food.

Lily *(Lilium)*
Season: All year (peaks in spring)
Available in every color except purple and blue, they have a royal look to them. Beware of the pollen; it can damage clothing.

Larkspur *(Delphinium)*
Season: Spring through summer
Available in white, dark blue, and lavender, larkspur is a stalk covered with flowers. It arranges well with lilies, daisies, and snapdragons for a country garden look.

Lily of the Nile *(Agapanthus africanus)*
Season: Mid-summer to early fall
Available in blue and white, this flower is dramatic and bold. There are no leaves on this long stalk, which is nice for a contemporary setting.

Marguerite Daisy *(Anthemis tinctoria)*
Season: All year
These flowers come in yellow and white. Before arranging, remove the foliage.

Marigold *(Tagetes)*
Season: Summer through fall
Available in pale yellow through gold, marigolds are hardy, nontoxic and trouble-free plants with dense, round flowers and tall or short stems. Many have strong scents; make sure to get the odorless varieties.

Pansy *(Viola cornuta)*
Season: Spring through summer
A five-petal flat flower with a dark center, pansies come in white, blue, yellow, pink, and purple and have a sweet scent.

Peruvian Lily *(Alstroemeria pelegrina)*
Season: May to mid-summer
Available in pink, yellow, red, apricot, rose, and rust, these lilies are a long-lasting flower.

Protea *(Protea)*
Season: All year
The flower sets on a woody stalk with petals that resemble a pinecone and are prickly at the ends like an artichoke. They come in many colors.

Rose *(Rosa hybriden)*
Season: All year
Available in a variety of colors, roses are fragrant, and they are beautiful alone or as mixers. It is a good idea to cut the stem under water for a longer lifespan. The nontoxic flowers can come in direct contact with food.

Statice *(Statice sinuata)*
Season: All year
Available in yellow, lavender, pink, white, and purple, they hold their color and are good for drying.

Stock *(Matthiola incana)*
Season: Spring through summer
They are very fragrant flowers that are available in many colors. They are fairly long-lasting.

Tuberose *(Polianthes tuberosa)*
Season: Summer through fall
These have a very sweet odor. Their white, waxy flower looks like a cluster of stars.

Tulip *(Tulipa gesneriana)*
Season: Winter through spring
They come in a variety of colors. Purchase them in bud form for a longer-lasting flower. They will last five to eight days.

Windflower *(Anemone cornaria)*
Season: Early spring to early fall
Windflowers are available in vibrant colors of red, purple, pink, lavender, and white on a leafless stem. Enjoy these while you can, because they are not long-lived.

Zinnia *(Zinnia elegans)*
Season: Late summer to early fall
Various colors are available, and flowers will last up to a week. They combine nicely with chrysanthemums, irises, or statice for an informal country bouquet.

Green Foliage for Arrangements

Coast Redwood *(Sequoia sempervirens)*
Season: All year
The leaves are flat, green, and feather-like, and grow out from the stem.

Evergreen Huckleberry *(Vaccinium ovatum)*
Season: All year
Huckleberry offers dark, lush, green leaves with white or pinkish flowers. In March through May, its berries are black and edible.

Galax *(Galax urceolata)*
Season: All year
Its shiny heart-shaped leaf turns a beautiful bronze color in the fall.

Ivy *(Hedera sp.)*
Season: All year
Its thick, leathery, heart-shaped leaves grow on a woody vine.

Japanese Aralia *(Fatsia japonica)*
Season: All year
The leaves are dark green in color and fanlike in shape. They give the appearance of being tropical and are nontoxic.

Leather Leaf Fern *(Rumohra adiantiformis)*
Season: All year
The triangular leaf is glossy green. It lasts a long time in arrangements.

Lemon *(Gaultheria shallon)*
Season: All year
The leaves are long and a bright, glossy green.

Ruscus *(Ruscus aculeatus)*
Season: All year
The deep, dark, waxy green foliage has leaves that are small.

Silver Dollar *(Eucalyptus polyanthemos)*
Season: All year
Its leaves are green or gray with a round or oval shape. The leaves cover a woody, barklike stem.

Silver Tree *(Leucodendron argenteum)*
Season: All year
Silvery white, silky leaves densely cover the branches. It is a foliage plant.

Umbrella Pine *(Sciadopitys verticillata)*
Season: All year
Glossy, dark green needles grow along branch ends and radiate out like the spokes of a bicycle wheel.

Decorating with Flowering Potted Plants

Azalea *(Rhododendrum)*
Season: Winter through spring
Azalea has a small, dark green leaf and is covered with delicate red, pink, orange, or salmon blossoms. It can also be cut and used in arrangements.

Chrysanthemum *(Chrysanthemum morifolium)*
Season: All year
It is a sturdy, upright plant with large blooms in many colors. Potted, it will last three to four weeks indoors. Keep the soil moist. It can also be cut and used in arrangements.

Coleus *(Coleus hybridus)*
Season: Winter
The foliage is multicolored and has a tropical look.

Cyclamen *(Cyclamen persicum)*
Season: All year
Available in crimson, red, salmon, purple, or white, their bloom is on a leafless stem with green kidney-shaped leaves at the base. They like cool nighttime temperatures.

Hydrangia *(Hydrangia macrophylla)*
Season: Winter to spring
Hydrangea has a large green leaf, and its long-lasting flowers come in white, pink, or blue. Its flowers can also be cut and used in arrangements, either fresh or dried.

Kalanchoe *(Kalanchoe blossfeldiana)*
Season: All year
Available in many colors, their leaves come from the stem and are thick, dark green. The flower blooms in a thick cluster above the leaves.

Narcissus *(Narcissus daffodil)*
Season: Winter through spring
A small white, yellow, or orange flower grows on an upright stem.

Poinsettia *(Euphorbia pulcherrima)*
Season: Winter
Large green leaves with inconspicuous yellow flowers are surrounded by colorful red, yellow, white, or pink petal-like bracts.

Snapweed or Touch-Me-Not *(Impatiens)*
Season: Summer annual
An erect plant, it has colorful flowers in white, pink, rose, lilac, and red. It is nontoxic and can be in direct contact with food.

Tulip *(Tulipa)*
Season: Winter through spring
Atop a delicate stem, the flower comes in a variety of bright colors. Since it is short-lived indoors, purchase it with the buds still tight.

Terms & Techniques

Acidated water   Water that has vinegar or lemon juice added to it. This is done to prevent certain fruits and vegetables from discoloring. When they are placed in it or cooked in it for a short period of time, discoloration can be avoided.

Almond paste   A paste made from blanched ground almonds, along with sugar and liquids. Marzipan is coarser in texture and sweeter than almond paste. Both are used in baked goods.

Ancho chiles   Sometimes called *poblano* or *pasilla*, they can be found fresh or dried and have a rich, herbal, earthy flavor. They are usually mild. When fresh, they are glossy green and resemble a somewhat flattened bell pepper. When dried, they are dark red, almost black.

Arborio rice   Italian short-grained rice used for making risotto; you can also substitute short-grained pearl rice for it. It produces a creamy dish, yet the rice grains retain a certain firmness.

Balsamic vinegar   A mellow Italian vinegar with a slightly sweet flavor found in gourmet shops or in markets that carry imported items. It is aged in wood barrels, much like wine.

Barbecue sauce (Chinese)   A thick, full-flavored sauce found in the Asian section of supermarkets. Use it as a seasoning in marinades and sauces, or brush it directly on foods, and barbecue or bake. Refrigerate indefinitely.

Blanching vegetables   Use this process to cook fully or partially, or just to soften vegetables. The cooking times vary with the degree of doneness desired. For instance, to loosen the skin of a tomato, blanch it for only a few seconds. To blanch vegetables, place them in a large pot of boiling salted water. Then remove them from the pot and either use them immediately or place them in ice water or under cold running water in a colander. This is referred to as *refreshing vegetables*. It stops the cooking process and locks in the vegetable's color and nutrients. This is a very practical technique that allows you to prepare in advance without overcooking. Restaurants commonly use this technique.

Brine   A solution of water and salt. Often sugar is added, which helps to prevent the brined food from being too salty. My formula is approximately ½ cup kosher or sea salt and ½ cup sugar per pound of meat, poultry, or seafood. Water is added to cover the meat. The amount of time to brine depends on the size of the meat. Delicate items such as shrimp or scallops require just an hour. Pork tenderloin and chicken breasts need about 2 hours. Larger items such as roasts or turkeys can be brined for up to 48 hours refrigerated. The point of brining is to produce juicier smoked or grilled items.

Bulgar   Cracked, toasted wheat found in supermarkets or health food stores. Cook it like rice or just soak it in water until it softens, and use in salads.

Cake flour   A high-starch, soft wheat flour that is very finely ground. It is especially well-suited for delicate cakes and pastries.

Calamata olives   Cured Greek black olives, they have a fabulous but salty flavor, which I find to be rich and winey.

Capers   The unopened flavor buds of the prickly caperbush plant. It grows on the mountain slopes bordering the Mediterranean Sea in Italy, Spain, and southern Greece. Capers are packaged in brine and are found in the pickle or import section of most supermarkets. I recommend rinsing before using them for the best results.

Caramelizing sugar   Place the sugar in a heavy saucepan over medium-low heat until the sugar is completely dissolved while holding the handle and swirling frequently. Increase the heat to medium-high for 1 to 2 minutes, until the mixture boils and has thick bubbles. Cook it until it turns a light, golden caramel color, swirling the pan frequently. Remove the pan from the heat and continue to swirl until the syrup turns a rich, deep caramel color. If the sugar is on the verge of being too dark, place the saucepan over a pan of cold water until the caramel cools slightly. Do not let it harden. At this point, if necessary, the pan can be placed over very low heat to maintain a liquid consistency. A word of caution: never let your skin come in contact with hot caramel. It burns instantly.

Celery root   This vegetable is also referred to as celeriac. It is an unattractive, light brown color and has a knobby shape. The exterior needs to be cut away. Celery root has an intense celery flavor and can be used raw or cooked.

To prevent it from discoloring, soak it either whole or sliced in water with lemon juice or vinegar. This is referred to as *acidated water.*

Chard   Also known as Swiss chard, it belongs to the beet family. The red variety has the most pronounced flavor, and it is available during the summer.

Chèvre cheese   A rich, herbal, French-style goat cheese. Feta cheese can often be substituted for chèvre cheese, because it is less expensive.

Chinese black bean sauce   This is a bottled Chinese sauce made from fermented black beans. It can be purchased in the Asian section of supermarkets or in Asian markets.

Chinese black fungus   Also known as wood ears, until very recently it was only available in dried form. When rehydrated, it has almost no flavor, but it provides a crunchy texture and black color. To rehydrate black fungus, place it in a small bowl and let it sit, covered with water, until it softens and expands. This will take about 30 minutes. To speed up this process, soften it in a pot of boiling water or in a bowl of water in a microwave. When used fresh, it has a delicate, earthy flavor. In folklore it is prized for its healthful properties, especially in preventing heart disease. I like to use it in rich menus to help balance the fats. It is my insurance policy against cholesterol and falls into the category of "it couldn't hurt."

Citrus zest   The flavorful, colored part of the citrus rind, not the bitter white portion. To remove and use the zest, use a vegetable peeler or a zester, which can be found any place that sells gourmet gadgets.

Cornichons   Small French sour pickles.

Couscous   Moroccan pasta (medium-grain semolina) that resembles pastina and cooks like bulgar.

Deglaze   Adding liquid to a hot, degreased cooking pan after sautéing or roasting food in it. The liquid is brought to a boil to capture all the flavor from the remaining brown bits and juices, which should be vigorously scraped. Use this liquid as a sauce or add to a final sauce.

Degrease   Removing the fat from a cooked liquid. One of the easiest methods is to refrigerate the item overnight. The next morning you will find a layer of solidified fat that can easily be removed. To remove the fat, immediately put ice cubes in the pan or pot with the liquid. It is easier if you are able to transfer the liquid to a bowl and then add the ice cubes.

Dried cherries   Delightfully tart, they are an interesting addition to both sweet and savory dishes, from salads to cookies.

Eggs   It seems as if there's always a new food villain. Currently the focus has been on eggs contaminated by *Salmonella* bacteria. This is of greater concern to pregnant women (because of the risk to the fetus), the elderly, and people already weakened by serious illness or whose immune systems are suppressed. According to the United States Department of Agriculture, the chances of a healthy person being affected are extremely small. They do, however, recommend not eating homemade foods containing raw or lightly cooked eggs. These foods range from mayonnaise to ice cream. The same items are risk free when commercially prepared because they are pasteurized, which kills the bacteria.

It is very important to follow the safe food handling practices listed below when using eggs:

- Buy only Grade A or AA eggs from a reputable market that keeps them under refrigeration. Open the carton to make sure the eggs are clean and crack-free. Do not purchase them if the expiration date has passed.

- Make sure you store your eggs in the refrigerator at a temperature no higher than 40 degrees F. Use them before the expiration date. Once they are hard-cooked, they should be used within one week. Leftover yolks and whites should be used within four days.

- When cooking, eggs should not be left at room temperature for more than 2 hours.

- Always wash your hands, utensils, and work surfaces with hot, soapy water when working with raw eggs.

You will find that some of my recipes could pose the risk of *Salmonella* infection. However, the recipes are so delicious and the risk so small that I could not eliminate them. Harold McGee, the author of *The Curious Cook,* provides a microwave method for eliminating *Salmonella* that you might want to look into. The bottom line is that the decision to make any of these dishes is yours, but it is important to be informed and to take into consideration the health of the people who will be enjoying your food.

Escarole   Also known as Batavian endive, this is a delightful green that can be used any way spinach is used. It has a fibrous texture and a slightly bitter flavor.

Fennel   See Herbs, page 16.

Flash freeze   A technique for freezing delicate foods and for conserving space in the freezer. It allows you to store foods in plastic bags rather than on trays. Place the item unwrapped on a cookie sheet or tray and freeze until firm. Then transfer it to plastic bags or containers and store in the freezer.

Fermented black beans   Also referred to as salted black beans or Chinese black beans, these have an intense salty flavor and contribute a rich, earthy quality when used as a seasoning. They can be found in Asian markets or in the Asian section of supermarkets. Refrigerate indefinitely.

Fresh ginger   A pungent root used as a seasoning. It is also recognized as having many healthful applications, ranging from digestive aid to anticarcinogen. It can only be refrigerated for about a week before it begins to mold. To preserve it in the freezer, store it whole or chopped in a plastic bag or container. To store it in the refrigerator, put it in a jar of sherry or rice vinegar, whole or chopped. It can be stored this way for at least six months. As a bonus, the liquid becomes infused with the flavor and can be used as a seasoning.

Green peppercorns   Immature pepper berries with less power and a more herbal flavor than mature black peppercorns. They come packed in brine or freeze-dried. Rinsing the brine-packed peppercorns in water before use is optional.

Gruyère cheese   A rich, nutty-flavored Swiss cheese.

Handling chiles   It is advisable to wear plastic gloves when working with chiles to prevent them from burning your skin. It is important not to touch any part of your body, especially your eyes, after touching chiles. Always wash your hands after handling them.

Hoisin sauce (Chinese)   A prepared Chinese sauce with a very thick consistency. Refer to Barbecue sauce for techniques, because it is used in the same manner. It's a great way to achieve bold flavors without adding fats or lots of calories.

Instant-read meat thermometer   A small, thin thermometer that is used to insert into meat or poultry to check for doneness, it almost instantly provides the temperature. It is not left in like the more common, thicker variety that leaves a larger hole and conducts heat, causing whatever you are baking to cook at two different rates.

Instantized flour   This processed flour offers hope to all those afflicted with lumpy sauces. It can be whisked into any liquid or sauce, and it never fails to dissolve and thicken.

Japanese persimmon   This is a squatty shaped persimmon that is eaten when firm like an apple.

Kirsch   A Swiss cherry-brandy liqueur.

Leeks   Resembling oversized green onions with a glandular problem, leeks have a more subtle flavor than onions or garlic but belong to the same family. Select smaller ones because they are more tender. They hold a lot of dirt inside the leaves. To clean, slit down from the top to the bottom and rinse well under running water.

Lemon grass   An Asian seasoning that has the appearance of a grass. It is gray-green with stalks about two feet long. Use the fibrous portion to flavor liquids, in the cavity of poultry, or to put under roasting meat. Mince or slice the tender inner portion and use in cooking.

Melting chocolate   Chocolate burns easily, which destroys its texture by making it stiffer. The safest method for up to 8 ounces is to melt chocolate pieces in the top of a double boiler set over several inches of water that has been brought to a boil and removed from the heat. Cover the saucepan and let it sit for about 5 minutes. Then stir the chocolate until it is smooth. If the chocolate still has not melted, return the double boiler to the burner over medium-low heat for several minutes more. Chocolate may also be melted in the microwave. I always set it on low power, and I usually start with 3 minutes, adding more time if needed.

Mizithera cheese   A very tasty white Greek grating cheese that is frequently difficult to find. Substitute Romano or Parmesan if Mizithera is unavailable.

Olive oil (for dipping bread)   Using olive oil rather than butter or (heaven forbid) margarine is not only healthier but also very country Italian. This custom has regained popularity. Make sure you use good extra virgin olive oil when doing this. Frequently, balsamic vinegar is also drizzled in the saucer with the olive oil. It is fun to get creative and flavor the olive oil with fresh or dried herbs and/or garlic.

Orzo   A rice-shaped pasta.

Pancetta   An Italian cured bacon, often coated with coarsely ground black pepper. It can be found at good delicatessens or butcher shops. Store it in the freezer for up to a year and cut off what you need while still frozen. Use it as a seasoning in small amounts.

Parmesan cheese   Parmigiano Reggiano is the Rolls Royce of Parmesan cheese. This type of cheese is a hard, dry, grating cheese that is produced in Modena or Parma, Italy, from skimmed milk. It has a rich, sharp flavor.

Pasilla chiles   These are dried chile peppers with a reddish brown color and an earthy flavor rather than a firey hot flavor. (See Ancho chiles.)

Pecorino Romano cheese   A grating cheese named after the city of Rome. The most distinguished variety is Pecorino Romano. It is a firm, sharp, tangy cheese.

Peeling carrots faster   If you are going to cook carrots, do not bother to peel them first. After they have been blanched or fully cooked, wipe off the peel while refreshing them in cold water. Sometimes it is necessary to use a knife to lightly scrape the skin off.

Peeling garlic faster   Just recently, raw garlic has become available already peeled in plastic jars (without preservatives). What a convenience! If this is not available to you, place heads of garlic in a paper or plastic bag. Hit it with a meat pounder or the bottom of a pan. This will separate it into cloves. Then put the cloves in boiling water for a few seconds. Remove them with a strainer and place them in the sink under cold running water. When cool enough to handle, the garlic will squeeze out of its skin.

Peeling tomatoes   First cut slits in an X shape at the core; then place the tomatoes in boiling water for about 30 seconds or until the skin can be removed easily. Immediately plunge them into cold water, then peel.

Pesto   An uncooked sauce made from fresh garlic, basil, pine nuts, Parmesan or Pecorino cheese, and olive oil. *Pesto* is Italian for "paste" and is often used to refer to other types of uncooked, herb-based sauces.

Pickled cactus (Nopales)   Commonly available in the Mexican section of the supermarket, this is thin strips of peeled, pickled cactus. I suggest rinsing it prior to using, because it improves the texture, which resembles that of okra.

Pickled ginger   Also referred to as sushi ginger, this is sliced ginger that is pickled in a solution of salt, sugar, and vinegar, which mellows it. It can be found in Asian markets or in the produce or Asian section of supermarkets. You may want to rinse it to remove some of the salt.

Pickled mango   An exotic condiment from India. It can be found in stores with an extensive import section or in specialty stores. Chinese plum sauce or a spicy chutney can be used in its place.

Pink peppercorns   These have a milder flavor than black peppercorns, and a beautiful color. Use them whole, ground, or crushed. They come freeze dried or in brine. Rinsing the brine-packed variety is optional. Pink peppercorns are popular in French cooking.

Plum sauce (Chinese)   A prepared sauce that can best be described as a plum jam with ginger and chiles. For information on its use and storage, refer to Barbecue sauce (Chinese). Using plum sauce achieves bold flavors without adding fats or a lot of calories. It can be found in Asian markets or in the Asian section of many supermarkets.

Porcini mushrooms   Also known as *bolete* or *cepe,* they have a very meaty texture when fresh. They resemble domestic mushrooms but are much larger. The caps are tan- to brown-colored, but the flesh is creamy white. Available fresh or dried, they are more commonly available dried, and have a fabulous earthy flavor. To rehydrate the dried variety, simply place them in a bowl and cover them with any liquid, from water to broth. Let sit at room temperature for about one hour or until soft. To speed up the process, place the mushrooms in a saucepan and boil until tender, or place them in a bowl of water and microwave.

Prosciutto   Specially cured Italian ham found at good delicatessens or butcher shops. It is used in small amounts as a seasoning, solo as an hors d'oeuvre, or with fresh fruit.

Pumpkin seeds (hulled)   Often called *pepitas*, they are a common ingredient in Mexican cooking. They can be used just as you would use any nut or seed. I roast them as I do with nuts and seeds and store them in the freezer. They can be purchased in health food stores.

Radicchio   An Italian red-leafed lettuce used in salads, pastas, and risottos. It is a member of the chicory family, which accounts for its bitter taste.

Red chard   This beautiful vegetable is a member of the beet family and is available during the summer.

Red jalapeño chiles   Small peppers with thick flesh, they are very hot but have a slight sweetness that makes them intriguing.

Reduce (or reduction)   This refers to the process of boiling cooking liquids down to intensify their flavors and/or thicken them.

Rice vinegar   A delightfully mellow and refreshing vinegar with a slightly sweet flavor. Cooking with rice vinegar is a great way to achieve bold flavors without adding fats or cholesterol. It is found in Asian markets or in the Asian section of many supermarkets.

Roasting garlic   To roast garlic, cut the top one-third from each head of garlic to expose the cloves. Using your hands, peel away some of the excess skin from around the garlic. Place the heads in a baking pan or heavy skillet and toss with a small amount of olive oil. You might also want to add some sherry wine and/or balsamic vinegar to the garlic. Cover with a lid and bake in a preheated 250 to 350 degree oven until the cloves are soft and buttery, about 2 hours. If you are lucky enough to be able to purchase prepeeled garlic cloves, simply toss them in olive oil and bake as directed above. Roasted garlic can be frozen for up to six months or refrigerated for at least five days.

Roasting peppers   Cut the peppers in half and remove the seeds and veins. Place them on an aluminum-foil-lined cookie sheet cut side down in a preheated 350 to 450 degree oven until the skin is charred. This will take 30 to 60 minutes. When cool enough to handle, remove and discard the skin. Use or store, wrapped, in the freezer for up to one year. Roasted red peppers are one of the most wonderful ingredients. I suggest you keep them on hand in your freezer. They will add instant magic to salads, dressings, sauces, and soups. One of my favorite hors d'oeuvres is chèvre, feta, or Brie placed in a skillet or ovenproof baking dish, topped with chopped, roasted red peppers, pine nuts, and chopped fresh basil. This is warmed in a preheated 350 degree oven for about 10 minutes and served with Garlic Crostini (page 66) or thinly sliced pieces of baguette.

Roasting shallots   Simply cut a small portion of the tip off of the shallot and proceed as directed in the technique for roasting garlic.

Rutabaga   A root vegetable that looks like a large, pale-lemon turnip and has a sweet flavor; it is a member of the cabbage family.

Saffron   A precious and costly spice, it is the stigma of autumn crocus and must be harvested by hand. It gives food a yellow-golden color and an exotic, earthy flavor. Always purchase saffron threads; the powdered form is not as flavorful and often is not pure.

Sesame oil (Chinese)   Use sesame oil very sparingly as a seasoning, not as a cooking oil. It has a rich and intensely nutty flavor and aroma. Store in the refrigerator to prevent it from becoming rancid; it will last for over a year. It can be found in Asian markets or in the Asian section of many supermarkets.

Shallot   A member of the onion family but with a more delicate flavor, it resembles a small onion with a brown skin.

Shiitake mushrooms   Also known as Black Forest mushrooms or Chinese mushrooms. Shiitake can be purchased fresh, but their flavor is more intense when dried. They have a rich, earthy flavor. They are always soaked in liquid to rehydrate before using. This will take about one hour. To speed up the process, place the mushrooms in a saucepan and boil them for several minutes, until tender. Never discard the soaking liquid. Strain it to remove any grit, reduce it, and use it in soups, stocks, and sauces.

Storing seeds or nuts   These items will get rancid if they are not stored in the freezer. They can be stored for at least six months this way.

Sun-dried tomatoes   Italian pear-shaped tomatoes that are salted and dried. They can be very expensive, especially if purchased marinated. I recommend buying them in bulk; just soften and marinate them yourself. To soften them for immediate use, place them in a plastic or glass jar with a few tablespoons of vinegar, wine, or water. Cover with a lid and place in the microwave for a few minutes until softened. To do this on the stove, place the tomatoes in a saucepan and add an equal amount of the liquid of your choice. Bring to a boil, then gently simmer until tender, about 10 minutes. Use as is or cover them with olive oil. Add garlic cloves, bay leaves, peppercorns, and/or fresh or dried herbs of your choice, and store in the refrigerator for up to one year. The oil becomes infused with the pungent tomato-herb essence and is wonderful used on bread or in cooking.

Sweetened chile sauce   This is a bottled Chinese sauce that is sweet and spicey. It can be purchased in the Asian section of supermarkets or in Asian markets.

Szechuan peppercorns   Peppercorns with an intriguing flavor that is a combination of menthol and heat. Use whole or crushed to flavor both Asian and non-Asian foods. They can be found in Asian markets, gourmet stores, or in the spice section of many supermarkets.

Tahini   A thick sesame seed paste.

Teleme cheese   An aged jack cheese with a softer texture and a more complex flavor than the regular jack.

Toasting seeds or nuts   Place on an aluminum-foil-lined cookie sheet in a preheated 350 degree oven until toasted. Watch carefully, shaking the pan from time to time to avoid burning; it should take 15 to 20 minutes.

Tomatillos   Also referred to as Mexican green tomatoes, they resemble a small green tomato and are covered with a greenish husk, which is not eaten. Used raw or cooked, they have a tart, lemonlike herbal flavor. When used raw, it tastes more acidic. When cooked, it adds some gelatinous texture.

Tonkatsu sauce   Japanese-style Worcestershire sauce. Refer to the entry for barbecue sauce for information on its usage and storage. It's a great way to add bold flavors to food without adding fats or cholesterol. It can be found in Asian markets or in the Asian section of many supermarkets.

Unmolding formed items   Dip a knife into hot water and run it around the perimeter of the mold or container, then place the container in warm water for a few seconds until the formed mixture can be jiggled away from the edge. Place a platter or plate on top of the mold and invert it. Sometimes it needs a tap to loosen it. For guaranteed, worry-free results, always oil the inside of the mold and line it with plastic wrap or cheesecloth. To unmold, simply pull it out.

White peppercorns   It is actually the inside of the black peppercorn. It has a milder, richer flavor than black peppercorns. They are widely used in delicate, light-colored sauces, since they do not add black flakes.

For further assistance with cooking terms and techniques, I recommend *The Way to Cook* by Julia Child and the *Food Lover's Companion* by Sharon Tyler Herbst.

Spring

Italian Sausage & Chard Burrito Brunch

*H*ere is a wonderful brunch that you are going to find a million reasons to stage. This party is especially well suited for those occasions when you need to serve large groups. The recipes can be easily increased. It will also serve you well as a lunch or dinner menu. This menu is abundant with big, bold, and earthy flavors. Vegetables are clearly the stars of this cast. Co-starring are delectable ingredients such as prosciutto and Italian sausages.

As for traditional brunch fare, this menu throws it to the wind. It is designed for a special occasion when nothing but the best will do.

Proscuitto and Basil Roulades, the hors d'oeuvre for this brunch, gets its inspiration from Thai cooking using rice paper.

The main course, Italian Sausage & Chard Burritos, marries an Italian filling with a Mexican tortilla along with a very Mediterranean sauce. The results are delicious and probably something you will also use for casual dinners.

For dessert: a divine, light, and very simple Zabaglione Mousse, which highlights the best of the season's offerings. In terms of "seasonizing," here is a party that can be adapted to any season with slight changes. For example, when basil is out of season, use prepared pesto rather than fresh basil for the roulades. For the dessert, frozen unsweetened berries are fine instead of fresh.

I recommend creating a bright look for the table. A bold green and white stripe or floral sheet for the cloth, with terra cotta flower pots for vases works well. Place glass jars in the pots and fill them with masses of white flowers and cuttings of leather fern. Shiny eggplants and lemons strewn down the center of the table complete the look. Instead of cut flowers, try pots with blooming bulbs for the ultimate spring look.

Menu

Prosciutto & Basil Roulades

Mediterranean Lentil Salad

Italian Sausage & Chard Burritos with Roasted Red Pepper Sauce

Zabaglione Mousse with Strawberries & Almonds

Faster & Flashier Menu

Prosciutto (wrapped around thin bread sticks)

Italian Sausage & Chard Burritos with Roasted Red Pepper Sauce

Strawberries on Vanilla Yogurt & Biscotti (purchased)

Sparkling Wine and/or Chardonnay

Sauvignon Blanc or Pinot Noir

Coffee and/or Sparkling Wine

TIMETABLE

Up to 2 weeks in advance	Balsamic Sun-Dried Tomato Vinaigrette
Up to 7 days in advance	Basil Cream Cheese
Up to 4 days in advance	Roasted Red Pepper Sauce
Up to 3 days in advance	Mediterranean Lentil Salad
Up to 2 days in advance	Zabaglione Mousse
Up to 1 day in advance	Set the table. Chill the wine.
Party day!	Assemble roulades. Heat burritos.

Prosciutto & Basil Roulades

*This hors d'oeuvre combines Asian and Italian ingredients to create
something very unique and delicious.*

Yield: About 48 pieces

24 rice paper circles,* about 8½ inches
    in diameter
12 thin slices of proscuitto, sliced in half
24 strips of roasted red peppers,
    skinned, seeded, and deveined

Basil cream cheese (recipe follows)
Extra virgin olive oil for brushing the
    roulades

1. Place several of the rice paper circles on a work surface and use a pastry
   brush to brush them with water on both sides. Let them sit for about 3
   minutes or until softened.
2. Spread one or two tablespoons of the Basil Cream Cheese on each of the
   softened rice paper circles. Top with a piece of prosciutto and red bell
   pepper.
3. Fold two sides toward the center, then form a roll by starting with the
   unfolded side and roll up the rice paper circle. Brush with olive oil. Repeat
   until all of the rice papers are used. Chill for several hours, then slice into
   ½-inch-thick logs.

FAST: Can prepare up to 6 hours in advance; cover tightly with plastic wrap
and refrigerate.

FLASHY: Serve chilled, garnished with a whole red pepper in the center of the
platter. Try lining the platter with large aralia* leaves for a great look.

FABULOUS: With minced green onions or alfalfa sprouts on top of the cream
cheese. With very soft, fresh flour tortillas or softened lavosh instead of rice
paper.

*Rice paper circles are brittle, paper-thin sheets made from rice and water. Before using as a wrapper, they
must be softened.

Basil Cream Cheese

Turns the ordinary into zesty!   **Yield: About 2½ cups**

1 8-ounce package cream cheese or
    low-fat or fat-free cream cheese
1 cup fresh, packed basil leaves
3 to 6 cloves garlic

¼ to ½ cup grated Parmesan cheese
Salt and white pepper, to taste
½ cup toasted walnuts, chopped

1. Combine the cream cheese with all the remaining ingredients, except for the walnuts, in a food processor fitted with the metal blade. Taste and adjust the flavors.
2. Add the walnuts, using several quick on-and-off motions so as not to destroy the texture.

FAST: Can prepare up to 7 days in advance and refrigerate, or freeze for up to 2 months.

FLASHY: Serve cold as a filling for cherry tomato halves, mushroom caps, or croustades. As a spread for crostini, French bread, and crackers.

FABULOUS: With 4 ounces cream cheese and 4 ounces chèvre or feta cheese instead of all cream cheese.

Mediterranean Lentil Salad

A marvelous rustic salad with a real nutritional bonus.   **Yield: Serves 8**

1 large eggplant, cut into 1-inch chunks
1 cup or more Balsamic Sun-Dried
    Tomato Vinaigrette (recipe follows)
1 pound cultivated mushrooms,
    quartered
2 large red, yellow, or white onions,
    quartered and thinly sliced
4 cups lentils, rinsed

8 cups water or chicken broth
    (homemade or canned)
½ cup balsamic vinegar
    Salt; freshly ground coarse black
    pepper; and fresh lemon juice,
    to taste
1 bunch Italian parsley, minced

1. Toss the eggplant with enough of the vinaigrette to coat the eggplant in a large baking pan. Place in a preheated 425 degree oven and bake until tender and slightly charred, about 30–45 minutes.
2. Meanwhile, place the mushrooms and onions in another baking pan and bake for about 20 minutes until the onions are tender and sweet.

3. Place the lentils in a large pot with the water, vinegar, and about 1 table-spoon salt. Bring this to a boil over high heat, cover with a lid, and reduce the heat to low. Cook just until tender; watch carefully so you don't end up with mushy lentils.
4. Pour the lentils through a fine wire mesh strainer in the sink to drain off any unabsorbed water.
5. Combine all the ingredients in a salad bowl and add more vinaigrette if needed. Season with salt, pepper, and fresh lemon juice to taste.

FAST: Can prepare up to 3 days in advance and refrigerate.

FLASHY: Served hot or cold. As an hors d'oeuvre with pita chips.

FABULOUS: With ½ cup chopped marinated artichoke hearts, 2 to 4 roasted red peppers (skinned, seeded, deveined, and cut into strips), 8 oz. crumbled feta and/or ¼ cup or more chopped fresh mint. With couscous, bulgar, and/or white beans instead of lentils.

Balsamic Sun-Dried Tomato Vinaigrette

Use this on anything except dogfood.

Yield: About 3 cups

2 cups extra virgin olive oil
½ cup sun-dried tomatoes, softened*
2 to 4 cloves garlic

⅔ cup balsamic vinegar
1 shallot
Salt and ground white pepper, to taste

1. Combine all the ingredients in a food processor fitted with the metal blade or in a blender until smooth. Taste and adjust the seasonings.
2. Store in a tightly covered jar in the refrigerator. Shake or stir before using.

FAST: Can prepare up to 2 weeks in advance and refrigerate, or freeze for up to 3 months.

FLASHY: As a dunk for raw vegetables, any crostini (page 66) or thinly sliced baguettes. Garnish by floating any nontoxic flower on it.

FABULOUS: As a marinade or sauce for vegetables, seafood, beef, poultry, and pork. On any salad.

*Refer to Terms & Techniques.

Italian Sausage & Chard Burritos with Roasted Red Pepper Sauce

Wow! If you are in the mood for something lighter, substitute fresh cooked salmon for the sausages.

Yield: 8+ servings

4 tablespoons olive oil and extra for brushing the burritos
2 to 3 yellow, white, or red onions, thinly sliced
3 to 6 cloves garlic, minced
1 pound cultivated mushrooms, thinly sliced
3 pounds fresh chard or frozen, thawed, and drained
2 pounds Italian sausages, casings removed (sweet, hot, or combo)
¼ cup fresh parsley, minced
1 cup ricotta cheese or low-fat or fat-free ricotta cheese
2 cups grated Monterey jack cheese
¼ to ½ cup freshly grated Parmesan cheese
Salt, white pepper, and grated nutmeg to taste
8 large flour tortillas
Roasted Red Pepper Sauce (recipe follows)

1. Sauté the onions and garlic in 2 tablespoons of the olive oil in a large pan or wok over medium heat until golden, about 15 minutes, or place in a large baking pan in a 300 degree oven until golden, about 30–45 minutes.
2. Add the mushrooms and chard, and sauté over medium-high heat until the liquid that the vegetables release is cooked away.
3. Meanwhile, break the sausage meat up with a fork and cook in a skillet or in the microwave. Blot on paper towels to remove any excess fat.
4. Stir in the cooked sausage to the vegetables along with the parsley and cheeses. Taste and adjust the seasonings.
5. Place a generous amount of the filling in the center of each tortilla. Fold them and place each burrito in an oiled baking dish, brush each burrito with olive oil, and cover with foil.
6. Bake in a preheated 350 degree oven for 20–30 minutes, until hot.

FAST: Can prepare up to 2 days in advance and refrigerate, or freeze for up to 3 months.

FLASHY: Serve with Roasted Red Pepper Sauce.

FABULOUS: Seasoned with fresh basil. With feta cheese instead of half or all of the jack cheese. With turkey or chicken sausages, or with fresh cooked salmon in place of the Italian sausages. As a filling for lasagna, pasta shells, or egg rolls.

Roasted Red Pepper Sauce

This is a favorite of mine. When I prepared it on national television, I splashed it all over the host, Gary Collins.

Yield: About 1½ cups or more

4 large red peppers, roasted,* peeled, and seeded
2 cloves garlic, or more
1 to 2 cups extra virgin olive oil or low-fat or fat-free sour cream

Salt, white pepper, and fresh lemon or lime juice, to taste

1. Combine all ingredients in a food processor fitted the with metal blade. Taste and adjust seasonings.

FAST: Can prepare up to 4 days in advance and refrigerate, or freeze for up to 6 months.

FLASHY: On anything from potatoes to fish.

FABULOUS: With heavy cream or chicken broth instead of oil, and served hot.

*Refer to Terms & Techniques.

Zabaglione Mousse with Strawberries & Almonds

A delicious and light way to end a big meal.

Yield: 8 servings

8 egg yolks or egg substitute, at room temperature
1 to 1½ cups granulated sugar, plus extra for the strawberries
¾ cup Marsala, Madeira, or sherry wine, warmed
Grated nutmeg to taste
Grated zest of 2 to 4 lemons
2 cups heavy cream or low-fat or fat-free sour cream

2 pints strawberries, hulled and halved or whole
Marsala, Madeira, or sherry for strawberries (optional)
8 ounces slivered almonds, toasted
Bittersweet chocolate, shaved or grated for garnishing

1. Process egg yolks or egg substitute with sugar in a food processor fitted with the metal blade, until lemon colored.

2. Add warm wine very slowly through the feed tube while machine is running.
3. Season with nutmeg, and briefly process in the lemon zest. Transfer to a saucepan placed over a pot of simmering water and whisk until completely thickened. Taste and add more sugar and/or wine if needed.
4. Transfer to bowl and chill in the freezer for about 30 minutes.
5. Whip the cream until it holds soft peaks and fold it into chilled mixture, or stir in the sour cream.
6. Chill in a mixing bowl, glass bowl, soufflé dish, or stemmed glasses until ready to serve.
7. To macerate strawberries, place them in a bowl, add sugar if needed, and some wine. Let sit at room temperature for several hours or refrigerate for up to 2 days.

FAST: Can prepare zabaglione up to 2 days in advance and refrigerate, or freeze for up to 1 month. Can prepare strawberries up to 2 days in advance and refrigerate.

FLASHY: Serve zabaglione in stemmed glasses or in a large glass bowl; spoon strawberries over it, sprinkle with almonds and some chocolate. Serve with Lemon Sesame Shortbread (page 281).

FABULOUS: On pound or angel food cake or on puff pastry. Use zabaglione to fill crepes, and top with strawberries, almonds, and chocolate. Substitute fresh cherries, peaches, or any berry for the strawberries.

FURTHER: Don't worry, there won't be any leftovers.

Hard-Boiled Eggs with Ham, Asparagus & Artichoke Hearts

*H*ard-boiled eggs once were a must at picnics and buffets but are not currently the culinary rage. This brunch uses hard-boiled eggs in a casserole, which is a variation of a provincial French dish. It is an extremely satisfying mixture of hard-boiled eggs, ham, asparagus, and artichoke hearts blended together in glorious cheese sauce, topped with grated Parmesan.

As for the accompaniments, what is the perfect complement to egg dishes? The answer, of course, is potatoes. This party has a marvelous rendition of breakfast potatoes full of herbs and onions. Next come sausages with two unique sauces. This is a real treat, especially in our fat-free world. Come on; let's live a little. Complete the menu with fresh fruit and homemade biscotti. There you have a delightful Sunday brunch with a cosmopolitan feel. If you are looking for a late-night get-together, say, "after the theater," this menu works well.

The table for this party is covered with a gray-and-white thin-striped sheet with napkins in light gray. A floral cloth in pastel colors is another option. For the centerpiece, a low-sided basket, spray-painted white, filled with 4-inch paper pots of white impatiens. The spaces between the plants can be filled with moss, leather ferns, and/or spears of raw asparagus or short cuttings of blossoms.

Menu

*Grilled Assorted Sausages with Gingered Dill Mustard Sauce
and Maple Mustard Sauce*

Hard-Boiled Eggs with Ham, Asparagus & Artichoke Hearts

Herbed Red Potatoes & Onions

French Bread

Fresh Fruit and Lemon Almond Biscotti

Faster & Flashier Menu

*Grilled Assorted Sausages with Dijon Mustard
and Maple Mustard Sauce*

Herbed Red Potatoes and Onions

Fresh Fruit and Biscotti (purchased)

Sparkling Wine

Sauvignon Blanc

Coffee

✄ TIMETABLE ✄

Up to 2 weeks in advance	Gingered Dill Mustard Sauce (or freeze for up to 6 months).
Up to 5 days in advance	Lemon Almond Biscotti. Maple Mustard Sauce.
Up to 2 days in advance	Hard-Boiled Eggs with Ham, Asparagus & Artichoke Hearts. Herbed Red Potatoes & Onions.
Up to 1 day in advance	Set the table. Chill the wines.
Party day!	Bake the potatoes. Grill sausages. Bake eggs right before serving.

Grilled Assorted Sausages with Gingered Dill Mustard Sauce & Maple Mustard Sauce

What a treat in our fat-free world!

Yield: 8+ servings

About 2 pounds of interesting sausages
Gingered Dill Mustard Sauce (recipe follows)
Maple Mustard Sauce (recipe follows)

1. Heat up the barbecue or preheat the oven to 400 degrees.
2. Prick the sausages with the tines of a fork to allow the fat to drain off. Thoroughly cook the sausages and remove them from the oven or barbecue. Let cool slightly and slice into chunks.

FAST: Cook right before serving.

FLASHY: Serve on a large wood or ceramic platter along with a bowl of the mustard sauce. Garnish with sprigs of fresh dill.

Gingered Dill Mustard Sauce

You will find a million uses for this wonderful sauce, ranging from a dip for cold shrimp to a sauce for anything grilled to asparagus.

Yield: About 2 cups

½ cup pickled ginger, drained
½ cup Dijon mustard
2 teaspoons dry mustard
3 to 4 tablespoons packed light or dark brown sugar

4 to 6 tablespoons rice vinegar
½ cup minced fresh dill, or to taste
⅓ to ⅔ cup canola or peanut oil (can substitute low-fat or fat-free sour cream)

1. Combine all the ingredients in a food processor fitted with a metal blade or in a blender. Taste and adjust the seasonings.

FAST: Can prepare up to 2 weeks in advance and refrigerate, or freeze for up to 6 months. Thaw in the refrigerator for 2 days or at room temperature for about 8 hours.

FABULOUS: With duck, lamb, poultry, or sausages. Use in sauces or marinades. Makes a great gift.

Maple Mustard Sauce

"Fast & Fabulous" at its best. . . . It's a must on baby back ribs.   **Yield: ¾ cup**

½ cup maple syrup
⅓ cup Dijon mustard
 1 teaspoon soy sauce, or more

1 clove garlic, minced
  Hot pepper sauce, to taste

1. Combine all ingredients in a small bowl.
2. Taste and adjust seasonings.

FAST: Can prepare up to 5 days in advance and refrigerate. Serve cold, at room temperature, or gently warmed.

FABULOUS: Seasoned with fresh lemon-thyme or dried thyme, fresh or dried rosemary, and/or sage. Use to glaze or as a sauce for anything broiled or grilled, from chicken to ribs.

Hard-Boiled Eggs with Ham, Asparagus & Artichoke Hearts

A change-of-pace, French-inspired casserole!   **Yield: Serves 8 to 10**

¼ cup unsalted butter, peanut oil, or
   cooking spray
2 bunches of green onions, thinly
   sliced
¼ cup all-purpose flour
2 cups milk or nonfat milk
2 cups chicken broth, homemade or
   canned
¾ cup medium sherry
   Salt and white pepper
1 teaspoon Dijon mustard, or more
4 to 8 ounces Muenster or jack cheese,
   cut up or grated
3 10-ounce packages frozen, chopped
   spinach, thawed and squeezed
   well to remove the excess
   moisture

½ cup sour cream or low-fat or fat-free
   sour cream
   Grated nutmeg, to taste
12 to 16 ounces smoked ham, cut into
   thin strips
1 14¾-ounce jar marinated or water-
   packed artichoke hearts, drained
   and cut into narrow slices
16 eggs, hard-boiled and peeled, cut in
   ½-inch-thick slices
1 pound asparagus, trimmed and cut
   into 1-inch lengths and blanched
½ cup freshly grated Parmesan cheese,
   or more
   Salt and white pepper, to taste

1. In a large, heavy skillet, melt butter and slowly sauté the onions until soft and tender.
2. Stir in the flour and mix well over medium heat. Cook over low heat for 2 minutes.
3. Whisk in all the liquid and stir well over high heat, until the sauce comes to a boil. Reduce the heat to medium, and whisk frequently until the sauce thickens.
4. Whisk in the mustard, nutmeg, and Muenster cheese. Taste and adjust the seasonings.
5. Combine the spinach, sour cream, white pepper, nutmeg, and grated Parmesan cheese, to taste. Place the mixture in the bottom of an oiled, buttered, or sprayed casserole. Top the spinach mixture with the ham, artichoke hearts, and asparagus. Then add a layer of the hard-boiled egg slices or halves. Spoon the sauce over the top and sprinkle with the desired amount of Parmesan cheese. Bake in a preheated 350 degree oven until hot, about 30 minutes.

FAST: Can assemble up to 2 days in advance and refrigerate. Bake before serving.

FLASHY: Serve hot with minced parsley sprinkled over the top. Lovely served in individual ramekins.

FABULOUS: With Canadian bacon or prosciutto instead of ham. With sautéed mushrooms and spinach. With any kind of cheese. As a filling for crepes or lasagna. With crab, clams, and/or shrimp instead of the ham.

Herbed Red Potatoes & Onions

These work for breakfast, lunch, or dinner!   ***Yield: 8+ servings***

2 pounds baby red potatoes, cubed or
    thinly sliced
4 tablespoons olive oil or unsalted
    butter, or more
2 yellow onions, chopped

2 tablespoons minced fresh rosemary,
    or more
Salt and freshly ground white
    pepper, to taste
¼ cup minced fresh Italian parsley

1. Place the potatoes in a large saucepan with boiling salted water. Cook until tender, about 8 minutes, over medium heat.
2. Meanwhile, in a large skillet, heat the olive oil or melt the butter over medium-low heat, and sauté the onions and rosemary until the onions are tender.
3. Drain the potatoes and add them to the skillet with the onions. Season with salt and pepper, and toss well. Place in a preheated 375 degree oven for about 40 minutes or until they reach the desired degree of crispness. Sprinkle the parsley over the top and serve.

FAST: Can boil potatoes and toss with remaining ingredients up to 2 days in advance and refrigerate. Bring to room temperature and bake before serving.

FABULOUS: With extra virgin olive oil instead of butter.

Lemon Almond Biscotti

One of my favorites and very low in fat!   ***Yield: About 7 dozen***

¾ to 1 cup granulated sugar
4½ cups all-purpose flour
   Grated nutmeg, to taste
½ teaspoon salt
1 teaspoon baking soda
4 large eggs or egg substitute

1 teaspoon vanilla extract
¼ cup fresh lemon juice
1½ cups almonds, toasted (page 13) and
   chopped
Grated zest of 3 lemons

1. Preheat the oven to 375 degrees.
2. Combine the sugar, 4 cups of the flour, the nutmeg, salt, and baking soda in a food processor fitted with the metal blade, or in a mixer.
3. Process in the eggs, vanilla, and lemon juice until the mixture forms a dough. Add water if the mixture is too dry and crumbly.
4. Add the almonds and zest. Process with several quick on-and-off motions so as not to destroy their texture.
5. Dust the work area with the remaining flour and lightly flour your hands. Divide the dough into thirds or fourths and form log shapes.
6. Place the logs on an oiled cookie sheet and bake until a tester inserted in the middle comes out clean, about 35–45 minutes.
7. Remove from the oven and let cool slightly. Cut the logs into ½-inch slices. You can cut each slice in half lengthwise for long narrow slices.
8. Return the slices to the cookie sheet, reduce the temperature to 300 degrees and bake until crisp, about 15–25 minutes more. Turn the oven off and leave the cookies in the oven with the door ajar for another 15 minutes.

FAST: Can prepare up to 14 days in advance and store in airtight jars or in plastic bags, or freeze for up to 6 months. Thaw in the refrigerator for 2 days or at room temperature for a few hours.

FLASHY: Serve on a platter with strawberries and garnish with sprigs of fresh mint.

FABULOUS: With half of each cookie dipped in melted milk chocolate or semisweet chocolate after baking.

Spring Lunch al Fresco

*C*old salmon, perfectly cooked, looks and tastes like spring. Small red potatoes, asparagus, and artichokes are more symbols of the season and make their presence felt at this party. We start off on a rich note: Camembert with Roasted Red Peppers, Spinach & Calamata Pesto. This wonderful hors d'oeuvre, along with some bread and wine, could be a lunch in itself. The salmon is simple and straightforward. It makes a marvelous dish for large or small groups. Once you taste the Spring Potato Salad you will be hard pressed to ever resort to the ho-hum pickle relish variety. This version combines cucumbers, marinated artichoke hearts, and asparagus with baby red potatoes bathed in an herbal Tarragon Cream Dressing. For a sinful conclusion, a Chocolate Espresso Loaf with Raspberries à la Mode. Need I say more?

For this party, I dressed the table in pastel plaid placemats with solid pink napkins that picked up several of the colors in the placemats. Any light-colored solid or patterned sheet would work as a tablecloth. Pick a complementary solid color for the napkins. A few square, Mexican, glass, votive candleholders were filled with casual bouquets of purple stock and pink cosmos mixed with fern leaves. The look was just as fresh and vibrant as the menu.

Menu

Camembert with Roasted Red Peppers, Spinach & Calamata Pesto
Cold Salmon & Baby Greens with a Caper Vinaigrette
Spring Potato Salad
Chocolate Espresso Loaf with Raspberries à la Mode

Faster & Flashier Menu

Camembert with French Bread
Cold Salmon & Baby Greens with a Caper Vinaigrette
New Potato Salad (purchased and mixed with artichoke hearts)
Dessert (purchased)

Sauvignon Blanc and/or Sparkling Wine
Coffee

TIMETABLE

Up to 7 days in advance	Tarragon Cream Dressing
Up to 5 days in advance	Dill Caper Vinaigrette
Up to 3 days in advance	Camembert with Roasted Red Peppers, Spinach & Calamata Pesto. Chocolate Espresso Loaf. Spring Potato Salad.
Up to 1 day in advance	Prepare the salmon. Set the table. Chill the wines.
Party day!	Prepare for fun!

Camembert with Roasted Red Peppers, Spinach & Calamata Pesto

A wonderful hors d'oeuvre that could easily be a lunch by itself.   **Yield: 8+ servings**

12 ounces roasted red peppers*
½ cup pitted calamata olives
3 bunches prewashed spinach
2 to 4 cloves garlic
 Fresh lime juice

½ cup extra virgin olive oil
 Salt and freshly ground, coarse black
  pepper, to taste
1 16-ounce wheel or wedge of
  Camembert, at room temperature

1. Combine all the ingredients except for the Camembert in a food processor fitted with the metal blade until the ingredients are chopped finely, using several quick on-and-off motions.
2. Place the Camembert on a platter, and top it with the pesto.

FAST: Can prepare up to 3 days in advance and refrigerate, or freeze for up to 3 months.

FLASHY: Serve at room temperature with thinly sliced baguettes and/or crostini (page 66).

FABULOUS: With 3 10-ounce packages frozen thawed spinach instead of fresh. With ½ cup roasted peanuts.

*Refer to Terms & Techniques.

Salmon & Baby Greens with a Dill Caper Vinaigrette

Light and herbal.   **Yield: 8 servings**

8 salmon filets
 Dill Caper Vinaigrette (recipe follows)
8 cups of baby greens, or more
 Fresh lemon juice, to taste
 Salt and white pepper, to taste

2 avocados, thinly sliced and squirted
  with lemon juice to prevent
  discoloring
24 strawberries, sliced

1. Place the salmon in a glass or ceramic baking dish and pour some of the vinaigrette over them. Let marinate at room temperature for up to 1 hour or in the refrigerator for up to 24 hours.
2. Bake in a preheated 350 degree oven for about 10 minutes, or microwave until cooked to your liking, about 4 minutes. (Plan on baking 10 minutes per inch of thickness.)
3. Toss the greens with the desired amount of vinaigrette, avocados, and strawberries.
4. Put about 1 cup of the salad on each plate and top each with a salmon filet. (The salmon can be hot or cold.) Serve with extra vinaigrette.

FAST: Can prepare the salmon up to 1 day in advance and refrigerate. Assemble before serving.

FABULOUS: With slices of mango, blanched asparagus spears, and/or toasted sesame seeds or nuts added.

Dill Caper Vinaigrette

Yield: About 1½ cups

1 cup extra virgin olive oil
⅓ cup red or white wine vinegar
1 to 2 cloves garlic, peeled
1 teaspoon Dijon mustard, or more

1 teaspoon salt
   White and black pepper, to taste
¼ to ½ cup capers, rinsed and drained
¼ to ½ cup minced fresh dill

1. Combine all ingredients in a food processor fitted with the metal blade or in blender.

FAST: Can prepare up to 5 days in advance and refrigerate.

FABULOUS: On potato, pasta, white bean, or seafood salads. To marinate or sauce vegetables, fish, seafood, poultry, and/or lamb.

Spring Potato Salad

This makes all other potato salads look uninspired.   **Yield: 8+ servings**

3 pounds small red potatoes, halved or
    quartered
1 cup thinly sliced, peeled cucumbers
1 cup asparagus tips, cut into 1-inch
    lengths and blanched
1 cup marinated artichoke hearts,
    drained

¼ to ½ cup green onions, minced
¼ to ½ cup Italian parsley, minced
    Tarragon Cream Dressing (recipe
    follows)
Salt and white pepper, to taste

1. Place the potatoes in a pot of salted cold water and bring to a boil. Reduce the heat and cook slowly until they are just tender. Remove the potatoes and place in a bowl.
2. Toss the potatoes with all of the ingredients and the desired amount of dressing.

FAST: Can prepare up to 3 days in advance and refrigerate.

FLASHY: Garnished with sprigs of fresh parsley and/or tarragon, a sprinkling of minced green onions, and/or any nontoxic flower.

FABULOUS: With hearts of palm instead of artichoke hearts; with sweet red onions instead of green onions; and with celery root, fennel, and/or celery.

Tarragon Cream Dressing   Yield: About 2½ cups

1 cup mayonnaise (homemade or
    purchased) or low-fat or fat-free
    mayonnaise
½ cup sour cream or fat-free sour cream
½ cup buttermilk or low-fat or fat-free
    buttermilk

Fresh lemon juice, to taste
2 shallots, minced
2 teaspoons dried tarragon or 1½
    tablespoons fresh
Salt and freshly ground, coarse black
    pepper, to taste

1. Combine all of the ingredients in a food processor fitted with the metal blade, in a blender, or mix by hand. Taste and adjust the seasonings.

FAST: Can prepare up to 7 days in advance and refrigerate.

FABULOUS: Seasoned with green peppercorns and fresh dill. Serve on anything from simple mixed greens to cooked vegetables to fish.

Chocolate Espresso Loaf with Raspberries à la Mode

Absolutely indulgent and very simple!   **Yield: 8+ servings**

4 ounces unsalted butter, or 4 ounces
    cream cheese, or low-fat or fat-free
    cream cheese
2 to 4 tablespoons brown sugar
2 to 4 tablespoons instant espresso
2 extra large eggs, or egg substitute
2 tablespoons vanilla extract
1 cup orange marmalade
⅓ cup sour cream or low-fat or fat-free
    sour cream
⅔ cup buttermilk or low-fat or fat-free
    buttermilk

1 teaspoon baking powder
1 cup oatmeal
1 cup all-purpose flour
8 to 10 ounces milk chocolate or
    bittersweet chocolate, broken into
    small pieces
  Vanilla ice cream or frozen yogurt
2 pints of raspberries
1 to 1½ cups toasted walnut pieces

1. Preheat the oven to 350 degrees and oil a 9-by-5-inch loaf pan.
2. Combine the butter or cream cheese, eggs, sugar, espresso, and vanilla in the food processor fitted with the metal blade.
3. Process in the marmalade, sour cream, and buttermilk.
4. Add the remaining ingredients, except for the walnuts, and process thoroughly. Stir in the walnuts.
5. Transfer to the prepared loaf pan and bake for about 1 hour, until a tester inserted into the middle comes out clean. Allow it to cool for about 10 minutes before inverting onto a plate.

FAST: Can prepare up to 3 days in advance and refrigerate or freeze for up to 3 months. Assemble right before serving.

FLASHY: Top each slice of cake with a scoop of ice cream and some raspberries.

Spring Picnic

This is the quintessential cosmopolitan picnic that can serve you well whether it's on the patio, on a tailgate, on the beach, or in a meadow full of wildflowers . . . with you by the proverbial brook. Hopefully, I have made my point. If you are caught by bad weather and want to raise spirits and encourage spring, you can even create this picnic on your living room cocktail table or in your dining room.

Picnics and pâtés are great team players. Unfortunately many of us suffer from pâté phobia. It is helpful to think of pâtés as just gussied-up meat loaves. Very often they are loaded with fat, which by the way makes them divine but deadly. This picnic is centered around a low-fat pâté that is as simple as . . . Have food processor, will cook. Poached Turkey & Scallop Sausage is actually called a sausage because of its shape, but it is a pâté. I know it sounds like culinary double talk, but let me assure you, it's delicious. When you experience it on a crostini topped with a dollop of Raspberry Mayonnaise, it's beyond words.

The other items on the menu are just as exciting. Besides which, all of the dishes can also be served as hors d'oeuvres. If you have not experienced bulgar or celery root, you are in for a treat. As for the cookies, try them; you'll love 'em.

No matter where you stage this picnic, a classic checkered cloth and napkins in any color are perfect. Add a white pitcher filled with daisies and that is it! To gild the lily, how about a plate with a wedge of Brie, maybe some Gorgonzola, and grapes? This menu works no matter where you are when you want an upscale, light-hearted picnic.

Menu

Mediterranean Stuffed Lettuce Leaves
Celery Root Pâté
Pickled Mushrooms
Garlic Crostini
Poached Turkey & Scallop Sausage with Raspberry Mayonnaise
Orange Chocolate Chip Nuggets

Faster & Flashier Menu

Mediterranean Stuffed Lettuce Leaves
(purchase tabouli at a deli and serve it in lettuce leaves)
Pâté with Assorted Mustards (purchased)
Cookies (purchased)

Sauvignon Blanc and/or Sparkling Wine

✄ TIMETABLE ✄

Up to 3 months in advance and freeze	Garlic Crostini
Up to 2 weeks in advance	Pickled Mushrooms
Up to 1 week in advance	Orange Chocolate Chip Cookies
Up to 4 days in advance	Celery Root Pâté. Raspberry Mayonnaise.
Up to 3 days in advance	Mediterranean Stuffed Lettuce Leaves
Up to 2 days in advance	Poached Turkey Scallop Sausage
Up to 1 day in advance	Chill the wines
Party day!	Enjoy!

Mediterranean Stuffed Lettuce Leaves

Full of fabulous flavors and interesting textures!   ***Yield: 8 servings***

1 cup bulgar (cracked wheat) soaked in 2 cups of water until tender and drained in a colander
⅓ cup extra virgin olive oil, or more
Fresh lemon juice, to taste
½ cup minced Italian parsley
½ cup minced green onions, or more
1 cup crumbled feta cheese
½ cup pitted, minced calamata olives
1 cup chopped, toasted walnuts
3 roasted red peppers, skinned, seeded, and chopped
Salt, freshly ground, coarse black pepper, and dried oregano, to taste
2 heads of butter lettuce, leaves separated and washed

1. Combine all the ingredients except for the lettuce in a large mixing bowl. Taste and adjust the seasonings.

FAST: Can prepare up to 3 days in advance and refrigerate.

FLASHY: To serve, place the bulgar salad in the middle of a large platter and surround with the lettuce leaves.

FABULOUS: With marinated artichoke hearts, pepperoncini, and/or shredded chicken added.

Celery Root Pâté

We are stretching the limits of a pâté with this recipe, but even my daughter loves it! You know how awful the word "spread" sounds.

Yield: About 2 cups, or 8 or more servings

½ cup mayonnaise, (homemade or purchased) or low-fat or fat-free mayonnaise

4 ounces chèvre cheese, cut into pieces

1 tablespoon coarse-grained or Dijon mustard, or more

3 to 6 green onions (scallions), white and green parts, minced

¼ cup sesame seeds, toasted (page 13) or to taste

Fresh lemon juice and/or apple cider vinegar, to taste

Salt and ground white pepper, to taste

1 medium-size celery root, peeled and finely grated

1. Combine all the ingredients, except the celery root, in a food processor fitted with the metal blade and process until smooth.
2. Add the celery root and process with several quick on-and-off motions so as not to destroy the texture.
3. Chill for at least 30 minutes. Pack into a terrine, soufflé dish, or serving bowl.

FAST: Can prepare up to 4 days in advance and refrigerate.

FLASHY: With pumpernickel squares, Pita Chips (page 112), or as a filling for Croustades (page 107) or raw mushroom caps. Garnished with toasted sesame seeds, parsley, and/or any nontoxic flower.

FABULOUS: With ¼ cup fresh dill or 1–2 tablespoons fresh tarragon and/or 1 cup fresh crabmeat.

Pickled Mushrooms

Great for picnics, barbecues, and hors d'oeuvres.

Yield: About 3 cups

1 cup white wine vinegar
½ cup chicken broth, homemade or
    canned
½ to 1 cup olive oil
2 to 4 cloves garlic, whole or minced
1 carrot, thinly sliced
4 to 8 green onions, cut into 1-inch
    pieces

¼ cup minced fresh parsley
    Dried marjoram, rosemary, and
        oregano, to taste
5 black peppercorns
½ bay leaf
1½ teaspoons salt, or to taste
1 pound small to medium-size
    mushrooms, stemmed

1. Combine all the ingredients, except the mushrooms, in a large saucepan and bring to a boil over high heat. Reduce the heat to medium-low and simmer for 5 mintues.
2. Add the mushrooms and simmer for 5–10 minutes. Taste and adjust the seasonings.
3. Cool. Transfer to a glass jar and refrigerate, covered, for several days to allow the mushrooms to absorb the flavors.

FAST: Can prepare up to 2 weeks in advance and refrigerate.

FLASHY: Serve with toothpicks and a sliced baguette.

FABULOUS: With about a pound of celery, fennel, artichoke hearts, carrots, green beans, zucchini, or peppers cut into bite-size pieces instead of the mushrooms.

Garlic Crostini

Yield: About 8 to 12 servings

2 sourdough or French baguettes,
    thinly sliced
1½ cups extra virgin olive oil
3 to 6 cloves garlic, minced, or to
    taste

¼ cup minced fresh Italian parsley
¼ to ½ cup apple cider or balsamic
    vinegar
Salt, to taste

1. Combine all the ingredients, except for the baguettes, in a food processor fitted with the metal blade or in a blender.
2. Place the baguette slices on a cookie sheet, brush with the olive oil mixture, and toast in a preheated 350 degree oven until crisp, about 15 minutes.

FAST: Can prepare the oil mixture up to 2 weeks in advance and refrigerate, or freeze for up to 3 months.

FLASHY: Serve at room temperature or warm in a napkin-lined basket or on a platter, garnished with green onion flowers (page 9), fresh oregano, and/or any nontoxic flower.

FABULOUS: With any herb. Experiment and have fun! All sorts of grated cheeses used as toppings, including feta, Parmesan, Gruyère, or bleu.

Raspberry Mayonnaise

Exquisite!   **Yield: About 1 cup**

⅔ cup walnut oil or peanut oil
 1 large egg yolk
 ½ teaspoon salt

White pepper to taste
2 tablespoons raspberry vinegar
2 teaspoons minced shallots

1. In a food processor fitted with the steel blade, add the yolks, salt, white pepper, vinegar, and shallots. Process until lemon-colored.
2. Very slowly add the oil.
3. Taste and adjust flavors and chill.

FAST: Can prepare up to 5 days in advance and refrigerate.

FLASHY: Serve cold or at room temperature.

FABULOUS: With the whipped egg whites folded into the mayonnaise to create a very light sauce. Seasoned with fresh dill, tarragon, and/or roasted garlic.

Poached Turkey Scallop Sausage with Raspberry Mayonnaise

A light pâté that happens to be low-fat.

Yield: 8 to 12 servings

Broth:
 4 green onions
 1 onion, sliced
 1 carrot, sliced
10 sprigs parsley
 1 cup dry white wine
 3 cups chicken stock
20 green peppercorns
 ½ teaspoon salt

 1 medium-size red potato
 ½ pound turkey breast

 ½ pound scallops
 1 tablespoon minced shallots
 ½ cup freshly grated Parmesan cheese
 2 to 4 tablespoons fresh minced dill
    Grated nutmeg, to taste
 1 egg plus 1 egg white
    Grated zest of 1 lemon
 ½ to 1 teaspoon salt and white pepper,
    to taste
 2 tablespoons dry sherry
    Cheesecloth

1. Bring all the ingredients for the broth to a boil and allow it to simmer for about 30 minutes.
2. Cook the potato in the simmering broth until tender. Remove the potato, peel it, and mash it. Reserve the broth.
3. In a food processor fitted with the steel blade, grind the turkey and scallops.
4. Add all the remaining ingredients, including the potato, except the cheese-cloth, and process briefly, just until combined.
5. Moisten cheesecloth and lay it out flat on work counter. Place mixture on cloth in a salami-like roll, about 2½ inches in diameter.
6. Wrap cheesecloth around roll and tie the ends with string.
7. Place the roll in the stock and bring it to a boil. Reduce heat to low and simmer covered for 30–45 minutes.
8. Remove from broth and unwrap when it is cool enough to handle. Chill.

FAST: Can prepare up to 2 days in advance and refrigerate.

FLASHY: Serve it on a bed of shredded spinach. Top the log with some of the mayonnaise and serve the rest on the side. Garnish the log with halved olives or fresh dill. The log should be sliced into ⅜-inch slices. Serve chilled on Garlic Crostini and topped with a dollop of Raspberry Mayonnaise.

FABULOUS: Seasoned with dried tarragon.

Orange Chocolate Chip Nuggets

The ultimate luxurious cookie!   **Yield: About 48 cookies**

 2 sticks unsalted butter, cut up
¼ cup confectioner's sugar
½ cup packed brown sugar
½ teaspoon salt
 2 teaspoons vanilla extract
 2 tablespoons orange-flavored liqueur

 2 jumbo eggs or egg substitute
 Zest of 3 lemons, finely grated
12 ounces semisweet chocolate chips
 2 cups all-purpose flour
 1 cup quick-cooking oatmeal
 2 cups toasted macadamia nuts

1. Combine the butter, sugars, salt, vanilla, liqueur, and sugar in a food processor fitted with the metal blade until well creamed.
2. Add the flour and process until thoroughly combined.
3. Add lemon zest, chocolate chips, and walnuts. Transfer to a floured work surface and mix all the ingredients in by hand as if kneading bread.
4. Using a tablespoon, form the dough into balls and place on ungreased cookie sheets. Press the balls down with the palm of your hand to flatten slightly.
5. Bake in a preheated 400 degree oven for 15–20 minutes until they are pale golden.

FAST: Can prepare up to 1 week in advance and store in an air-tight container or in plastic bags, or freeze for up to 3 months.

FABULOUS: With pecans, walnuts, or almonds instead of macadamia nuts. Try dipping them in chocolate.

Spring Linguini Dinner

Shrimp, scallops, strawberries, and asparagus are the perfect foods for welcoming spring. This party uses all of these elements with simplicity and great style. It is a light menu with a strong focus on vegetables that can easily be transformed into a vegetarian meal. The Italian Spinach Salsa is an excellent example of the glorification of vegetables. The salad furthers this theme and is equally noteworthy. I ask you, have you ever experienced an escarole salad, which has a bit of refreshing bitterness, with sweet strawberries and asparagus? I'm convinced this dish was definitely sent to me by divine inspiration. As for the party's star, picture this: a medley of pasta tossed with a generous amount of basil, pistachios, baby corn, sun-dried tomatoes, shrimp, and scallops enlivened with tangy feta and Romano cheeses. If it's a vegetarian party you are looking for, just omit the seafood. For the finale, there is yet another simple seasonal indulgence. It is a parfait with a divine chocolate sauce and raspberries.

The look for this party should be fresh and crisp. A peach-colored, striped sheet or tablecloth with peach-colored, checked napkins set the scene. Potted azaleas or geraniums can be used instead of a more formal centerpiece. Add lots of white candles and you are ready for a fabulous spring evening. For a touch of whimsy, I use bunches of asparagus wrapped with rafia scattered down the center of the table.

Menu

Italian Spinach Salsa with Garlic Crostini
Escarole Salad with Strawberries & Asparagus
Seafood Linguini with Sun-Dried Tomatoes, Pistachios & Basil
Aphrodite's Parfait

Faster & Flashier Menu

Italian Spinach Salsa
(prepared with frozen spinach) with Sliced Baguettes

Salad with Strawberries & Asparagus
(prepared with prewashed lettuce)

Seafood Linguini with Sun-Dried Tomatoes, Pistachios & Basil

Aphrodite's Parfait (with prepared chocolate sauce)

Sauvignon Blanc and/or Sparkling Wine

TIMETABLE

Up to 3 months in advance and frozen	Garlic Crostini. Brandied Chocolate Sauce.
Up to 5 days in advance	Salad Dressing
Up to 2 days in advance	Italian Spinach Salsa. Sauce for linguini.
Up to 1 day in advance	Whip the cream. Set the table. Chill the wines.
Party day!	Assemble the salad. Assemble the parfait. Finish the linguini.

Italian Spinach Salsa

Fresh choice.

Yield: About 3 cups

2 to 3 bunches fresh, prewashed
   spinach, or 2 8-ounce packages
   frozen spinach, thawed and
   drained
1 cup extra virgin olive oil
¼ cup pine nuts, toasted

½ to 1 shallot
½ teaspoon dried, mixed Italian herbs
   or fresh basil, to taste
Fresh basil and/or any nontoxic
   flower for garnishing

1. Combine all the ingredients in a food processor fitted with the metal blade or in a blender. Taste and adjust the seasonings.
2. Chill for at least 30 minutes before serving.

FAST: Can prepare up to 2 days in advance and refrigerate.

FLASHY: As a dunk for vegetables, Bagel Chips, or Pita Chips. Garnish with fresh basil and/or any nontoxic flower.

FABULOUS: As an entrée sauce for fish, seafood, chicken, or pasta. Seasoned with fresh or dried rosemary, capers, pitted and chopped calamata olives, and/or lemon juice.

Escarole Salad with Strawberries & Asparagus

What a salad! It is a true experience.

Yield: 8 servings

½ cup walnut oil
½ cup olive or peanut oil
⅓ cup sherry wine vinegar
 1 teaspoon Dijon mustard, or more
½ to 1 shallot, minced
½ to 1 teaspoon salt
½ cup toasted walnuts, chopped, or
   more

⅓ to ⅔ cup pitted calamata olives,
   minced
 1 large head of escarole
   Freshly ground, coarse black pepper,
   to taste
 1 pint strawberries, hulled
½ pound blanched asparagus tips, cut
   into 1-inch lengths

1. Combine oils, vinegar, mustard, shallots, and salt in a food processor fitted with the metal blade.
2. Process in the nuts and olives with two quick on-and-off motions, using care not to destroy the texture. Taste and adjust the seasonings.
3. Tear escarole into bite-size pieces and toss with the desired amount of dressing, strawberries, and asparagus.

FAST: Can prepare the dressing up to 5 days in advance and refrigerate. Can assemble salad 6 hours in advance and refrigerate. Toss before serving.

FABULOUS: With chopped nuts tossed into the salad. With chèvre, Parmesan, or Gorgonzola cheese instead of the olives.

Seafood Linguini with Sun-Dried Tomatoes, Pistachios & Basil

Yield: 8+ servings

4 tablespoons plus 1 cup extra virgin olive oil
3 shallots, minced
6 cloves garlic, minced, or more
2 cups minced basil, stemmed, or more
½ to 1 cup minced Italian parsley
2 cups sun-dried tomatoes, softened and cut into strips
1 to 2 pounds shrimp, shelled and deveined

1 to 2 pounds scallops
1 8-ounce can of baby corn, cut up
1 cup toasted pistachios, or more
Feta cheese, crumbled, to taste
Freshly grated Romano cheese, to taste
Fresh lemon juice, salt, and freshly ground, coarse black pepper, to taste
2 pounds linguini

1. Combine 1 cup of the olive oil with the shallots, garlic, basil, parsley, sun-dried tomatoes, and pistachios in a food processor fitted with a metal blade.
2. Heat the 4 tablespoons of olive oil in a large skillet or wok and quickly sauté the seafood. (I use two woks or do it in two batches rather than overcrowding the pan.) When the seafood turns opaque, it's done.
3. Meanwhile, cook linguini until al dente, drain and toss it in a large bowl with the seafood and basil mixture. Add the cheeses, taste and adjust the seasonings, and enjoy.

FAST: Can prepare Step 1 up to 4 days in advance and refrigerate, or freeze for up to 6 months.

FLASHY: Serve hot or cold.

FABULOUS: With Parmesan instead of feta and Romano cheeses. Without the shrimp and/or scallops.

Aphrodite's Parfait

As soon as you taste this, you'll understand why I dedicated it to the goddess of love.

French vanilla ice cream or fat-free vanilla frozen yogurt
Brandied Chocolate Sauce (recipe follows)

Walnuts, toasted
Orange-flavored liqueur, to taste
2 pints of fresh raspberries
Whipped cream

1. Combine raspberries with liqueur in glass bowl. Let them macerate for about 1 hour at room temperature, or up to 1 day refrigerated, and spoon into goblets.
2. Next add desired amount of ice cream.
3. Top with Brandied Chocolate Sauce, walnuts, and whipped cream.

FAST: Can prepare whipped cream up to 1 day in advance and refrigerate. Assemble right before serving.

FLASHY: Serve with Lemon Sesame Shortbread (page 281) or purchased butter cookies.

FABULOUS: With any kind of berries instead of raspberries. With chunks of brownies, cookies, or cake layered in.

Brandied Chocolate Sauce

This makes a great Christmas gift and is pure heaven!   **Yield: About 3 cups**

2 cups heavy cream
⅔ cup sugar, or more, to taste
  Grated zest of 2 oranges
⅓ cup brandy
16 ounces semisweet chocolate chips or
  bittersweet chocolate, broken up

2 teaspoons vanilla extract
2 tablespoons orange-flavored liqueur
  Grated nutmeg, to taste

1. Combine first 3 ingredients in a saucepan and bring to a boil. Cook until sugar dissolves.
2. Meanwhile, chop chocolate in a food processor fitted with the metal blade.
3. Add cream mixture through feed tube while machine is running.
4. Process in vanilla, orange-flavored liqueur, and nutmeg.

FAST: Can prepare up to 2 weeks in advance and refrigerate, or freeze for up to 1 year.

FLASHY: On ice cream, pound cake, brownies, strawberries, and so on.

FABULOUS: Substitute any kind of liqueur for the brandy.

Herbed Rack of Lamb Dinner

This dinner party ushers in the season with great style. For the opening act, a sublime Smoked Salmon Sauce makes a perfect dipping sauce for crisp raw vegetables. Following this comes an elegant and refreshing Cream of Celery Soup. Roast Herbed Rack of Lamb is this party's star attraction. It is encased with an herb-studded mustard crust and sauced with a Raspberry Beurre Blanc. A beurre blanc sauce is one of those sinful things we order out and are usually frightened of preparing at home. It's simple! This dish is a show stopper. Beautifully sautéed asparagus enlivened with lemon, garlic, sesame seeds, and a touch of anchovy paste complement the rack and provide a unique alternative to plain boiled asparagus. Pilaf is another natural match for lamb, but too often it is treated with a ho-hum attitude. I guarantee that my pilaf has a personality of its own and will stand up nicely to the starring rack of lamb.

After this menu, there is no room left for a heavy finale, but a decadent ending is a must! A Chilled Champagne Mousse with Strawberries will do well.

The table for this party must be as special as the menu. The background of a purple, pink, or peach tablecloth sets the scene. Purple iris in thin glass vases, purple candles, and purple napkins help to complete the look. Several cuttings of branches with blossoms can just be strewn down the table. This creates a dramatic table for a fabulous party.

Menu

Smoked Salmon Sauce with Pea Pods,
Jicama Spears & Broccoli Flowerets
Cream of Celery Soup
Herbed Rack of Lamb with Raspberry Beurre Blanc Sauce
Shiitake Mushroom Pilaf
Sesame Asparagus Sauté
Chilled Champagne Mousse with Strawberries

Faster & Flashier Menu

Smoked Salmon Sauce with Pea Pods,
Jicama Spears & Broccoli Flowerets
Herbed Rack of Lamb
Rice with Lemon
Blanched Asparagus with Dilled Mayonnaise
Dessert (purchased)

Sparkling Wine and/or Chardonnay
Sauvignon Blanc and Pinot Noir or Zinfandel
Sparkling Wine and/or Coffee

❦ TIMETABLE ❦

Up to 4 days in advance	Cream of Celery Soup
Up to 3 days in advance	Smoked Salmon Sauce. Start Raspberry Beurre Blanc.
Up to 2 days in advance	Champagne Mousse. Set the table.
Up to 1 day in advance	Prepare rack of lamb through Step 3. Blanch asparagus. Chill the wines.
Party day!	Finish sauce, rack of lamb, asparagus. Shiitake Mushroom Pilaf.

Smoked Salmon Sauce

A delightful indulgence. **Yield: About 1½ cups**

6 to 8 ounces smoked salmon, minced,
  or more
¾ cup sour cream or low-fat or fat-free
  sour cream
2 tablespoon capers, drained

1 tablespoon shallots, minced
Grated zest of 1 lemon
White pepper and fresh lemon juice,
  to taste
Fresh dillweed, minced, to taste

1. Combine all of the above ingredients in a mixing bowl or in a food processor fitted with the metal blade. Taste and adjust the seasonings.
2. Chill and serve with jicama spears, broccoli flowerets, and pea pods.

FAST: Can prepare up to 3 days in advance and refrigerate.

FLASHY: Serve in a bowl on a platter surrounded with pea pods, jicama spears, and broccoli flowerettes. Garnish with fresh dill and/or any nontoxic flower.

FABULOUS: As a dressing on pasta, rice, potatoes, or spinach salads. It also makes a lovely sauce for hot or cold artichokes, asparagus, broccoli, or grilled fish. With finely chopped cucumber mixed in.

Cream of Celery Soup

Delicious any time of the year. Trust me, it's better than the canned version.

3 cups celery, stringed and minced
   Celery leaves, minced
2 cloves garlic, minced
2 to 4 tablespoons unsalted butter
4 tablespoons flour (optional)
1 onion, chopped
5 cups chicken broth, homemade or
   canned

1 cup heavy cream or low-fat or fat-
   free sour cream
1 bay leaf
¼ to ½ cup Madeira
½ to 1 teaspoon celery seeds
   Salt, white pepper, freshly grated
   nutmeg, and thyme, to taste

1. Melt the butter in a large saucepan and sauté onion until soft, not brown.
2. Add the celery, celery leaves, and garlic. Sauté covered until tender.
3. Stir in the flour and cook for 1 minute. Add the broth, cream, and seasonings, and simmer for about 15 minutes until the flavors have developed. Purée this mixture in a food processor fitted with the metal blade, in a blender, or using a blender on a stick. If using sour cream, just mix it in at the end. Cook over low heat; never boil or it will curdle.
4. Reheat the soup and add the wine. Taste and adjust the seasonings.

FAST: Can prepare up to 4 days in advance and refrigerate, or freeze for up to 6 months.

FLASHY: Garnish with a lemon slice, minced green onion, or chopped almonds that have been sautéed with garlic and parsley.

FABULOUS: With any vegetable instead of celery, or with any herbs. Enriched with 2 tablespoons of cold butter swirled in before serving.

Roast Herbed Rack of Lamb

Luscious!   ***Yield: 8 servings***

2 to 3 8-rib racks of lamb
   Garlic, peeled and cut into slivers (as
     much as you like!)
   Dijon-style mustard, to coat the lamb
4 slices sourdough bread (made into
     crumbs in a food processor fitted
     with the metal blade)
½ to 1 teaspoon dried thyme, crumbled

2 to 4 tablespoons minced parsley
   Grated, minced zest of 2 lemons
4 tablespoons fresh minced rosemary
4 tablespoons fresh minced mint
   Salt and freshly ground, coarse black
     pepper, to taste
   Raspberry Beurre Blanc (recipe
     follows)

1. Preheat oven to 400 degrees. Combine the bread crumbs with the thyme, parsley, lemon zest, rosemary, and mint.
2. Trim fat layer on lamb to ¼ inch. Using a sharp paring knife, insert garlic slivers into the lamb.
3. Combine the breadcrumbs, thyme, parsley, lemon zest, rosemary, and mint in a mixing bowl.
4. In a skillet, place lamb fat side down. Brown lamb well (about 10 minutes). Cool slightly.
5. Spread mustard over the fat side of the lamb, and pat the breadcrumb mixture on top of the mustard. Sprinkle with salt and pepper.
6. Roast, coating side up, for 15–20 minutes for rare in a 400 degree oven (25–30 minutes for medium). Allow lamb to rest for 5–10 minutes before carving. Serve with Raspberry Beurre Blanc.

FAST: Can prepare through Step 3 up to 1 day in advance and refrigerate. Before roasting, allow lamb to come to room temperature.

FLASHY: Serve on a platter. Garnish with fresh rosemary sprigs.

FABULOUS: Have fun with the herbs and create your own combinations.

Raspberry Beurre Blanc

A perfect sauce for a splurge! This is the simple
food-processor version.

Yield: About 1¼ cups

2 parsley sprigs
1 clove garlic
4 medium shallots
4 tablespoons raspberry vinegar, or to
   taste

1 cup dry white wine
   Salt and white pepper, to taste
1 cup hot, melted, unsalted butter

1. Mince the garlic, shallots, and parsley in a food processor fitted with the metal blade. Transfer this to a small (nonaluminum) saucepan. Add the wine and simmer uncovered until it reduces to ¼ cup.
2. Strain the mixture and add raspberry vinegar, salt, and white pepper.
3. Place the strained mixture in a food processor fitted with the metal blade. While the machine is running, slowly add the hot melted butter. Process 10 seconds after all the butter has been added. Add more salt, white pepper, and more raspberry vinegar if needed.

FAST: Can prepare through Step 2 up to 3 days in advance and refrigerate. Can fully prepare and keep warm over hot water or in a thermos for up to 4 hours.

Sesame Asparagus Sauté

Yield: 8 servings

2 pounds thin asparagus, cut into
  2-inch pieces (if only the thick
  ones are available, cut into thin,
  matchstick slices)
¼ cup unsalted butter
3 tablespoons olive oil
2 to 4 cloves garlic, minced

6 tablespoons minced parsley
4 tablespoons toasted sesame seeds,
  or more
½ to 1 teaspoon anchovy paste
  Juice of 1 lemon, or to taste
  Salt and white pepper, to taste

1. Melt butter with the olive oil over medium heat in a large skillet. Add
   garlic and asparagus, and sauté until just tender.
2. Add seasonings and serve.

FAST: For added convenience, blanch asparagus up to 1 day in advance and
refrigerate. Bring to room temperature and sauté briefly before serving.

Shiitake Mushroom Pilaf

Uptown rice.

Yield: 8 servings

2 to 4 tablespoons unsalted butter or
  olive oil
1 shallot, minced
1¾ cups raw, long-grain rice (can use
  basmati rice)
¼ cup bulgar
16 shiitake mushrooms (or more),
  rehydrated, stemmed, and thinly
  sliced

3 cups chicken broth, homemade or
  canned
1 cup dry white wine
1 bay leaf
  Salt and white pepper, to taste

1. Melt butter in a saucepan and sauté the shallots until soft.
2. Add the rice and bulgar and sauté until the rice becomes opaque.
3. Add the mushrooms, broth, wine, and seasoning. Bring to a boil.
4. Reduce heat to low, cover with a lid, and simmer for 20 minutes.

FAST: Can prepare through Step 3 up to 6 hours in advance and leave at room
temperature. Simmer before you are ready to serve.

FLASHY: Garnish with minced parsley or green onion.

Chilled Champagne Mousse

Light and luscious.   **Yield: 8 servings**

1 cup sparkling wine, dry or sec
8 large eggs, separated (at room
    temperature), or egg substitute and
    8 large egg whites
1 to 1½ cups sugar

Pinch salt
1 cup heavy cream, beaten until it holds
    stiff peaks or low-fat or fat-free
    sour cream
Fresh strawberries, at least 16

1. Place the yolks or egg substitute, sugar, and salt in a food processor fitted with the metal blade, and combine until they are a pale yellow color.
2. Transfer the yolk mixture to the top of a double boiler and, while whisking, add 1 tablespoon of the champagne at a time. Continue whisking 3–5 minutes until the mixture triples in volume and holds soft peaks. (You may wish to use an electric mixer.)
3. Place the mixture in a bowl and set it in the freezer to chill. Stir from time to time.
4. Meanwhile, beat the whites until they hold stiff peaks.
5. Fold in the cream, or mix in the sour cream and then the whites into the chilled mixture.
6. Spoon the mousse into parfait or stemmed glasses with the strawberries. Chill for at least 1 hour or until set.

FAST: Can prepare up to 2 days in advance and refrigerate, or freeze for up to 1 month.

FLASHY: To gild the lily, garnish with shaved chocolate.

FABULOUS: Delicious with almost any fresh fruit, especially berries.

Summer

A Summer Brunch al Fresco

As far as I'm concerned, basil is the scent of summer. This brunch begins by paying homage to this delightful herb. The hors d'oeuvre is Italian Basil Salsa, a simple mixture of luscious seasonal ingredients along with some good olive oil and garlic. It is served with crisp crostini. This salsa is not just a delicious starter but also a great cold sauce, whether you use it on fish or on pasta. I have a hunch that it will probably become a staple in your kitchen.

The Salami & Egg Salad with Grilled Polenta, Vegetables & Mango is a unique idea for a one-dish brunch entrée. All the components of the dish can be prepared days in advance. Besides which, it incorporates grilled items that provide a real summer feel. Needless to say, this entrée also can be served for lunch or dinner.

A cold Berry Soufflé with Lemon Shortbread provides a cool and refreshing finish.

This brunch was staged on my patio. I used a lavender plaid tablecloth with deep purple napkins. My centerpiece consisted of an earthenware paella pan brimming over with several varieties of eggplant, zucchini, and tomatoes. The table was surrounded by lovely potted plants on my patio.

Menu

Italian Basil Salsa with Garlic Basil Crostini

*Salami & Egg Salad with Grilled Polenta,
Vegetables & Mango*

French Bread with Olive Oil

Cold Berry Soufflé

Faster & Flashier Menu

Salsa (purchased) with Fresh Basil (added) and chips

Salami & Egg Salad with Roasted Red Peppers (bottled)

French Bread with Olive Oil

Dessert

*Dry White or Sparkling Wine
and/or Bloody Marys*

Coffee

✄   TIMETABLE   ✄

Up to 7 days in advance	Garlic Basil Crostini. Red Wine Vinaigrette.
Up to 5 days in advance	Italian Basil Salsa
Up to 3 days in advance	Grilled Polenta Triangles. Grilled Japanese Eggplant and Red Onions.
Up to 2 days in advance	Prepare all the salad components. Cold Berry Soufflé.
Up to 1 day in advance	Set the table. Chill the wine.
Party day!	Assemble the salad.

Italian Basil Salsa

The taste of summer.

Yield: About 2 cups

8 to 10 ripe, pear-shaped tomatoes,
   seeded and chopped
2 to 4 cloves garlic, minced
½ to 1 bunch fresh basil, stemmed and
   minced
¼ to ½ cup minced fresh Italian parsley

¼ cup extra virgin olive oil
   Juice of ½ to 1 lemon or lime
½ cup freshly grated Parmesan cheese,
   or more
   Salt and freshly ground black pepper,
   to taste

1. Combine all the ingredients in a food processor fitted with the metal blade
    and process, using several quick on-and-off motions so as not to destroy all
    the texture, or combine in a bowl. It should be chunky. Taste and adjust
    the seasonings.

FAST: Can prepare up to 5 days in advance and refrigerate, or freeze for up to
6 months.

FLASHY: As a dunk for French bread, or any melba/crostini. Garnish with fresh
basil leaves and /or any nontoxic flower.

FABULOUS: As an entrée sauce for fish, chicken, beef, pork, pasta, potatoes, or
vegetables. With capers, chopped marinated artichoke hearts, pickled peppers,
or minced anchovies to taste mixed in. With chopped cooked shrimp,
scallops, or crabmeat mixed in. To go tropical, add chopped mango or papaya.

Garlic Basil Crostini

Definitely addictive.   ***Yield: About 140 crostini***

2 sourdough or French baguettes,
    thinly sliced
1½ cups extra virgin olive oil
⅓ cup apple cider vinegar

2 to 6 cloves garlic, minced, or to taste
¼ cup minced fresh Italian parsley
¼ cup minced basil, or more
    Salt, to taste

1. Combinee all of the ingredients, except for the bread, in a food processor fitted with the metal blade, or in a blender.
2. Place the baguette slices on a cookie sheet and brush with the olive oil mixture. Toast in a preheated 350 degree oven until crisp, about 15 minutes.

FAST: Can prepare the olive oil mixture up to 14 days in advance and refrigerate. Can completely assemble up to 7 days in advance and store in plastic bags or jars, or freeze for up to 3 months.

FLASHY: Serve at room temperature or warm in a napkin-lined basket or on a platter, garnished with fresh oregano sprigs and/or any nontoxic flower.

FABULOUS: With any herb. Experiment and have fun! All sorts of grated cheeses used as toppings, including feta, Parmesan, Gruyère, or bleu cheese. Vegetables, fish, seafood, poultry, or meats can be sautéed in the olive oil mixture.

Salami & Egg Salad with Grilled Polenta, Vegetables & Mango

This is a marvelous summer salad that makes a wonderful entrée for brunches, lunches, and light dinners.

Yield: 8 servings

8 cups assorted baby salad greens
½ pound thinly sliced Italian salami, cut into thin strips
  Red Wine Vinaigrette (recipe follows)
8 large hard-boiled eggs, sliced
  Grilled Japanese Eggplant & Red Onions (recipe follows)
4 to 6 roasted red peppers*

1 to 2 mangos, peeled and cut into slices
8 to 16 Grilled Polenta Triangles (recipe follows)
½ cup toasted pine nuts, or more
  Salt and freshly ground, coarse black pepper, to taste

1. Toss the salad greens, salami, and hard-boiled eggs with the desired amount of vinaigrette and arrange on a large platter or on individual plates.
2. Surround with the Polenta Triangles and top with the grilled vegetables. Scatter the pine nuts on top.

FAST: Can have all the components prepped up to 3 days before serving. Toss and arrange at serving time or up to 1 hour in advance.

FLASHY: Garnish with fresh herbs and/or any nontoxic flower.

FABULOUS: With any fresh herb, walnuts instead of pine nuts, shaved or grated Parmesan cheese, or crumbled feta cheese. To reduce the fat, substitute ham or smoked turkey for the salami.

*Refer to Terms & Techniques.

Grilled Polenta Triangles

Italian soul food!   **Yield: 8+ servings**

3 cups instant polenta
8 cups chicken broth, homemade or
    canned
1 cup dry white wine

4 to 10 cloves garlic, minced
2 bay leaves
    Salt and white pepper, to taste

1. Add all the ingredients to a large stockpot. Bring to a boil. Lower the heat. Stir frequently, using a large wooden spoon. Cook until the polenta comes away cleanly from the sides of the pot, about 15 minutes. Remove and discard the bay leaves.

   To prepare the polenta in the microwave, combine the ingredients in a glass, plastic, or ceramic bowl. Stir in the polenta. Cover with plastic wrap and puncture to allow the steam to escape. Microwave for about 15 minutes, until fully cooked. Remove and discard the bay leaves.

2. Oil a cookie sheet and transfer the polenta mixture onto it. Cool to room temperature, and place in the refrigerator or freezer, if necessary, until firm.

3. Cut triangles into the desired size.

4. Oil the grill of your barbecue, brush the polenta with oil, and grill until hot, or place on an oiled cookie sheet and broil for a few minutes.

FAST: Can prepare up to 3 days in advance and refrigerate.

FLASHY: Serve hot or cold.

FABULOUS: Seasoned with any fresh or dried herb.

Grilled Japanese Eggplant & Red Onions

The ultimate summer veggie dish for any occasion.   **Yield: 8+ servings**

4 Japanese eggplants, cut into ¼-inch-
  thick circles or long slices
2 large red onions, cut into ½-inch-thick
  slices

Olive oil, as needed
Kosher or sea salt, as needed

1. Sprinkle eggplant and onion slices with salt. Place in a colander in the sink or in a bowl and let drain for 30–60 minutes to remove the bitter juices.
2. Rinse off the eggplant and onion slices and blot dry.
3. Place eggplant and onions on a large platter, drizzle olive oil over the top, and sprinkle with garlic. Cover with plastic wrap and marinate for 1 hour at room temperature or up to 48 hours in the refrigerator.
4. Oil the barbecue grill and put the slices on when coals turn white-hot. Grill for several minutes, until cooked on one side. Turn and grill on the other side.

FAST: Can prepare up to 3 days in advance and refrigerate.

FLASHY: Serve hot or at room temperature.

FABULOUS: As a salad with roasted red peppers and a Basil Vinaigrette, in hot or cold pasta, as a topping or condiment for grilled fish, seafood, chicken or meats, and chopped as an hors d'oeuvre.

Red Wine Vinaigrette

A classic!

½ cup good-quality red wine vinegar
2 cups extra virgin or pure olive oil
2 cloves garlic, or to taste

Salt, ground white and black pepper,
and minced fresh or dried herbs, to
taste

1. Combine all the ingredients in a food processor fitted with the metal blade or in a blender. Process in the blender, or whisk together in a bowl. Taste and adjust the seasonings.
2. Store in a tightly covered jar in the refrigerator. Shake or stir before using.

FAST: Can prepare up to 2 weeks in advance and refrigerate, or freeze for up to 3 months.

FLASHY: Garnish by floating fresh parsley and/or any nontoxic flower on top.

FABULOUS: With ¼ to ½ cup crumbled bleu, feta, or grated Parmesan cheese. Using different oils, herbs, and vinegars. Adding 2 teaspoons mustard. As a marinade, sauce, or dunk for vegetables, seafood, beef, lamb, poultry, and pork. On any salad. To reduce the fat, replace half of the olive oil with low-fat or fat-free sour cream.

Cold Berry Soufflé

Light and luscious.   ***Yield: 8+ servings***

4 egg yolks or egg substitute
1 cup brown sugar, packed well
2 envelopes unflavored gelatin
4 tablespoons triple sec
2 to 4 tablespoons Marsala or Madeira wine
  Grated zest of 2 limes and juice, to taste

1 cup sour cream or low-fat or fat-free sour cream
4 ounces cream cheese or low-fat cream cheese
1 pound boysenberries (may substitute any fresh fruit)
½ cup shaved chocolate and extra berries for garnish

1. Oil a 1½-quart soufflé or loaf pan.
2. Combine the eggs and brown sugar in a saucepan. Place this saucepan over a saucepan of simmering water, whisking frequently until the sugar dissolves and the mixture thickens.
3. Add the gelatin, triple sec, and Marsala.
4. Meanwhile, in a food processor fitted with the metal blade, add the grated zest, sour cream, cream cheese, berries, and lime juice. Process until well mixed.
5. Transfer the egg yolk mixture into the mixture in the food processor, and combine thoroughly. Transfer this to the prepared soufflé pan. Cover with plastic wrap and chill until set, about 4 hours.

FAST: Can prepare up to 3 days in advance and refrigerate. It's best when made at least 24 hours before serving.

FLASHY: Garnish with shaved chocolate, mint leaves, berries, and some whipped cream, if desired. This can also be served in individual stemmed glasses and garnished.

FABULOUS: With any kind of berry or soft fruit.

Lentil & Mango Salad with Marinated Smoked Pork Tenderloin Lunch

S alads are sensational in summer. I consider iceberg lettuce and bottled dressings to be less than thrilling, while the possibilities for creating innovative salads are limitless. You will find the salad in this menu a delicious example of an interesting summer salad. Our Lentil & Mango Salad with Grilled Eggplant is an exotic mixture of ingredients with diverse culinary influences. Lentils are an ancient European legume, while mangos bring a tropical influence, and the grilled eggplant adds a strong Mediterranean touch. To say the least, this salad is anything but ho-hum. It is truly an experience.

As an added bonus, we have Marinated & Smoked Pork Tenderloin. Although our menu is complete without it, I urge you to go for it. Lemon Sherry Biscotti and fresh fruit conclude the lunch.

As for the table, I used blue-and-white paisley placemats with matching napkins. Stems of zinnias in several small bud vases were my centerpiece. The look was definitely summer.

Menu
Lentil & Mango Salad with Grilled Eggplant
Marinated & Smoked Pork Tenderloin (optional)
French Bread and Olive Oil
Lemon Sherry Biscotti
Fresh Fruit

Faster & Flashier Menu
Salad (purchased from a deli)
Smoked Meat (purchased from a deli)
French Bread and Olive Oil
Biscotti (purchased) and Fresh Fruit

Dry White Wine

❦   TIMETABLE   ❦

Up to 14 days in advance	Lemon Sherry Biscotti
Up to 4 days in advance	Marinate the pork.
Up to 3 days in advance	Lentil & Mango Salad
Up to 1 day in advance	Smoke the pork. Set the table. Chill the wine.
Party day!	Enjoy!

Lentil & Mango Salad with Grilled Eggplant

Lentils offer us a powerhouse of nutrition and flavor. A meal in itself!   **Yield: 8 servings**

2 cups dry lentils
5 cups chicken broth, homemade or
    canned
4 to 6 Japanese eggplants, sliced into
    ½-inch slices
Sesame oil
½ red onion, thinly sliced
1 bunch of cilantro, minced

2 to 4 green onions, minced
1 to 2 red bell peppers, seeded and
    thinly sliced
½ cup sesame seeds, toasted
    Chinoise Vinaigrette (recipe follows)
1 to 2 mangoes, cut into small cubes
8 ounces feta cheese, crumbled, or
    more

1. Place the lentils and chicken broth in a saucepan and bring to a boil.
2. Cover the saucepan and cook over very low heat until just tender, not soggy, about 30 minutes.
3. Drain any remaining liquid off the lentils and transfer to a salad bowl. Toss with all the remaining ingredients, except for the eggplant and feta. Use only as much dressing as needed.
4. Meanwhile, salt the eggplant slices and place in a colander. Set over a bowl to drain for about 30 minutes. Blot the slices with paper towels.
5. Brush the slices with the sesame oil and place on an oiled grill over hot coals or on an oiled baking sheet in a 400 degree oven. Cook until just tender.
6. Toss the eggplant and the feta into the salad. Taste and adjust the seasonings.

FAST: Can prepare up to 3 days in advance and refrigerate. It's best when made at least 24 hours before serving.

FLASHY: Garnish with cilantro sprigs and fresh mint leaves.

FABULOUS: With cooked Chinese sausages tossed in. These sausages can be purchased at Asian supermarkets, either fresh or frozen.

Chinoise Vinaigrette

Yield: About 1¾ cups

1 cup peanut oil, less 2 tablespoons
⅓ cup Chinese rice vinegar
1 tablespoon red wine vinegar
2 cloves garlic, or more
¼ cup pickled ginger, or to taste

2 tablespoons Chinese sesame oil
1 to 2 tablespoons fermented black
   beans
Szechuan peppercorns, to taste

1. Combine all the ingredients in a food processor fitted with the metal blade. Taste and adjust the seasonings.

FAST: Can prepare up to 2 weeks in advance and refrigerate.

FLASHY: To serve, place the lentil salad on individual plates or a platter and surround with the eggplant slices. Sprinkle crumbled feta cheese over the top.

FABULOUS: As a sauce for broiled or grilled fish, chicken, or pork. As a sauce for noodles and vegetables.

Marinated & Smoked Pork Tenderloin

Fabulous flavor.

Yield: 8+ servings

4 pounds whole pork tenderloins
2 to 3 cups smoke chips, soaked in
    warm water for at least 1 hour or
    microwaved for 15 minutes

The Brine* (optional)
1 cup kosher or sea salt
1 cup white or brown sugar
  Water to cover the pork

The Marinade: A "World-Class" Marinade.
Use it on ribs, turkey, or chicken.
 1 cup hoisin sauce*
10 cloves garlic
½ cup soy sauce
 1 cup cream sherry or Mirin wine*
⅓ to ½ cup fresh minced mint
⅓ to ½ cup fresh minced lemon
    verbena or grated zest of 3 to 4
    lemons
  1-inch piece of ginger root, minced
 1 cup orange marmalade
  Freshly ground black pepper, to taste

1. Place the pork in a nonmetal pan or plastic container and add all the brining ingredients. Let sit at room temperature for 1 hour.
2. Combine all the ingredients for the marinade.
3. Place the pork in a glass, ceramic, or plastic container and add all the marinade. Cover with the plastic wrap and let sit at room temperature for up to 1 hour or refrigerate for up to 3 days.
4. Remove the smoke chips from the soaking liquid and scatter them over hot coals. Place the pork on the grill, cover, and let smoke for about 20 minutes, or until the pork is no longer pink.

FAST: Can fully prepare the pork up to 3 days in advance and refrigerate. Can prepare the marinade up to 3 months in advance and refrigerate.

FLASHY: Serve hot or cold, thinly sliced, with French bread and assorted mustards.

FABULOUS: With fresh rosemary added to the marinade.

*Refer to Terms & Techniques.

Lemon Sherry Biscotti

If you are a biscotti fan, you will love this.   ***Yield: About 70***

1 to 1½ cups sugar
½ teaspoon salt
1 teaspoon baking soda
4 large eggs or egg substitute
2 teaspoons vanilla extract

½ cup cream sherry, or more as
   needed
4½ cups all-purpose flour
   Grated zest of 2 to 4 lemons
   Grated nutmeg, to taste

1. Preheat the oven to 350 degrees.
2. Combine the sugar, salt, and baking soda until fluffy in a food processor fitted with a metal blade, or in a bowl with an electric mixer.
3. Add the zest, eggs, sherry, and nutmeg while the machine or mixer is running.
4. Process in 4 cups of the flour and continue until a soft dough forms. If too dry, add more cream sherry.
5. Dust the work surface with the remaining flour and lightly flour your hands. Divide the dough in fourths and form into four cylinders about 2 inches wide. Place on an oiled cookie sheet and bake until the tester comes out clean, about 35 minutes.
6. Let cool and cut each loaf into ½-inch-thick slices at an angle. Cut each slice in half lengthwise and return to the cookie sheet.
7. Reduce the oven temperature to 300 degrees and bake until crisp, for 15–20 minutes more. Turn the oven off and let sit for 15 minutes more, with the door open.

FAST: Can prepare up to 14 days in advance and store in an airtight jar or plastic bag, or freeze for up to 6 months. Thaw at room temperature for a few hours.

FABULOUS: With any chopped nut mixed in or dipped in chocolate.

Summer Cocktail Party
(Taster's Heaven)

If you are lucky enough to live in a climate where you can stage this party outside, by all means do. Instead of using one huge table for the hors d'oeuvres, I recommend using several. You will find that this will help the traffic flow as well as create more visual excitement. Cloths or sheets in bright bold colors such as purple, bright orange, and hot pink work well. Hurricane lanterns with pillar candles on every table are practical and attractive. French tin flower pails holding gladiolas are great, especially when they are surrounded by ripe tomatoes, eggplants, and bell peppers. I think it is boring to place everything flat on the table. There are several ways to create a variety of levels. For example, go to a restaurant supply store, or just look around your house, and you will find all sorts of gizmos to raise dishes. Try using terra cotta pots, bricks, stemmed glasses, or upside-down bowls for a more unconventional way to achieve different heights. Cover up any less-than-attractive bases with coordinating fabric.

Menu
(For 30 to 50)

Hearts of Palm, Avocado & Artichoke Croustades

Tomato Cheese Croustades

*Spicy Pork Sausages in Grape Leaves with
Plum Vinegar Sauce & Mango Vinegar Sauce*

Italian Basil Salsa & Hummus with Pita Chips

*Cold Shrimp & Jicama Sticks with
Mexican Cream Sauce*

Marinated Feta with Pasilla Chiles & Tomatoes

TIMETABLE

Up to 3 months in advance and frozen	Croustades. Pita Chips. Mexican Cream Sauce.
Up to 1 month in advance and refrigerated	Plum Vinegar Sauce
Up to 5 days in advance	Italian Basil Salsa. Marinated Feta with Pasilla Chiles & Tomatoes.
Up to 4 days in advance	Mango Vinegar Sauce
Up to 3 days in advance	Tomato Cheese Croustades (filling). Hearts of Palm, Avocado & Artichoke Croustades (filling).
Up to 2 days in advance	Spicy Pork Sausages in Grape Leaves. Hummus. Shrimp.
Up to 1 day in advance	Work on the displays and presentation.
Party day!	Assemble and garnish.

Hearts of Palm, Avocado & Artichoke Croustades

Cool and refreshing

Yield: About 60 croustades

6 to 8 canned hearts of palm, sliced
   into thin rounds
1 cup drained marinated or water-
   packed artichoke hearts, chopped
1 to 2 bunches watercress leaves
¼ to ½ cup minced fresh Italian parsley
1 cup diced jicama
4 to 8 green onions (scallions), white
   and green parts, minced

¼ cup capers, drained and rinsed
2 large, ripe avocados, peeled, pitted,
   and chopped
½ cup Tarragon Caper Vinaigrette
   (recipe follows), or to taste
About 60 croustades (recipe follows)

1. Toss the first 8 ingredients together.
2. Add the vinaigrette and toss. Taste and adjust the seasonings.
3. Fill the croustades.

FAST: Can prepare through Step 2 up to 3 days in advance and refrigerate. Can assemble up to 2 hours in advance.

FLASHY: Serve chilled on a platter with a whole raw artichoke in the center and garnish with johnny jump-ups or any other nontoxic flower and/or fresh herb sprigs.

FABULOUS: With cooked lobster, tuna, crab, or chicken instead of the shrimp. With minced papaya and/or mango mixed in. With ½ cup sour cream or mayonnaise mixed in.

Tarragon Caper Vinaigrette   *Yield: About 2¼ cups*

½ cup tarragon wine vinegar
¼ cup capers, drained, rinsed
1¼ cups peanut, canola, or olive oil

¼ cup fresh lemon juice
Salt, ground white pepper, and fresh
   or dried tarragon to taste

1. Combine all the ingredients in a food processor fitted with the metal blade or in a blender and process, or whisk together in a bowl. Taste and adjust the seasonings.
2. Store in the refrigerator in a tightly covered jar. Stir or shake before using.

FAST: Can prepare up to 2 weeks in advance and refrigerate, or freeze for up to 3 months.

FLASHY: On any combination of greens.

FABULOUS: As a marinade or sauce for vegetables, seafood, beef, lamb, poultry, and pork. On any salad. To reduce the fat, replace half of the olive oil with low-fat or fat-free sour cream.

Tomato Cheese Croustades

1 large, ripe tomato, peeled, seeded,
  and chopped
¾ to 1½ cups softened, sun-dried
  tomatoes,* minced
8 ounces crumbled feta cheese, or to
  taste, plus extra feta for topping
2 to 4 tablespoons freshly grated
  Parmesan or Romano cheese
½ cup packed fresh basil, minced, or
  1 to 2 tablespoons dried
2 cloves garlic, minced, or more

¼ cup minced fresh Italian parsley, or
  to taste
2 tablespoons capers, drained and
  rinsed
¼ cup sour cream or low-fat or fat-free
  sour cream
Salt, ground white pepper, and
  grated nutmeg, to taste
Extra virgin olive oil for drizzling
About 60 croustades (recipe follows)
½ cup pine nuts, toasted

1. Preheat the oven to 400 degrees.
2. Combine all the ingredients, except the pine nuts, olive oil and croustades, in a food processor fitted with the metal blade, or in a bowl by hand until well mixed. Add the pine nuts and combine. Taste and adjust the seasonings.
3. Fill the croustades, and place on an ungreased cookie sheet; top with more grated cheese, if desired, and drizzle olive oil over the top of each croustade.
4. Bake until hot and bubbly, 10–15 minutes.

FAST: Can assemble up to 3 hours in advance, leave at room temperature, and bake just before serving. Can prepare the filling up to 3 days in advance and refrigerate, or freeze for up to 3 months.

FLASHY: Serve hot on a platter and garnish with fresh basil leaves and/or a whole raw tomato.

FABULOUS: Use the fillings in omelets or to stuff raw mushroom caps. With fresh or dried rosemary instead of the basil. With chopped calamata olives and/or marinated artichoke hearts added.

*Refer to Terms & Techniques.

Croustades

This is a quick, low-cholesterol alternative
to rich pastry tartlets.

Yield: About 35 croustades

1 cup extra virgin olive oil
2 to 4 cloves garlic, minced
½ teaspoon salt, or to taste

1 large loaf sliced sourdough bread
(very fresh)

1. Preheat the oven to 350 degrees.
2. Combine the olive oil with the garlic and salt in a food processor fitted with the metal blade, in a blender, or in a bowl.
3. Using a cookie cutter or a wine glass, cut the bread into rounds about 2½ inches wide.
4. Roll the bread rounds out with a rolling pin.
5. Brush the garlic oil on mini-muffin tins. Press the bread rounds into the cups and brush them with garlic oil.
6. Bake until completely crisp, about 15 minutes. Now they are ready to be filled.

FAST: Can store in airtight jars or plastic bags for up to 1 week, or freeze for up to 3 months. No thawing is needed.

FLASHY: Filled with anything.

FABULOUS: With fresh or dried herbs added to garlic oil. Made with any combination of peanut, canola, and/or olive oil. To reduce the fat, use nonstick mini-muffin tins and do not brush with olive oil.

Spicy Pork Sausages in Grape Leaves

Unusual and exotic, but simple!

Yield: About 48 sausages, 20 or more servings

2 pounds lean ground pork
2 tablespoons pickled mango,* or to taste
½ cup minced fresh mint

4 to 8 tablespoons Chinese plum sauce*
About 48 preserved grape leaves*
Olive oil

1. Mix together all the ingredients, except the grape leaves and olive oil, in a bowl using a wooden spoon or your hands. Fry 1 teaspoon of the mixture until cooked all the way through to check the seasonings.
2. Form the mixture into small sausage shapes about 1½ inches long.
3. Wrap each sausage in a grape leaf, placing the shiny side of each leaf toward the work surface. Fold the sides toward the center and roll up the sausages as tightly as possible.
4. Brush the wrapped sausages with olive oil and grill over a medium-hot fire, or place in a baking dish or on a baking sheet and bake in a preheated 350 degree oven until the mixture is no longer pink, about 15 minutes.

FAST: Can prepare through Step 3 up to 2 days in advance and refrigerate, or freeze for up to 6 months. Thaw in the refrigerator overnight.

FLASHY: Serve hot on a platter and garnish with fresh herbs and/or nontoxic flowers or leaves. With Plum Vinegar Sauce and Mango Vinegar Sauce (recipes follow).

FABULOUS: With minced cilantro (fresh coriander) mixed in.

*Refer to Terms & Techniques.

Plum Vinegar Sauce

A delightful, fat-free Asian sauce.

Yield: About 1 cup

½ cup Chinese plum sauce*
½ cup Chinese rice vinegar*

1. Combine the ingredients in a food processor fitted with the metal blade, or in a blender, or whisk together in a bowl. Taste and adjust the flavors.

FAST: Can prepare up to 1 month in advance and refrigerate.

FLASHY: As a dunk for Spicy Pork Sausages in Grape Leaves, any pork, ribs, chicken wings, or almost any Asian hors d'oeuvre. Garnish with toasted sesame seeds,* minced green onions, and/or cilantro.

FABULOUS: As a marinade for fish, chicken, seafood, or pork. As an entrée sauce on noodles, pork, chicken, fish, or seafood.

*Refer to Terms & Techniques.

Mango Vinegar Sauce

A fresh and tropical fantasy that is also low-fat.   **Yield: About 2 cups**

1 medium- to large-size ripe mango,
   peeled and pitted
½ cup balsamic vinegar
2 tablespoons minced fresh ginger

½ cup packed fresh basil leaves
½ cup water or orange juice
½ to 1 teaspoon pickled mango*
   Salt, to taste

1. Combine all the ingredients in a food processor fitted with the metal blade or in a blender, and process until smooth. Taste and adjust the seasonings.

FAST: Can prepare up to 4 days in advance and refrigerate, or freeze for up to 6 months.

FLASHY: Serve at room temperature or hot in a bowl, and garnish with a sprinkling of toasted sesame seeds. With Spicy Pork Sausages in Grape Leaves.

FABULOUS: As a dunk for grilled sausage and skewers of seafood, pork, fish, chicken, or beef.

*Refer to Terms & Techniques.

Hummus

A bit of Middle Eastern exotica that can be served whenever you would serve guacamole.

2 cups (one 16-ounce can) chick peas or dried chick peas prepared according to the package instructions
½ cup extra virgin olive oil or to taste
¼ to ½ cup tahini*
⅓ cup fresh lemon juice, or to taste

2 cloves garlic, or more
¼ cup minced fresh mint leaves, or more
¼ cup minced cilantro (fresh coriander), or more
Salt, hot pepper sauce, and ground white pepper, to taste

1. Process all the ingredients in a food processor fitted with the metal blade or in a blender until smooth. Taste and adjust the seasonings.

FAST: Can prepare up to 2 days in advance and refrigerate, or freeze for up to 6 months.

FLASHY: Garnish with minced fresh parsley or cilantro and serve with Pita Chips (recipe follows).

FABULOUS: With ½ cup or more toasted walnuts (page 13) substituted for the tahini and with 1 cup fresh basil leaves instead of the cilantro and mint. To reduce the fat, replace some or all of the olive oil with water.

*Refer to Terms & Techniques.

Pita Chips

An addictive chip!

Yield: About 96 chips

1 package pita bread, each bread
   separated in half, forming two
   separate rounds
1 cup olive oil
⅓ cup red wine vinegar

Optional Seasonings:
  Minced fresh garlic
  Minced fresh basil

Minced cilantro (fresh coriander)
Minced fresh rosemary
Dried oregano
Minced fresh dill
Freshly grated Parmesan cheese
  (optional)
Salt

1. Preheat the oven to 350 degrees.
2. Combine the olive oil and vinegar with the garlic and other optional seasonings in a food processor fitted with the metal blade or in a bowl until well mixed.
3. Brush each half with the seasoned oil.
4. Stack the pita bread rounds and cut them into triangles using a Chinese cleaver or chef's knife.
5. Transfer the pita triangles to an ungreased cookie sheet.
6. Sprinkle them with Parmesan and/or salt if desired.
7. Bake until crisp, 10–20 minutes.

FAST: Can prepare up to 1 week in advance and store in airtight jars or plastic bags, or freeze for up to 3 months.

FLASHY: Serve in a napkin-lined basket.

FABULOUS: Prepared with any combination of your favorite oils or herbs. To reduce the fat, omit the oil, and just cut the pita bread and bake it plain.

Cold Shrimp

A classic!

½ lemon, sliced
½ onion, sliced
2 teaspoons salt

1 tablespoon pickling spice
1 quart water
1 pound shrimp

1. Bring water to a boil over high heat, and add all of the seasonings. Boil for about 5 minutes, until the broth is flavorful.
2. Add the shrimp and continue to cook over high heat just until the shrimp turn pink, about 2 minutes.
3. Drain the shrimp in a colander and put in cold water to stop the cooking process.
4. Drain, shell, and enjoy.

FAST: Shrimp can be cooked up to 2 days in advance and refrigerated, or frozen for up to 1 month.

FLASHY: Serve on a large platter with a bowl of Mexican Cream Sauce in the middle. Garnish with sprigs of cilantro and/or whole raw chiles.

Mexican Cream Sauce

If this is your first encounter with tomatillos, you'll be delighted with their tangy, lemonlike flavor.

Yield: About 2¼ cups

6 medium to large tomatillos,* husked and quartered

5 canned whole green chiles,* seeded and deveined

½ to 1 medium- to large-size ripe avocado, peeled and pitted

¾ cup sour cream or low-fat or fat-free plain yogurt or sour cream

3 to 6 green onions (scallions), white and green parts, cut up

2 cloves garlic

¼ cup minced cilantro (fresh coriander), or more, to taste

Salt, ground white pepper, ground cumin, and fresh lemon juice, to taste

1. Combine all the ingredients in a food processor fitted with the metal blade or in a blender, and purée. Taste and adjust the seasonings.

FAST: Can prepare up to 3 days in advance and refrigerate, or freeze for up to 3 months.

FLASHY: As a dunk for Tortilla Chips, Jicama Sticks, poultry, lamb, pork, beef, fish, or seafood. Garnish with minced cilantro, green onions, and/or any nontoxic flower.

FABULOUS: As an entrée sauce for beef, pork, poultry, seafood, pasta, or rice. With chopped, cooked salmon, shrimp, or crabmeat mixed in.

*Refer to Terms & Techniques.

Marinated Feta with Pasilla Chiles & Tomatoes

Yield: 10 servings

1 pound feta cheese
½ to 1 cup extra virgin olive oil
3 to 4 tablespoons minced fresh
 rosemary
4 to 8 cloves garlic, minced

2 to 3 dried pasilla chiles,* rehydrated,*
 stemmed, seeded, and minced or
 puréed
3 to 4 medium-size ripe tomatoes,
 seeded and minced or chopped

1. Place the feta in an attractive, small, ovenproof pan or au gratin dish. Cover with the olive oil and scatter in the rosemary and garlic. Mix in the chiles and tomatoes.
2. Let marinate for at least 1 hour at room temperature, or refrigerate for up to 5 days. Warm in a preheated 350 degree oven until the cheese begins to melt, about 15–20 minutes.

FAST: Can prepare up to 5 days in advance and refrigerate, or freeze for up to 1 month.

FLASHY: Serve with thinly sliced baguettes, assorted crackers, crostini (page 66), or Pita Chips (page 112). Garnish with fresh rosemary, whole fresh chiles, and/or any nontoxic flower.

FABULOUS: With toasted sesame seeds* or nuts scattered over the top. With ½ cup minced sun-dried tomatoes instead of the fresh tomatoes.

*Refer to Terms & Techniques.

Grilled Skewers
of Lamb Dinner

*T*his party captures the wonderful carefree spirit that summer evokes. It is simple and full of fresh vitality. As for ease of preparation, this menu is a dream. The party opens with a Greek Pesto and Pita Chips. This dish is totally unique and exploits grapes leaves for all the flavor and character they offer. I suspect that you will find tons of uses for this mixture. Just as unique as this is the salad. Its use of papaya makes it very refreshing and digestive. The menu's stars are the skewers of beautifully marinated tender lamb, grilled and sauced with a sweet and smoky Roasted Red Pepper Sauce and a Tarragon Mayonnaise Sauce. Both sauces are too simple for words, faster than a speeding bullet, and just as versatile. Are you sold? The Lemon Couscous also fits this description. As for the Green Beans with Capers and Basil, it reflects my eternal struggle to treat vegetables with inspiration. Most of us remember the days when a party vegetable always involved a can of cream soup and a can of French onion rings. Thank goodness we have evolved.

As for the table, I used a black-and-white sheet with a pattern that resembles granite, and white napkins. Terra cotta pots painted gloss white, planted with white impatiens, ran down the center of the table. White candles in glass candlesticks were interspersed along with shiny leaves.

Menu

Greek Pesto

Papaya, Mushroom, Cucumber & Red Onion Salad

Skewers of Lamb with Roasted Red Pepper Sauce
& Tarragon Mayonnaise Sauce

Lemon Couscous

Green Beans with Capers & Basil

Peach & Boysenberry Cobbler

Faster & Flashier Menu

Hors D'Oeuvres (purchased salsa with dried oregano
and crumbled feta mixed in)

Tossed Salad with Greek Vinaigrette

Skewers of Lamb with Tarragon Mayonnaise Sauce

Lemon Couscous

Dessert (purchased)

Sauvignon Blanc and Pinot Noir or Merlot

Sparkling Wine and/or Coffee

TIMETABLE	
Up to 4 days in advance	Roasted Red Pepper Sauce. Tarragon Mayonnaise Sauce.
Up to 3 days in advance	Lemon Couscous. Marinate the lamb.
Up to 2 days in advance	Papaya, Mushroom, Cucumber & Red Onion Salad. Peach & Boysenberry Cobbler.
Up to 1 day in advance	Blanch the green beans. Set the table. Chill the wines.
Party day!	Grill the lamb. Bake the cobbler. Finish the green beans and couscous.

Greek Pesto

If you haven't tasted grape leaves before, you're in for a treat.   **Yield: About 1¾ cups**

4 to 6 grape leaves, jarred
1 cup almonds, toasted
½ cup extra virgin olive oil
1 to 4 tablespoons fresh mint leaves, minced

2 to 4 tablespoons parsley, minced
1 to 6 cloves garlic, minced
Freshly ground, coarse black pepper and fresh lemon juice, to taste

1. Combine all the ingredients in a food processor fitted with the metal blade or in a blender. Taste and adjust the seasonings.

FAST: Can prepare up to 5 days in advance and refrigerate, or freeze for up to 6 months.

FLASHY: As a spread with Pita Chips (page 112), crackers, thinly sliced baguettes, French bread, or any crostini (pages 66 and 192).

FABULOUS: With fresh oregano and/or basil. As an entrée sauce for chicken, seafood, pork, or lamb. With ½ cup sour cream or low-fat yogurt added. On pasta, rice, or beans. To reduce the fat, replace some or all of the olive oil with low-fat or fat-free sour cream or plain yogurt.

Papaya, Mushroom, Cucumber & Red Onion Salad with Feta

Almost a meal in itself . . . definitely a lunch.   **Yield: 8 servings**

2 large papaya, peeled, seeded, and thinly sliced
1 large sweet red onion, thinly sliced
1½ pounds mushrooms, halved
8 ounces feta cheese, crumbled

1 large European-style cucumber, thinly sliced
Greek Vinaigrette (recipe follows)
Sprigs of cilantro and/or lettuce leaves for garnishing

1. Combine all the ingredients, except for the dressing, in a mixing bowl.
2. Toss with the desired amount of dressing and let sit for at least 1 hour, at room temperature, or up to 2 days in the refrigerator.

FAST: Can prepare up to 2 days in advance and refrigerate.

FLASHY: Arrange on salad plates or on a platter and garnish with sprigs of cilantro, or serve on lettuce leaves.

FABULOUS: With shrimp, crab, or lobster added.

Greek Vinaigrette

1 cup extra virgin olive oil
Juice of about 2 lemons, or to taste
2 teaspoons red wine vinegar, or to taste
2 cloves garlic

4 anchovy fillets
½ teaspoon dried oregano
Freshly ground, coarse black pepper, to taste

1. Combine all the ingredients in a food processor fitted with the metal blade. Taste and adjust the flavors.

FAST: Can prepare up to 14 days in advance and refrigerate.

FLASHY: On any combination of tossed greens.

FABULOUS: As a sauce or marinade for chicken, fish, or lamb.

Skewers of Lamb with Roasted Red Pepper Sauce

Simple but exotic, with brilliant flavors!

Yield: 8 servings

4 to 6 pounds boned leg of lamb, cut into 1¼-inch cubes, trimmed
Roasted Red Pepper Sauce (recipe follows)
Sprigs of fresh thyme, parsley, mint, and/or rosemary for garnishing

The Marinade:
5 to 8 cloves garlic
1 cup olive oil or low-fat or fat-free plain yogurt
¼ cup Italian parsley, minced
1 red onion, cut up
¼ cup soy sauce
4 tablespoons Dijon mustard
¼ cup fresh lemon juice, or more
Fresh rosemary, dill, thyme, and mint, minced, to taste
Salt and freshly ground, coarse black pepper, to taste

1. Place garlic in saucepan with salted water, bring to a boil, and drain. Repeat this process once. This will mellow the garlic.
2. Combine all ingredients for the marinade, including garlic, in a food processor fitted with the metal blade.
3. Place lamb in glass or ceramic pan with marinade. Cover with plastic wrap and refrigerate for 4–36 hours.
4. Skewer the lamb and grill over hot coals until browned on the outside but still pink on the inside, about 8 minutes. Can also broil.

FAST: Can marinate up to 3 days in advance and refrigerate. Can prepare marinade up to 2 weeks in advance and refrigerate, or freeze for up to 6 months.

FLASHY: Serve on a puddle of half Roasted Red Pepper Sauce and half Tarragon Mayonnaise Sauce. Garnish with sprigs of fresh parsley, mint, thyme, and/or rosemary.

FABULOUS: With chicken or pork instead of lamb. With rehydrated shiitake mushrooms added to skewers.

FURTHER: Use leftovers cold in a salad with couscous, rice, or bulgar.

Roasted Red Pepper Sauce

This is a favorite of mine. When I prepared it on national
television, I splashed it all over Gary Collins.

Yield: About 2 cups

4 red bell peppers, roasted,* peeled, and
    seeded
2 cloves garlic
1 to 2 cups extra virgin olive oil or low-
    fat or fat-free sour cream or plain
    yogurt

Salt and freshly ground white pepper,
    to taste
Fresh lemon or lime juice, to taste

1. Purée all the ingredients in a food processor fitted with the metal blade or
   in a blender.
2. Taste and adjust the seasonings.

FAST: Can prepare up to 4 days in advance and refrigerate, or freeze for up to
6 months. Thaw in the refrigerator for 2 days or at room temperature for
about 4 hours.

FLASHY: Serve on anything from potatoes to fish.

FABULOUS: Serve hot with heavy cream or chicken broth instead of the oil.

*Refer to Terms & Techniques.

Tarragon Mayonnaise Sauce

Fantastic flavors and a real no-brainer to prepare!   ***Yield: About 1¾ cups***

½ cup mayonnaise or low-fat or fat-free
   mayonnaise
½ cup yogurt or nonfat yogurt
2 tablespoons tarragon vinegar, or
   more

4 ounces cream cheese (optional) or
   fat-free cream cheese
Fresh minced tarragon (optional)
Fresh, coarse, cracked black, red,
   and/or green peppercorns, to taste

1. Combine all the ingredients in a bowl by hand, or in a food processor fitted with the metal blade.

FAST: Can prepare up to 7 days in advance and refrigerate.

FLASHY: Use as a sauce for cooked or raw vegetables, fish, lamb, pork, or poultry.

FABULOUS: With fat-free yogurt instead of mayonnaise to reduce the calorie count.

Lemon Couscous

A delicious alternative to rice pilaf.

Yield: About 8 servings

4 tablespoons extra virgin olive oil
2 to 4 shallots, minced
¼ cup parsley, minced
2 7-ounce jars marinated or water-packed artichoke hearts, drained
2 cups uncooked couscous

Juice of 1 lemon
3½ cups chicken broth, homemade or canned
½ cup dry vermouth
1 bay leaf
Salt and white pepper, to taste

1. Heat the olive oil in a large sauté pan, and sauté the shallots and parsley over medium-high heat for about 2 minutes until the shallots are tender.
2. Add the remaining ingredients and bring to a boil over high heat. Cover with a lid, reduce the heat to the lowest setting, and cook for about 10 minutes until the liquid is absorbed.

FAST: Can prepare fully up to 3 days in advance and refrigerate, or freeze for up to 3 months. Reheat in a 350 degree oven, covered, for about 20 minutes until hot, or microwave for about 10 minutes on a medium setting.

FLASHY: Garnish with minced parsley and/or extra artichoke hearts.

FABULOUS: With ½ cup freshly grated Parmesan cheese or crumbled feta cheese mixed in.

FURTHER: As a salad or as a filling for stuffed tomatoes or eggplant.

Green Beans with Capers & Basil

A lovely way to treat green beans!   **Yield: 8 servings**

2 pounds green beans, stringed
4 tablespoons unsalted butter or olive oil
2 shallots, minced
4 tablespoons capers, rinsed and drained

Salt, white pepper, fresh lemon juice, fresh or dried thyme, and grated nutmeg, to taste
1 bunch of basil leaves, chopped or cut into thin strips

1. Blanch green beans in large pot of boiling, salted water, until barely tender. Remove beans and place in strainer or colander. Run under cold running water until no longer warm. Drain well.
2. In large skillet, melt butter or heat the olive oil and sauté shallots until tender.
3. Add capers, green beans, and seasonings. Toss over medium-high heat with basil leaves until beans are hot. Taste and adjust seasonings. Serve.

FAST: Can blanch beans up to 1 day in advance and refrigerate. Bring to room temperature before sautéing.

FABULOUS: With walnuts, sesame seeds, hazelnuts, pecans, almonds, or other nuts.

Brandied Peach & Boysenberry Cobbler

A real homey treat!   ***Yield: 8 servings***

The Filling:
- 6 pounds peaches, pitted and sliced
- 1 pound fresh boysenberries or frozen, unsweetened boysenberries
- 6 tablespoons instant tapioca
- 3 tablespoons fresh lemon juice
- ¼ cup brandy
- ¼ cup brown sugar

The Pastry:
- 6 tablespoons unsalted cold butter, cut into pieces
- 2 cups oatmeal
- 1 teaspoon baking powder
- ¾ teaspoon ground cinnamon
- Ground nutmeg, to taste
- ¼ teaspoon salt
- ½ cup buttermilk or low-fat or fat-free buttermilk
- 1 teaspoon vanilla extract
- ½ cup toasted, sliced almonds, or more
- Grated zest of 2 lemons

1. Preheat the oven to 350 degrees. Butter a 10-inch square glass baking dish.
2. In a large mixing bowl, combine the peaches, boysenberries, tapioca, and lemon juice. Combine and let stand for about 10 minutes.
3. Meanwhile, combine 4 tablespoons butter with the oatmeal, baking powder, cinnamon, nutmeg, and salt in a food processor fitted with the metal blade, using several quick on-and-off motions until the dough resembles a coarse meal.
4. Process in the buttermilk and vanilla until a smooth dough is formed.
5. Transfer the fruit to the buttered pan.
6. Drop the dough on top of the fruit using a tablespoon. Sprinkle the almonds on top.
7. Place on a cookie sheet and bake for about 30 minutes until the pastry is golden and the fruit bubbles.

FAST: Can prepare through Step 6 up to 2 days in advance, or freeze for up to 6 months. Bake before serving.

FLASHY: Serve with a big scoop of vanilla ice cream or frozen yogurt.

FABULOUS: With any fruit.

Marinated Grilled Chicken Breasts with Zucchini & Two Sauces

*H*ere's a Southwestern party menu with a real contemporary summer feel. It could not be any simpler to prepare or more delicious. It is definitely stylish but casual! We make no attempt to organize the dinner into traditional courses. Our party begins with a marvelous guacamole that is molded into a soufflé. This makes a dramatic presentation. From hors d'oeuvres we progress right into the main event. Let's spend just a minute talking about chicken breasts. I'd rather not eat than experience another dry, tasteless chicken breast. In this recipe the chicken is marinated to perfection. By the way, try this marinade on fish and seafood as well. The zucchini also gets soaked in this liquid magic and grilled. Now for the sauces; they are equally simple, yet wild with flavor. You will also get a great deal of mileage from them. The only other accompaniment is a Southwestern Black Bean & Hominy Salad. It functions both as the salad and the starch. For a grand conclusion, Chocolate Espresso Charlotte with Walnuts & Double Berry Sauce, a chocolate lover's dream!

I wanted the table to be just as stylish and casual as the menu. My table was dressed in a golden yellow cotton bedspread from an import store. Red chile strands ran down the center of the table. Tall Mexican wrought-iron candlesticks held white pillar candles. Spanish green glass pots held a mixture of brilliant flowers interspersed with herb cuttings.

Menu

Cold Guacamole Soufflé with Chips

*Marinated Grilled Chicken Breasts with Zucchini
& Two Sauces*

*Southwestern Black Bean & Hominy Salad
with Cilantro Vinaigrette*

*Chocolate Espresso Charlotte with Walnuts
& Double Berry Sauce*

Faster & Flashier Menu

Guacamole (purchased)

Black Bean Salad (using canned beans)

*Marinated Grilled Chicken Breasts with Zucchini
& Two Sauces*

Double Berry Sauce & Ice Cream

Margaritas, Beer, or Dry White Wine

Sauvignon Blanc

Sparkling Wine and/or Coffee

✄	TIMETABLE	✄
Up to 7 days in advance	Cilantro Vinaigrette	
Up to 5 days in advance	Double Berry Sauce. Double Pepper Mayonnaise Sauce.	
Up to 3 days in advance	Black Bean Salad. Cilantro Pesto.	
Up to 2 days in advance	Chocolate Espresso Charlotte with Walnuts. Cold Guacamole Soufflé.	
Up to 1 day in advance	Marinate the chicken and zucchini. Set the table. Chill the wines.	
Party day!	Grill the chicken and zucchini.	

Cold Guacamole Soufflé

A refreshing, cool, summer hors d'oeuvre.   **Yield: About 4 cups**

2 envelopes unflavored gelatin
¼ cup fresh lemon juice, or to taste
1 cup mashed ripe avocado (about 2 to
  3 avocados)
1 cup sour cream or low-fat or fat-free
  sour cream
1 cup Salsa, homemade or purchased
½ cup chopped fresh cilantro
¼ to ½ cup minced green onions
2 to 4 dried pasilla chiles, rehydrated,
  stemmed, seeded, and minced

2 cloves garlic, minced
1 cup grated sharp cheddar cheese
  Salt and freshly ground white pepper,
    to taste
  Ground cumin, to taste
  Minced fresh cilantro, black olives,
    marigolds, and/or sour cream for
    garnish

1. Oil a 4- to 6-cup soufflé dish, flan tin, or container of your choice.
2. Dissolve the gelatin by sprinkling it over the lemon juice in a small bowl
   set in a larger bowl of hot water, or dissolve it in a microwave set on low
   power.
3. Combine the avocado, sour cream, salsa, and dissolved gelatin in a food
   processor fitted with the metal blade, or in a large bowl.
4. Process in the remaining ingredients with several quick on-and-off
   motions, using care not to destroy their texture, or combine with the
   ingredients in the bowl. Taste and adjust the seasonings.
5. Pour the mixture into the prepared mold and chill until firm, about 2 hours
   in the refrigerator or 1 hour in the freezer.

FAST: Can prepare up to 3 days in advance and refrigerate.

FLASHY: Garnish with a dollop of sour cream on top and a sprinkling of
minced cilantro or a marigold and/or black olives.

FABULOUS: With minced fresh or dried chiles of your choice. To reduce fat
content, substitute low-fat yogurt for the sour cream.

Southwestern Black Bean & Hominy Salad

Yield: 8+ servings

1 pound dry black beans or 2 15-ounce cans of black beans
1 15-ounce can hominy
1 7-ounce can whole green chiles, deveined, seeded, and chopped
½ to 1 bunch green onions, minced
1 small head purple cabbage, shredded
1 bunch cilantro, minced
8 ounces feta cheese, crumbled, or more
1 6-ounce can pitted black or calamata olives, drained

Sweet red onion, halved and thinly sliced

Optional Seasonings for Beans while Cooking:
1 ham hock
Cumin, to taste
Chile powder, to taste
Garlic cloves, peeled and smashed

Sour cream, to taste, or low-fat or fat-free sour cream
Cilantro Vinaigrette (recipe follows)

1. Soak beans according to instructions on bag.
2. Drain beans and place in a large pot of cold, salted water with any or all of the seasoning ingredients desired. Bring water to a boil, reduce heat to lowest setting, cover pot, and allow to cook for about 20 minutes. Use care not to overcook the beans; they should be lightly al dente.
3. When beans are barely tender, remove from water and place in a large salad bowl. Toss well with desired amount of the vinaigrette and all of the remaining ingredients, except for the sour cream and guacamole. (You may wish to reserve some for garnishing.)

FAST: Can prepare the salad up to 3 days in advance and refrigerate. Can freeze the cooked beans up to 6 months in advance. This salad is best when prepared a day before serving.

FLASHY: Place the salad on a large platter or on individual salad plates, top with a generous dollop(s) of sour cream and guacamole and a sprinkling of any of the ingredients with which you wish to garnish.

FABULOUS: With any kind of beans.

Cilantro Vinaigrette

Yield: About 1½ cups

1 cup olive oil
⅓ cup white wine vinegar
½ to 1 teaspoon salt
½ teaspoon chile powder, or to taste

½ teaspoon cumin, or to taste
2 cloves garlic
½ to 1 bunch cilantro

1. Combine all of the above ingredients in a food processor fitted with the metal blade.
2. Taste and adjust the seasonings.

FAST: Can prepare up to 7 days in advance and refrigerate.

FABULOUS: Use as a marinade or sauce for vegetables, chicken, pork, or fish. To reduce the fat, replace half of the oil with low-fat or fat-free sour cream. With 4 to 6 tomatillos added to the vinaigrette.

Marinated Grilled Chicken Breasts with Zucchini & Two Sauces

Yield: 8 servings

4 to 5 large chicken breasts, boned, skinned, and separated in half
2½ to 3 pounds zucchini, blanched, refreshed, and sliced into ¼-inch-thick long slices

The Marinade:
4 cloves of garlic, minced
2 tablespoons fresh oregano, minced, or dry oregano, to taste
½ cup lime juice

½ cup extra virgin olive oil or low-fat or fat-free plain yogurt
8 tomatillos, husked and cut up
6 to 8 green onions, minced
½ cup cilantro, minced
2 teaspoons sugar
2 teaspoons salt, or more
Cilantro Pesto (recipe follows)
Double Pepper Mayonnaise Sauce (recipe follows)

1. Purée all the ingredients for the marinade in a food processor fitted with the metal blade. Taste and adjust the seasonings.
2. Place the chicken in a glass or ceramic pan and top with the marinade. Cover with plastic wrap and marinade in the refrigerator for up to 24 hours.
3. Place the zucchini in a separate pan and drizzle with the extra marinade. Let sit for at least 1 hour at room temperature or refrigerate for up to two days.
4. Have your coals red hot, sprinkle with smoke chips, and grill the breasts for about 3 minutes on each side, just until no longer pink.
5. Meanwhile, place the zucchini around the edges of the grill while the chicken is cooking. Grill just long enough to heat the zucchini.

FAST: Can marinate or fully prepare up to 2 days in advance and refrigerate.

FLASHY: Serve hot or at room temperature on a large platter, with the chicken breasts interspersed with the zucchini. Garnish with whole green chiles and strips of red bell pepper. Serve with a dollop of the Cilantro Pesto and Double Pepper Mayonnaise.

FABULOUS: With eggplant instead of zucchini.

Cilantro Pesto

Yield: About 3½ cups

3 bunches cilantro
½ cup almonds, toasted
½ to 1 cup olive oil or low-fat or
    fat-free sour cream
½ to 1 fresh chile, seeded, or use
    several canned chiles

2 to 4 cloves garlic
  Salt, to taste
1 tablespoon red wine vinegar or
    fresh lemon or lime juice

1. Combine all the ingredients in a food processor fitted with the metal blade. Taste and adjust the seasonings.

FAST: Can prepare up to 3 days in advance and refrigerate, or freeze for up to 3 months.

FLASHY: Serve at room temperature in a bowl, or place a dollop directly on the chicken.

FABULOUS: With sour cream or mayonnaise mixed in, and served as a sauce for hors d'oeuvres. With 4 to 6 tomatillos and/or ½ cup nopales added. Add to marinades, salad dressings, or soups. Serve on pasta, rice, fish, chicken, or pork.

Double Pepper Mayonnaise Sauce

A fabulous and versatile condiment!   ***Yield: About 2 cups***

3 to 6 dried pasilla chiles, rehydrated, stemmed, and seeded
2 roasted red peppers, skinned and seeded
½ cup mayonnaise or low-fat or fat-free mayonnaise

½ cup yogurt or low-fat or fat-free yogurt
Fresh lemon or lime juice, to taste
½ cup cloves roasted garlic, optional (recipe follows)

1. Combine all of the ingredients in a food processor fitted with the metal blade or in a blender. Taste and adjust the seasonings.

FAST: Can prepare up to 5 days in advance and refrigerate.

FLASHY: Serve as a dunk for cold chicken, seafood, or veggies, or as a cold sauce for fish, vegetables, chicken, pork, or seafood. Add your favorite vinegar and use as a salad dressing for any kind of salad.

FABULOUS: With all fat-free yogurt in place of the mayonnaise to reduce the fat and calories.

Chocolate Espresso Charlotte with Walnuts & Double Berry Sauce

A chocolate lover's dream and a wonderful splurge.   **Yield: 8+ servings**

Chocolate Espresso Filling:
5 jumbo egg yolks or egg substitute
1 cup granulated sugar
1 tablespoon instant espresso
1 cup unsweetened cocoa
¼ cup confectioners sugar
1 cup heavy cream
5 ounces bittersweet chocolate, broken
    or cut up
8 ounces milk chocolate chips

1¼ cups heavy cream
¼ cup brandy
½ cup Kahlua
    Grated nutmeg and cinnamon, to
    taste
    Zest from 3 oranges, finely grated
2 cups walnut halves, toasted

30 ladyfingers (purchased), split in half

1. Place the egg yolks in a food processor fitted with the metal blade and process with the sugar until they turn a light lemon color.
2. Process in the espresso and cocoa.
3. Meanwhile, put 1 cup heavy cream, chocolate, brandy, and Kahlua in a bowl and microwave, using medium power, until the chocolate melts, or place in the top of a double boiler over medium heat.
4. Add the melted chocolate mixture to the food processor with the other ingredients. Process thoroughly and season to taste with nutmeg and cinnamon. Transfer this mixture to a bowl and chill it in the freezer for about 15 minutes.
5. Fold the whipped cream with orange zest and walnuts into the chocolate mixture.
6. Line a 1-quart charlotte mold with plastic wrap and then with ladyfinger halves. Fit them together very closely, with the split side facing inside. To line the bottom of the mold, place ladyfingers in a spike shape toward the center, fitting them as tightly as possible. It may be necessary to trim or shape them.
7. Add a layer of walnuts, then the filling. If the ladyfingers extend past the rim of the mold, trim them. Cover with plastic.

8. Chill for at least 4 hours in the refrigerator.
9. Unmold the charlotte on a platter, and remove and peel off the plastic wrap.

FAST: Can prepare up to 2 days in advance and refrigerate, or freeze for up to 3 months.

FLASHY: Serve with the Double Berry Sauce and with extra walnuts. For an attractive presentation, place the sauce in a squirt bottle and drizzle a pattern on the plate before placing a piece of the charlotte mold on top. Garnish with extra whole berries and fresh mint leaves.

Double Berry Sauce

Yield: About 2½ cups

½ pound boysenberries
½ pound blueberries
¼ cup orange-flavored liqueur

Sugar, to taste
Lemon juice, to taste

1. Purée all but 1 cup of the berries in a food processor fitted with the metal blade.
2. Stir in the orange-flavored liqueur, lemon juice, and sugar.
3. Strain the sauce and stir in the reserved berries.

FAST: Can prepare up to 5 days in advance and refrigerate, or freeze up to 6 months.

FABULOUS: Serve on vanilla ice cream or frozen yogurt.

Asian Jerked Rib Dinner

his dinner party is loaded with diverse culinary influences and jubilant flavors. As an added bonus, all the dishes except for the ribs and corn are served cold or at room temperature, which means that it is ideal for large groups. The party starts off with an upscale rendition of black beans that have been gelled into a cold soufflé. From hors d'oeuvres we move on to the main event. The Asian Jerked Ribs are marinated in a tasty combination of Chinese ingredients and further enlivened with some Jamaican jerk seasoning paste. If you haven't ever had jerk, you're in for a treat. These ribs are so spectacular that they don't need any sauces. Having said that, and with my passion for gilding the lily, I have a very simple mustard sauce for the ribs. Grilled corn is the perfect partner for ribs and another spiritual summer experience. A made-in-advance salad with an Indian influence rounds out this menu of great flavors.

My table captured this excitement by using a tablecloth with a black background and abstract flowers in hot pink, yellow, green, orange, and blue. My napkins were bright yellow and hot pink. The centerpiece consisted of a mixture of summer annuals. I'm not talking cut flowers. What I mean is using six-packs from the nursery crammed artistically into a high-sided basket. To fill in the spaces and make everything appear lush, use leather ferns or any greenery. Along with my flowers were lots of votive candles.

Menu

Cold Black Bean Soufflé

Asian Jerked Ribs

Curried Rice & Pea Pod Salad

Grilled Corn

Nectarine Bombé with Sauce

Faster & Flashier Menu

Black Bean Dip (homemade or purchased)

Asian Jerked Ribs

Corn

Salads (purchased from the deli)

Ice Cream (with purchased sauce)

Margaritas and/or Beer

Pinot Noir and Coffee

✄   TIMETABLE   ✄

Up to 1 month in advance and frozen	Nectarine Bombé
Up to 2 weeks in advance	Prepare the Asian Jerked Marinade. Plum Mustard Sauce.
Up to 4 days in advance	Raspberry Sauce
Up to 3 days in advance	Curried Rice & Pea Pod Salad
Up to 2 days in advance	Cold Black Bean Soufflé. Marinate the ribs.
Up to 1 day in advance	Set the table.
Party day!	Grill the ribs. Grill the corn.

Cold Black Bean Soufflé

Uptown beans!

½ cup canned green chiles, deveined,
   seeded, and chopped
4 to 6 pasilla chiles, rehydrated,
   stemmed, and seeded
8 ounces cream cheese or low-fat or
   fat-free cream cheese
3 cups cooked black beans, drained, or
   canned beans
2 packages unflavored gelatin dissolved
   in ¼ cup water or sherry

1 15-ounce jar pickled cactus* (nopales)
1 bunch cilantro, chopped
1 bunch green onions, chopped
  Salt, ground cumin, and hot pepper
   sauce, to taste
  Sour cream, chopped green onions,
   tomatoes, and/or cilantro, radishes,
   and/or green onions for garnishing

1. Combine the first 4 ingredients in a food processor fitted with the metal blade.
2. Process in the dissolved gelatin.
3. Add the remaining ingredients and process with several quick on-and-off motions, using care not to destroy all of the texture. Taste and adjust the seasonings.
4. Transfer the mixture into an oiled 6- to 8-cup bowl or mold. Refrigerate until firm, about 2 hours. Unmold and enjoy!

FAST: Can prepare up to 2 days in advance and refrigerate, or freeze for up to 3 months.

FLASHY: Garnish with any or all of the garnishes, and serve with warm tortillas, tortilla chips, and/or thinly sliced baguettes.

FABULOUS: With canned, refried beans or cooked pinto beans.

*Refer to Terms & Techniques.

Curried Rice & Pea Pod Salad

Always make this dish with rice that has been prepared
at least a day in advance and refrigerated.

Yield: 8+ servings

3 cups cooked and chilled long-grain
    white or brown rice
½ to 1 sweet red onion, chopped
8 ounces pea pods, blanched
1 cup roasted peanuts, chopped or
    whole
2 cups cantaloupe chunks

½ cup sour cream or low-fat or fat-free
    sour cream
½ cup Curried Vinaigrette, or to taste
    (recipe follows)
    Salt and freshly ground, coarse black
    pepper, to taste

1. Place the rice in a large mixing bowl and toss with all the ingredients. Taste
   and adjust the seasonings.

FAST: Can prepare up to 3 days in advance and refrigerate.

FLASHY: Serve in hollowed-out tomatoes or in cantaloupe halves.

FABULOUS: With cooked chicken, crab, and/or shrimp added.

Curried Vinaigrette

Yield: About 2¼ cups

1 cup peanut or canola oil
1 cup seasoned rice vinegar
3 to 4 teaspoons curry paste
    (purchased)

¼ cup fresh mint leaves, or to taste
2 cloves garlic
    White pepper and/or hot pepper
    sauce, to taste

1. Combine all the ingredients in a food processor fitted with the metal blade.
   Taste and adjust the seasonings.

FAST: Can prepare up to 14 days in advance and refrigerate.

FLASHY: On any combination of tossed greens.

FABULOUS: As a marinade or sauce for fish, chicken, or pork.

Grilled Corn

A religious summer experience.

Yield: 8+ servings

8 ears of corn, or more, husked
½ to 1 cup hickory chips, soaked
Extra virgin olive oil

Salt and freshly ground, coarse black
pepper

1. Bring a large pot of salted water to a boil. Add the corn and cook for about 3–5 minutes, until barely tender.
2. While the ribs are being cut up for serving, place the hickory chips on the coals and the corn on the grill. Brush the corn with the olive oil and season with the salt and pepper. Place the cover over the barbecue and smoke for about 15 minutes over a very low fire until hot.

FAST: Can boil the corn up to 6 hours in advance, brush it with olive oil, salt it, and refrigerate. Grill before serving.

FABULOUS: Try cutting the corn into coins.

Marinated Asian Jerked Ribs

Exotically spicy!   **Yield: 8 servings**

¼ to ½ cup Jamaican jerk
¾ cup Chinese Black Bean Sauce*
   prepared
1½ cups Chinese Lemon or Plum
   Sauce,* prepared

1½ cups fresh mint, minced
3 cups cream sherry
8 to 12 pounds baby back pork ribs,
   trimmed well to remove the fat

1. Combine all of the ingredients, except for the ribs, in a food processor fitted with the metal blade or in a blender.
2. Place the ribs in a plastic, ceramic, or glass pan and cover with the marinade. Let sit at room temperature for 2 hours or marinate in the refrigerator for up to 3 days.
3. To barbecue, have the coals hot and set them on each side of a kettle-type barbecue. For a smokier flavor, add several handfuls of smoke chips before putting the ribs on. Cover and let cook for about 45 minutes or until fully cooked. The cooking time will vary greatly, depending on the meatiness of the ribs. Serve with Plum Mustard Sauce and/or Maple Mustard Sauce.

FAST: Can prepare the marinade up to 2 weeks in advance and refrigerate, or freeze for up to 6 months. Can marinate the ribs up to 3 days in advance and refrigerate.

FABULOUS: As a marinade for ribs, chicken, swordfish, halibut, tuna, beef, pork, lamb, or vegetables. As a cold sauce mixed with sour cream or yogurt (½ cup mixed with 2 cups sour cream).

*Refer to Terms & Techniques.

Plum Mustard Sauce

Yield: About 2 cups

½ cup Dijon mustard
¾ to 1 cup Chinese Plum Sauce
¼ to ½ cup Balsamic vinegar

1. Combine all the ingredients. Taste and adjust the seasonings.

FAST: Can prepare up to 3 months in advance and refrigerate.

FLASHY: Serve cold or hot as a sauce or dip.

FABULOUS: With fresh, chopped mint leaves.

Nectarine Bombé with Raspberry Sauce

Cool and beautiful, this is a molded, flavored ice cream dessert.   *Yield: 8 to 12 servings*

1 quart French vanilla ice cream,
    softened, or fat-free vanilla ice
    cream or frozen yogurt
6 large nectarines, peeled, pitted, and
    puréed (about 1½ cups of purée)
4 ounces bittersweet chocolate, shaved
    or chopped

2 cups almonds, toasted and chopped
⅔ cup orange-flavored liqueur
⅓ cup brandy
    Freshly grated nutmeg, to taste
    Raspberry Sauce (recipe follows)
    Whipped cream and sprigs of fresh
        mint for garnish

1. Oil 2-quart mold with vegetable or other flavorless oil.
2. Combine all the ingredients, except the Raspberry Sauce and garnishes, in
    a large bowl, blending well.
3. Pour ingredients into the prepared mold. Cover with plastic wrap and
    freeze until firm, at least 3 hours. Let sit at room temperature for about 15
    minutes before serving.

FAST: Can prepare up to 1 month in advance and freeze.

FLASHY: To serve, run a sharp knife dipped in hot water around the mold. Dip the bottom of the mold in hot water quickly and invert onto a platter. Top with Raspberry Sauce and whipped cream. Garnish with sprigs or leaves of mint.

FABULOUS: With peaches, cantaloupe, bananas, papaya, kiwi, and/or mangos instead of the nectarines.

Raspberry Sauce

Make large batches of this wonderful sauce and freeze it so you can enjoy the taste of summer any time.   **Yield: About 4½ cups**

3 cups (1½ pints) fresh or unsweetened frozen raspberries, puréed and strained
½ cup orange-flavored liqueur

¼ cup brandy
½ cup sugar, or to taste

1. Combine all the ingredients, except the cream, in a food processor fitted with the metal blade or in a bowl.

FAST: Can prepare up to 4 days in advance and refrigerate, or freeze for up to 6 months. Thaw in the refrigerator for 2 days or at room temperature for about 8 hours.

FABULOUS: Prepared with any berry and seasoned with fresh mint leaves.

Grilled Bourbon Tri-Tip

The typical '90s carnivore eats very little meat. On those special occasions when they do, both quality and creativity is important. Most of us have transcended the days when a plain unseasoned piece of beef was barbecued to grayness and slapped on a plate. I prefer beef that has been submerged in a luscious marinade, grilled to a perfect pinkness, and topped with a sauce or condiment. The Grilled Bourbon Tri-Tip is topped with an Onion & Bleu Cheese Salad, which provides great flavors and textures. If you are a tri-tip lover, this menu is for you.

It goes without saying that a great grilled beef menu must have potatoes. If it's French fries or a lovely foil-wrapped baked potato you crave, disappointment awaits. Crisp, Roasted Garlic Potatoes complement the luscious tri-tip.

Red onions, peaches, and sprigs of rosemary are the stars of this table. In the center of the pastel plaid tablecloth is a medium-size terra cotta flowerpot turned upside down. It holds a low-sided basket filled with peaches. The onions are placed directly on the cloth surrounding the flowerpot. Rosemary sprigs and votive candles are interspersed.

Menu

Chard Pesto on Saint André Cheese

Crostini

Grilled Bourbon Tri-Tip

Onion & Bleu Cheese Salad

Crisp, Roasted Garlic Potatoes

Garlic Rosemary Bread

Peach Almond Egg Rolls with French Vanilla Ice Cream

Faster & Flashier Menu

Brie Smothered in Roasted Red Peppers (purchased)

Grilled Bourbon Tri-Tip

Sliced Onions & Tomatoes with Bleu Cheese Dressing (purchased)

Baked Potatoes

French Bread

Dessert (purchased)

❧ TIMETABLE ❧

Up to 7 days in advance	Tri-Tip Marinade. Red Wine Vinaigrette.
Up to 5 days in advance	Peach Almond Egg Rolls
Up to 4 days in advance	Chard Pesto. Onion & Bleu Cheese Salad.
Up to 3 days in advance	Marinate the tri-tip.
Up to 1 day in advance	Assemble the potatoes. Set the table.
Party day!	Bake the potatoes. Grill the tri-tip. Broil the egg rolls.

Chard Pesto on Saint André Cheese

*This, combined with a baguette of bread and
a bottle of wine, makes a lovely lunch.*

Yield: 8+ servings

1 large bunch of red chard, with the
  stalks reserved for another use
1 to 2 large onions
4 to 8 cloves garlic
½ cup extra virgin olive oil, or more
½ cup freshly grated Parmesan cheese,
  or more

Salt, freshly ground, coarse black
  pepper and fresh lemon juice, to
  taste
1 cup walnuts, toasted (page 13)
½ pound Saint André cheese, at room
  temperature

1. Place the chard in a large pot or wok over medium heat and cover with a
   lid. Cook for about 5 minutes or until just wilted.
2. Drain off any excess liquid and transfer to a food processor fitted with the
   metal blade.
3. Add all the remaining ingredients, except the walnuts and Saint André
   cheese, and process until finely chopped.
4. Add the walnuts and process, using several quick on-and-off motions so as
   not to destroy the texture of the walnuts. Taste and adjust the seasonings.
5. Place the Saint André cheese on a plate and surround or top the cheese
   with the pesto.

FAST: Can prepare the pesto up to 4 days in advance and refrigerate, or freeze
for up to 3 months.

FLASHY: Serve with thinly sliced baguettes and/or crostini (page 66).

FABULOUS: With feta instead of Parmesan cheese and/or with Brie or
Camembert instead of Saint André cheese.

Onion & Bleu Cheese Salad

A flavorful duo!　　　　　　　　　　　　　　　　**Yield: 8+ servings**

2 large white onions, sliced thinly
2 large red onions, sliced thinly
2 teaspoons sugar, or more
　Red Wine Vinaigrette (page 93)

½ cup parsley, minced
8 ounces or more bleu cheese, crumbled
　Salt and freshly ground, coarse black
　pepper, to taste

1. Bring a pot of salted water to a boil. Add the onions and sugar. Blanch for just a few seconds. Remove onions to a colander. Place in sink under cold running water. Drain well.
2. Transfer onions to a bowl. Toss with desired amount of vinaigrette, parsley, and bleu cheese. Taste and adjust seasonings.

FAST: Can prepare up to 4 days in advance and refrigerate.

FLASHY: Serve instead of a sauce with meat, lamb, chicken, or swordfish.

FABULOUS: With any kind of onions, with fresh dill or rosemary. When the onions are chopped, this mixture can be used as an hors d'oeuvre served with crostini.

Grilled Bourbon Tri-Tip

This is beef at its best!   **Yield: 8+ servings**

4 to 6 pounds tri-tip

Bourbon Marinade:
2 large red onions
½ cup fresh rosemary
½ cup fresh mint leaves

½ cup bourbon
1 tablespoon salt
¾ to 1 cup balsamic vinegar
2 cups tomato juice
6 to 12 garlic cloves
½ cup soy sauce

1. Combine all of the ingredients for the marinade in a food processor fitted with the metal blade.
2. Place the tri-tip in a glass, ceramic, or plastic pan and pour the marinade over it. Let sit for 2 hours at room temperature or up to 3 days refrigerated.
3. To grill, have the coals hot and set them on each side of a kettle-type barbecue. For a smokier flavor, add several handfuls of soaked smoke chips to the hot coals. Place the meat on the grill and cover with the lid. Grill for about 30 minutes or until a meat thermometer inserted into the center reaches 120 degrees for rare or 130 degrees for medium.

FAST: Can prepare the marinade up to 7 days in advance and refrigerate. Can marinate for up to 3 days refrigerated.

FLASHY: Serve on a wood platter garnished with sprigs of fresh rosemary or marigolds.

Crisp, Roasted Garlic Potatoes

This is as close to a religious experience as any potato lover can get.   **Yield: 8+ servings**

3 pounds russet potatoes, or your
    favorite variety
1 cup olive, peanut, or canola oil

¼ to ½ cup garlic cloves
Salt and white pepper, to taste

1. Bring a large pot of salted water to a boil and preheat the oven to 400 degrees.
2. Meanwhile, scrub and thinly slice the potatoes into rounds.
3. Combine the oil, garlic, salt, and pepper in a food processor fitted with the metal blade or in a blender.
4. Place the potatoes in the boiling water until barely tender. Watch carefully to avoid overcooking. Remove the potatoes to a colander in the sink and drain thoroughly. Blot with paper towels.

5. Place the potatoes in a large bowl and gently coat with the oil mixture.
6. Line several baking pans with foil and transfer the potatoes to them, spreading the potatoes out to form a thin, even layer.
7. Bake for at least 30 minutes or until the potatoes are crisp enough.

FAST: Can prepare through Step 6 up to 1 day in advance and refrigerate. Bake before serving.

FABULOUS: With fresh or dried rosemary, oregano, or basil added to the oil.

Peach Almond Egg Rolls with French Vanilla Ice Cream
Yield: 8 servings

1 package egg roll wrappers
French vanilla ice cream

The Filling:
¼ cup rum
¼ to ½ cup sugar, extra for sprinkling
½ cup peach preserves

Zest of 1 to 2 lemons, grated
2½ to 3 pounds peaches, pitted and thinly sliced
Freshly grated nutmeg and ground cinnamon, to taste
⅓ cup melted, unsalted butter
1 cup slivered almonds, toasted

1. Place all the filling ingredients, except for the melted butter, almonds, and peaches, in a heavy skillet over high heat to dissolve the sugar and preserves.
2. Mix in the almonds and peaches. Taste and adjust the seasonings.
3. Place several tablespoons of the filling at an angle in the center of an egg roll wrapper. Roll up like an envelope, lightly moistening the edges with water to seal. Place seam-side down on a buttered baking sheet. Repeat until the filling is used.
4. Brush the tops of the egg rolls with the melted butter and sprinkle with the extra sugar.
5. Place under a preheated broiler until golden, about 5 minutes.

FAST: Can prepare the filling up to 4 days in advance and refrigerate or freeze for up to 6 months. Can prepare through Step 4 up to 1 day in advance and refrigerate, or flash freeze for up to 3 months.

FLASHY: Serve hot with a scoop of ice cream and garnish with fresh mint.

FABULOUS: With almost any fresh fruit.

Seafood Barbecue Dinner

*T*his party calls for a luxurious al fresco setting. Try a bright summer-white or cream-colored cloth or possibly a blue-and-white-striped sheet. Spread fish netting down the center of the table with scattered seashells, and set out terra cotta saucers in a variety of sizes, filled with sand holding white candles. For visual variety, use some terra cotta pots turned upside down to place some of the sand-filled saucers on. For the centerpiece, white stattice in a small tin pail looks wonderful. You might consider painting the saucers and pots white. This creates a dramatic monochromatic look.

Our menu is luxurious and stylish, with strong Mediterranean influences. For openers, my Feta & Roasted Red Pepper Torta. This hors d'oeuvre combines such delicacies as roasted red peppers, pine nuts, garlic, and herbs layered between a feta-based cheese mixture. It is molded to perfection, creating a bold and dramatic presentation.

Next comes a delicious version of a Greek Salad. Combine this salad with a grilled or broiled piece of fish, chicken, lamb, or beef and you have dinner—simply delicious!

Perfectly grilled Seafood Skewers, along with a very refreshing and unique Fresh Fruit Salsa are complemented by Lemon & Pine Nut Bulgar, which is a lovely alternative to rice pilaf. Bulgar is extremely convenient and full of flavor, not to mention high in nutrition. Our vegetable dish offers us another very flavorful way to make good use of zucchini. Dinner culminates on another simply delicious note—Mango & Berry Tart. From start to finish, this party is the ultimate in stylish simplicity!

Menu

Feta & Roasted Red Pepper Torta
Summer Greek Salad
Seafood Skewers with Fresh Fruit Salsa & Italian Basil Salsa
Lemon & Pine Nut Bulgar
Baked Zucchini with Artichoke Hearts
Mango & Berry Tart

Faster & Flashier Menu

Feta Cheese topped with chopped Roasted Red Peppers
Summer Greek Salad
Seafood Skewers with Fresh Fruit Salsa
Lemon & Pine Nut Bulgar
Vanilla Ice Cream with Mango & Berries

Sauvignon Blanc and/or Beer
Coffee

✃ TIMETABLE ✃

Up to 5 days in advance	Salad dressing. Prepare the seafood marinade. Feta & Roasted Red Pepper Torta.
Up to 4 days in advance	Prepare the pastry cream or glaze.
Up to 3 days in advance	Fresh Fruit Salsa
Up to 2 days in advance	Baked Zucchini with Artichoke Hearts
Up to 1 day in advance	Prep the salad. Marinate the seafood. Lemon & Pine Nut Bulgar. Tart shell.
Party day!	Toss the salad. Heat up the bulgar.

Feta & Roasted Red Pepper Torta

A celebration of summer.   **Yield: About 3½ cups**

¾ pound feta cheese
  1 8-ounce package cream cheese or
      low-fat or fat-free sour cream, at
      room temperature
½ pound (2 sticks) unsalted butter or
      half-fat butter, cut into pieces
  2 to 4 tablespoons fresh lemon juice

1 shallot, minced
1 to 2 cloves garlic, minced
  Ground white pepper, to taste
4 large red bell peppers, roasted,* peeled,
      seeded, and minced, or to taste
1 cup walnuts, toasted (page 13)
2 cups packed fresh basil leaves, minced

1. Combine the cheeses, butter, lemon juice, shallot, garlic, and pepper in a
   food processor fitted with the metal blade and process until smooth, or
   combine in a bowl.
2. Oil a 4- to 5-cup straight-sided mold, bowl, or pâté terrine. Line with
   plastic wrap.
3. Add a layer of the roasted red peppers with the desired amount of basil
   and walnuts to the mold. Top with a layer of the cheese mixture. Alternate
   until the mold is filled, ending with a layer of the cheese mixture.
4. Fold the plastic wrap over the top and gently press down to compress the
   layers.
5. Refrigerate until firm, at least 1 hour before unmolding. To unmold,
   remove the plastic wrap and place on a serving plate.

FAST: Can prepare up to 5 days in advance and refrigerate, or freeze for up to
3 months.

FLASHY: Serve with Bagel Chips (page 272), thinly sliced French bread, or
pumpernickel squares. Garnish with fresh basil leaves, pine nuts, minced
fresh parsley, and/or any nontoxic flower or leaves.

FABULOUS: Create a caviar torta by layering 4–6 ounces caviar with the
minced green onions and zest from 2–3 lemons instead of the roasted red
peppers. To further reduce the fat, replace all or half of the butter with feta
cheese.

FURTHER: Use leftovers tossed into hot pasta or rice, or instead of a sauce on
fish or poultry.

*Refer to Terms & Techniques.

Summer Greek Salad

Use this salad as a luncheon entrée.

Yield: 8 servings

2 to 4 cloves garlic
Capers, to taste
½ cup parsley, minced
¼ cup fresh mint leaves, minced
Oregano, dried, to taste
Lemon juice, to taste (about ⅔ cup)
2 cups extra virgin olive oil
8 cups Romaine lettuce leaves, torn
6 to 8 radishes, thinly sliced
21 Greek olives, or more
2 tomatoes, cut into thin wedges
2 to 3 red peppers, roasted, peeled, seeded, and thinly sliced, or use purchased roasted red peppers
½ to 1 sweet red onion, cut into thin rings
1 cucumber, peeled and thinly sliced
4 to 8 anchovies
½ pound feta cheese, crumbled
Kosher salt and freshly ground, coarse black pepper

1. Rub a clove of the garlic and a teaspoon of salt in a wooden salad bowl using a fork.
2. Combine the remaining garlic along with the capers, parsley, mint, oregano, lemon juice, olive oil, salt, and pepper in a food processor fitted with the metal blade or in a blender. Taste and adjust the seasonings.
3. Add all the salad ingredients to the bowl, except for the dressing.
4. Toss in the desired amount of the dressing along with the feta cheese. Taste and adjust the seasonings.

FAST: Can prepare the dressing up to 5 days in advance and refrigerate. Have all vegetables and ingredients prepped and refrigerated up to 1 day in advance. Toss right before serving.

FLASHY: Serve as the main course for lunch or dinner with plenty of crusty French bread.

Seafood Skewers with Fresh Fruit Salsa & Italian Basil Sauce

Yield: 8 servings

32 to 48 large sea scallops (4 to 6 per person)

8 to 16 large shrimp (1 to 2 per person), shelled and deveined

The Marinade:

1 cup olive oil or low-fat or fat-free plain yogurt

¼ cup parsley, minced

½ cup fresh, packed basil

2 shallots

4 cloves garlic

Fresh lemon or lime juice

Salt and white pepper, to taste

8 bamboo skewers

Fresh Fruit Salsa (recipe follows)

1. Place scallops and shrimp in a large glass or ceramic pan.
2. Combine all ingredients for the marinade in a food processor fitted with the metal blade. Taste and adjust seasonings.
3. Pour marinade over seafood, cover with plastic wrap, and let marinate in refrigerator for up to 1 day.
4. Skewer seafood.
5. Heat up barbecue or broiler and cook very briefly, just until the shrimp turns opaque.

FAST: Can prepare the marinade up to 5 days in advance. Can marinate up to 1 day in advance.

FLASHY: Serve skewers on top of sauce or with sauce drizzled on top.

FABULOUS: With chunks of swordfish, salmon, and/or tuna added to skewers.

Fresh Fruit Salsa

A show stopper!

Yield: About 4 cups

1 red Fresno chile, stemmed, seeded, and cut up
1 medium-size red onion, peeled and cut into about 8 small pieces
½ cup fresh mint leaves

2 mangos, peeled, pitted, and cut up
2 pints strawberries, hulled and halved
Salt, to taste
½ cup raspberry vinegar

1. Combine all of the ingredients in a food processor fitted with the metal blade, using several quick on-and-off motions so as not to destroy all the texture. Taste and adjust the seasonings.

FAST: Can prepare up to 3 days in advance and refrigerate.

FLASHY: Serve with anything grilled.

FABULOUS: With ½ cup fresh basil or cilantro. With a variety of fresh, seeded, and minced chiles.

Lemon & Pine Nut Bulgar

This is a great change of pace from rice.

Yield: 8 servings

2 to 4 tablespoons unsalted butter or
   olive oil
2 shallots, minced
2½ cups bulgar
 ½ cup dry vermouth
 5 cups chicken broth, homemade or
   canned

Grated zest of 2 lemons
¼ to ½ cup pine nuts, toasted
   Salt and white pepper, to taste
   Minced parsley for garnishing

1. Melt butter in saucepan and sauté shallots until tender.
2. Add bulgar and sauté over low heat, while stirring, until it is well coated with butter. Do not brown.
3. Stir in wine, broth, and zest. Bring to boil, reduce heat to low, and cover with a lid. Cook until it is absorbed. This will take about 10–15 minutes.
4. Taste and add more liquid if bulgar isn't tender enough.
5. Stir in pine nuts.

FAST: Can prepare up to 1 day in advance and refrigerate. Reheat in microwave using medium heat for about 5 minutes or in a preheated 350 degree oven for about 15 minutes.

FLASHY: Garnish with sprinkling of minced parsley.

FABULOUS: Prepared with equal amounts of couscous, orzo, and bulgar. With sautéed mushrooms and seasoned with any fresh or dried herb.

Spring Hard-Boiled Eggs with Ham, Asparagus & Artichoke Brunch
Fresh Fruit *(top left)*, Hard-Boiled Eggs with Ham, Asparagus & Artichokes *(top center)*,
Bagels & Lemon Almond Biscotti *(top right)*, Herbed Red Potatoes & Onions *(bottom left)*, Grilled Sausages with Gingered Dill Mustard Sauce & Maple Mustard Sauce
(bottom center).

Summer Lentil & Mango Salad Lunch
Fresh Fruit *(top left)*, French Bread with Olive Oil *(top right)*, Marinated & Smoked Pork *(bottom left)*, Lentil & Mango Salad *(bottom right)*.

Fall Chicken Breast with Shiitake, Shallot & Pear Sauce Dinner
Roasted Garlic Decadence from Heaven and Roasted Garlic Decadence from Hell
with Rosemary Garlic Crostini *(top center)*, Chocolate Cheesecake Mousse Chee Wow
Wa *(top right)*, Chicken Breast with Shiitake, Shallot & Pear Sauce *(middle right)*,
California Chile Soup *(left center)*, Couscous with Carrots *(bottom)*.

Winter Osso Bucco Dinner
Roasted Garlic & Balsamic Pesto with Pita Chips *(top right)*, Chard with Sweet
Onions *(bottom right)*, Osso Bucco surrounded by Saffron Barley & Brown Rice Risotto
(bottom left), Almond Pear Cake topped with Brandied Chocolate Sauce *(top left)*.

Baked Zucchini with Artichoke Hearts

A wonderful vegetable dish that is equally at home at a picnic as an elegant dinner.

Yield: 8 servings

2 to 2½ pounds zucchini, trimmed and cut into 1-inch cubes
  Salt, to taste
2 6-ounce jars marinated artichoke hearts (reserve the marinade)
4 cloves garlic, minced, or to taste
1 red onion, thinly sliced

2 tablespoons capers, rinsed and drained
¼ cup minced fresh parsley
¼ minced fresh basil, or to taste
¼ to ½ cup pumpkin seeds, toasted
  Fresh, ground white pepper, to taste
  Fresh lemon juice, to taste

1. In a large bowl, combine the zucchini and artichoke hearts and their marinade, garlic, and onions. Place in a baking pan and bake in a preheated 425 degree oven until tender, about 10–30 minutes.
2. Add the remaining ingredients, then taste, and adjust the seasonings.

FAST: Can prepare up to 2 days in advance and refrigerate. (For best results, undercook for about 15 minutes if you are planning on reheating and serving this hot.) Reheat in a microwave, using medium power for about 10 minutes, or in a preheated 350 degree oven for about 15 minutes.

FLASHY: Serve at room temperature for this menu or serve hot for more elegant dinners.

FABULOUS: With eggplant instead of zucchini, and with roasted red peppers mixed in. With freshly grated Parmesan cheese.

FURTHER: Use leftovers in soups, or in lettuce, rice, or pasta salads. Toss into hot pasta.

Mango & Berry Tart

Great colors, flavors, and shapes! This recipe looks involved
but is totally do-able and delicious.

Yield: 1 11-inch tart

The Walnut Pastry:
4½ teaspoons sugar
 ¼ teaspoon salt
1½ cups all-purpose flour
 ¼ pound (1 stick) unsalted frozen
    butter, and cut into small pieces
 2 tablespoons ice water
 ½ cup walnuts, toasted (page 13) and
    chopped

The Glaze:
 ½ cup apricot preserves or orange
    marmalade
 2 tablespoons liqueur, rum, brandy,
    bourbon, or Scotch

The Pastry Cream:
 1 cup heavy cream, less 2 tablespoons
 1 tablespoon unflavored gelatin
 1 large egg or egg substitute
 2 large egg yolks or egg substitute
 ⅓ cup sugar
 2 tablespoons cornstarch
    Finely grated zest of 1 lemon
 2 tablespoons Scotch
 1 teaspoon vanilla extract
    Freshly grated nutmeg, to taste
 1 to 2 mangos, peeled and sliced
 1 pint berries (blueberries,
    strawberries, raspberries, or other)
    Sprigs of fresh mint for garnish

1. Place the sugar, salt, flour, and butter in a food processor fitted with the
   metal blade and process until the mixture resembles a coarse meal.
2. While the machine is running, slowly add the water through the feed tube.
   Process until the dough begins to form a ball. To prepare without using a
   food processor, combine the sugar, salt, and flour in a bowl. Add the butter
   (chilled, not frozen) and cut it in, using two knives or a pastry blender,
   until the mixture resembles coarse meal. Stir in the ice water until the
   mixture holds together and can be gathered into a ball.
3. Take the dough from the processor, form into a ball, and roll it out on
   a lightly floured surface so it is 2 inches larger than the diameter of an
   11-inch tart pan.
4. Fold the dough in half and place it in the pan. Unfold and lightly press it
   into the pan. Prick the bottom with a fork and scatter the walnuts over the
   pastry, gently pressing them in.
5. Refrigerate for 30 minutes. Preheat the oven to 400 degrees.
6. Line the crust with aluminum foil and fill with uncooked beans, pastry
   weights, or with another plate.
7. Bake for 12 minutes.

8. Meanwhile, make the glaze by heating the preserves with the liqueur in a microwave or in a small saucepan over low heat until the preserves melt. Strain through a fine mesh strainer or use as is.

9. Remove the foil and lightly brush the pastry with the glaze. Bake for 12 minutes more or until golden. Let the crust cool a while.

10. For the pastry cream, bring the cream and gelatin to a boil over medium-high heat in saucepan.

11. Combine the egg, egg yolks, sugar, cornstarch, zest, and Scotch in a food processor fitted with the metal blade, or in a mixing bowl using an electric mixer.

12. Process several tablespoons of the hot cream through the feed tube while the machine is running, or beat it with an electric mixer.

13. Transfer the contents of the food processor or mixing bowl to the saucepan containing the cream, whisking all the while.

14. Cook, while whisking, over medium heat until the mixture is thickened, about 3–8 minutes. Do not let it boil.

15. Stir in the vanilla and nutmeg.

16. Cool for at least 30 minutes before filling the tart shell. Use the freezer to speed up the process.

17. Fill tart shell with pastry cream and arrange fruit on top. Brush glaze over the fruit. Enjoy!

FAST: Can prepare pastry cream and glaze up to 4 days in advance and refrigerate, or freeze for up to 3 months. Prepare the tart shell up to 1 day in advance and hold covered with plastic wrap at room temperature, or freeze for up to 3 months.

FLASHY: Garnish with sprig of fresh mint.

FABULOUS: Use pastry cream as a filling for crepes or cakes. Flavor the pastry cream with any liqueur, bourbon, or rum; minced dried apricots or chocolate; or with any fruit.

Fall

Herbed Scrambled Eggs &
Polenta Florentine Brunch

*I*f you avoid serving scrambled eggs to groups of people because you hate to be tied up in the kitchen rather than out with your company, you will love this method for preparing eggs in advance. Along with the Herbed Scrambled Eggs is a delicious version of polenta with spinach instead of potatoes. As a matter of fact, there is nothing predictable about this brunch. Rather than just serving sausages, we prepare a melange of Italian sausages and chicken livers enlivened with green onions, mushrooms, and Madeira wine. Fear not; if chicken livers are not your passion, omit them and go heavy on the mushrooms. For the grand finale, there is fresh fruit and pumpkin muffins.

For this brunch, I dressed my table in purple placemats. A low-sided basket, filled with purple heads of cabbage surrounded with Brussels sprouts created the centerpiece. Between the heads of cabbage I placed persimmons. This centerpiece has great colors and shapes along with a sense of seasonal whimsy.

Menu

Polenta Florentine

Sautéed Chicken Livers with Sausages

Herbed Scrambled Eggs

Fresh Fruit and Sin-Free Pumpkin Muffins

Faster & Flashier Menu

Polenta Florentine (using purchased, prepared polenta topped with thawed frozen spinach)

Herbed Scrambled Eggs

Fresh Fruit and Muffins (purchased)

Brut Sparkling Wine

Juices

Coffee

❧   TIMETABLE   ❧

Up to 3 days in advance	Sin-Free Pumpkin Muffins
Up to 2 days in advance	Polenta Florentine. Sautéed Chicken Livers with Sausages.
Up to 1 day in advance	Herbed Scrambled Eggs. Set the table. Chill the wines.
Party day!	Reheat everything!

Polenta Florentine

This is definitely a dish you could make a meal out of.   ***Yield: 8+ servings***

2 to 4 tablespoons olive oil
1 cup chopped white or yellow onions
¼ cup minced Italian parsley
2 pounds frozen spinach, thawed
2½ cups chicken broth, homemade or
   canned

½ cup dry vermouth
1½ cups uncooked instant polenta
   Salt, white pepper, and grated
   nutmeg, to taste

1. Place the olive oil, onions, and parsley in a pot and sauté over medium heat until the onions are tender, about 10 minutes, stirring from time to time.
2. Meanwhile, squeeze out the excess moisture from the spinach and add it to the pot with the onions.
3. Add all the remaining ingredients to the pot and bring it to a boil, stirring constantly.
4. Reduce the heat to medium-low and continue to stir from time to time until the liquid is absorbed and the polenta pulls away from the sides of the pan when stirred, about 10–20 minutes.
5. Transfer the polenta to an oiled glass or ceramic loaf pan and let stand at room temperature until cool. Refrigerate until firm enough to slice. Cut into ½-inch-thick slices or into triangles.
6. Place the polenta slices on an oiled cookie sheet and heat in a 350 degree oven for about 15 minutes, until hot.

FAST: Can prepare through Step 5 up to 2 days in advance and refrigerate.

FLASHY: For another way of forming the polenta: Put the still-hot polenta in oiled custard or cupcake cups and chill in the refrigerator. When firm, unmold.

FABULOUS: With chard, kale, or escarole instead of spinach. Serve with a tomato sauce.

FURTHER: Use leftovers cut up and added to salads or soups.

Sautéed Chicken Livers with Sausages

This also makes a lovely entrée served with rice, pasta, or polenta.
Chicken liver phobics, relax! Omit them and go heavy on the mushrooms.   **Yield: 8 servings**

1 pound chicken livers
  Milk for soaking the liver
1½ to 2 pounds Italian or low-fat Italian
  sausages (mild, hot, or a combo)
1 large yellow or white onion, thinly
  sliced
1 pound domestic mushrooms
3 ounces shiitake mushrooms,
  rehydrated and sliced
2 tablespoons unsalted butter

2 to 4 cloves garlic, minced
  Flour for dredging the liver
¼ to ½ cup Madeira wine
½ to 1 teaspoon dried thyme
½ cup chicken broth, homemade or
  canned
¼ to ½ cup minced Italian parsley
  Salt and freshly ground pepper,
  to taste
½ cup minced green onions

1. Clean the livers and soak them for at least 1 hour in milk. Drain the livers and discard the milk before using. (These can soak for up to 24 hours refrigerated.)
2. Pierce the sausages with a fork to allow the fat to cook away. In a skillet, brown the sausages and cook until no longer pink. (This can also be done in a microwave.) Remove them and cut into slices. Pour off all the fat but 2 tablespoons and sauté the onion and mushrooms until the onions are tender.
3. In another skillet, melt the butter and garlic. Dredge the liver in flour and sauté until brown on the outside and pink on the inside. Remove the liver and set aside.
4. Add sausages, mushrooms, Madeira, seasonings, and stock to the skillet. Bring to a boil, stir in the parsley, and cook until the liquid is slightly thickened.
5. Taste and adjust the seasonings.

FAST: Can prepare up to 2 days in advance and refrigerate. Bring to room temperature and reheat, covered, in a 350 degree oven or in a microwave. For best results, undercook the liver if you plan to reheat it.

FLASHY: Garnish with a scattering of green onions.

FABULOUS: Seasoned with fresh or dried rosemary, marjoram, and/or sage. Served as an entrée on rice, pasta, mashed potatoes, or soft polenta.

FURTHER: Toss leftovers into hot pasta or rice.

Herbed Scrambled Eggs

*This egg recipe was designed specifically to be made in advance.
There's nothing worse than scrambling eggs at the last minute when
a bunch of people are ready to eat.*

Yield: 8+ servings

16 extra-large eggs or egg substitute
½ cup milk or low-fat or fat-free milk
½ teaspoon salt, or more
  White pepper, to taste
8 tablespoons unsalted or half-fat
  butter

½ cup fresh minced Italian parsley
½ cup minced green onions
8 ounces herbed cream cheese or
  chèvre, cut into tiny cubes

1. Beat the first 3 ingredients together until just combined.
2. Melt the butter in a large skillet and add the parsley and green onions.
   Sauté until the onions are wilted.
3. Add the eggs and chèvre or cream cheese and scramble over very low heat.
   When they reach the very runny stage, you can remove them from the
   heat and hold until you are ready to eat. At that time, resume scrambling
   over low heat.

FAST: Can prepare up to the runny stage up to 1 day in advance and refrigerate. Finish right before serving.

FABULOUS: With sautéed mushrooms, peppers, and/or artichoke hearts scrambled in.

Sin-Free Pumpkin Muffins

These are so delicious, it is hard to believe that they are low-fat.   **Yield: About 24 muffins**

1 cup canned pumpkin purée
⅓ cup orange marmalade
⅔ cup brown sugar, packed
2 extra-large egg whites or egg
    substitute
Pinch of salt
1 teaspoon baking soda

1½ teaspoons pumpkin pie spice
1 tablespoon vanilla extract
½ cup low-fat buttermilk
1 cup quick-cooking oatmeal
1⅓ cups cake flour
Extra brown sugar and all-bran
    cereal for a topping (optional)

1. Preheat the oven to 350 degrees and oil a muffin tin.
2. Combine the first 9 ingredients in a food processor fitted with the metal blade.
3. Add the oatmeal and flour and process in until just combined.
4. Fill the muffin tin cups with the batter and top with the brown sugar and bran cereal (optional). Bake for 30 minutes or until a tester inserted into a muffin comes out almost clean.

FAST: Can prepare up to 3 days in advance and refrigerate, or freeze for up to 3 months.

FABULOUS: With banana instead of pumpkin.

Dilled Celery Root & Smoked Turkey Egg Roll Brunch

*I*t just takes one quick glance to realize that this is not a typical brunch menu. No apologies necessary. This meal can consist of anything from eggs to roast beef. By definition, brunch is unconventional. Relax, if you are searching for a lunch or dinner menu, this will easily fit the bill. Add a salad, a cooked vegetable, and candles, and this brunch is transformed into a lovely dinner party.

For decorations, I recommend using fresh rosemary cuttings down the center of the table, interspersed with shiny red apples and heads of garlic. Your table will have a very distinctive look that will nicely complement the menu.

The Dilled Celery Root & Smoked Turkey Egg Rolls are as unusual as they are delicious. The textures range from the firm and crisp celery root to the creamy beans and cheeses. These rolls can be made as sin-free as you wish by simply substituting fat-free cheeses and sour cream.

The Roasted Garlic & Shallot Potatoes with Yams are nirvana for all of you potato and garlic lovers. I am positive that this dish will become a regular part of your repertoire.

Moving on to the grand finale, the Triple Sec Chocolate Chunk Cake meets all my dessert criteria: quick and sinful, with interesting adult flavors, but *not* overly sweet.

168

Menu

Apples with Cold Madeira Bleu Cheese Sauce

*Dilled Celery Root & Smoked Turkey Egg Rolls
with Garlic Dill Sauce*

Roasted Garlic & Shallot Potatoes with Yams

Rolls with Butter

Triple Sec Chocolate Chunk Cake

Fresh Fruit

Faster & Flashier Menu

*Dilled Celery Root & Smoked Turkey Egg Rolls
with Marinara Sauce (bottled)*

Roasted Garlic & Shallot Potatoes with Yams

Dessert (purchased)

Fresh Fruit

Dry White or Sparkling Wine and Coffee

TIMETABLE

Up to 5 days in advance	Cold Madeira Bleu Cheese Sauce
Up to 4 days in advance	Garlic Dill Sauce (or freeze for up to 3 months)
Up to 3 days in advance	Dilled Celery Root & Smoked Turkey. Rolls (or freeze for up to 1 month).
Up to 2 days in advance	Roasted Garlic & Shallot Potatoes with Yams. Triple Sec Chocolate Chunk Cake (or freeze for up to 3 months).
Up to 1 day in advance	Set the table. Chill the wine.
Party day!	Slice the apples and squirt with lemon. Finish the potatoes. Heat the turkey rolls.

Cold Madeira Bleu Cheese Sauce

Wicked on chicken wings, great on steak or almost anything!   ***Yield: About 2½ cups***

5 ounces bleu cheese, or to taste
¼ cup Madeira wine
1 cup mayonnaise, homemade or
    purchased, or low-fat or fat-free
    mayonnaise
1 cup sour cream or fat-free cream
    cheese

1 to 2 cloves garlic
1 to 2 shallots
    Salt and ground white pepper, to taste
    Dash of hot pepper sauce
    Dash of Worcestershire sauce
    Grated zest of 2 lemons

1. Combine all the ingredients, except for the lemon zest, in a food processor fitted with the metal blade, in a blender, or in a mixing bowl. Process until smooth.
2. Add the zest and process or blend briefly, so as not to destroy all the texture. Taste and adjust the seasonings.

FAST: Can prepare up to 5 days in advance and refrigerate, or freeze for up to 3 months.

FLASHY: Serve with apple slices to dip in. Squirt the slices liberally with lemon juice to prevent discoloring. Or serve as a dunk for vegetables, cooked hot or cold beef, seafood, turkey, or chicken wings. Garnish with any nontoxic flower, fresh parsley sprigs, and/or strips of lemon zest.

FABULOUS: In hollowed-out, boiled baby red potatoes, cherry tomatoes, or raw mushroom caps. As an entrée sauce with grilled steaks or roast beef. With pink or green peppercorns added.

Dilled Celery Root & Smoked Turkey Rolls

Crisp egg roll wrappers encase a delightfully smoky filling.

Yield: About 16 rolls;
8+ servings

1 medium-size celery root*
2 tablespoons white or red wine
 vinegar
3 cups cooked white beans,
 fresh-cooked or canned
1 pound smoked turkey, cubed
½ cup sour cream or low-fat or fat-free
 sour cream
½ cup ricotta cheese or low-fat or fat-
 free ricotta cheese

3 to 6 green onions, minced
¼ to ½ cup minced fresh dill
¼ to ½ cup freshly grated Parmesan
2 to 3 cloves garlic
1 cup grated jack cheese (optional)
 Salt and white pepper, to taste
 Egg roll wrappers
 Olive oil

1. Grate the celery root by hand or in a food processor fitted with the metal blade. Put it in a mixing bowl and toss it with the vinegar.
2. Toss in the turkey and beans.
3. Combine all the remaining ingredients, except for the egg rolls, olive oil, and sauce. Taste and adjust the seasonings.
4. Place some of the filling in the center of the egg roll wrapper. Lightly moisten the edges with water and fold it like an envelope, or just roll it and press the edges together to seal it. Repeat until you have made the desired amount.
5. Place the filled egg rolls in an oiled baking pan, brush the top with olive oil, and place in a preheated 350 degree oven for about 30 minutes, until hot.

FAST: Can prepare up to 3 days in advance and refrigerate, or flash freeze for up to 1 month.

FLASHY: Serve hot with Garlic Dill Sauce.

FABULOUS: With ham instead of turkey. With Marinara Pronto (page 247) instead of Garlic Dill Sauce. This filling can also be used to fill Croustades (page 107) for hors d'oeuvres.

*Refer to Terms & Techniques.

Garlic Dill Sauce

*On anything from fish to vegetables, this is a wonderfully
versatile sauce.*

Yield: About 2¼ cups

2 tablespoons unsalted or half-fat
  butter
3 to 6 cloves garlic, minced
1 tablespoon minced shallots
  Stems from 1 bunch fresh dill,
  minced
2 tablespoons all-purpose flour
1 teaspoon anchovy paste, or more

½ cup dry vermouth
1¾ cups chicken broth, homemade or
  canned
½ cup minced fresh dill
  Salt and freshly ground white
  pepper, to taste
  Fresh lemon juice, to taste

1. Melt the butter in a medium-size saucepan over medium-low heat and
   sauté the garlic, shallots, and dill stems briefly; do not brown.
2. Whisk in the flour and anchovy paste and cook over low heat for several
   minutes, continuing to whisk.
3. Turn the heat to high, whisk in the vermouth and broth, and bring to a
   boil while whisking.
4. Reduce the heat to medium-low and simmer for about 5 minutes.
5. Strain the sauce through a fine mesh strainer into another saucepan. Add
   the minced dill, salt, pepper, and lemon juice. Simmer until flavors are
   pleasing, about 5 minutes.

FAST: Can prepare up to 4 days in advance and refrigerate, or freeze for up to
3 months. Thaw in the refrigerator for 2 days or at room temperature for
about 8 hours.

FLASHY: Serve on anything from pasta to fish.

FABULOUS: Seasoned with any fresh or dried herb. With ¼ cup freshly grated
Parmesan and/or 1 cup grated mozzarella or jack cheese and ¼ cup heavy
cream added at Step 5.

Roasted Garlic & Shallot Potatoes with Yams

The ultimate fall potato experience!   **Yield: 8 servings**

4 to 6 pounds baking potatoes
2 medium to large yams

Seasoned Olive Oil Mixture:
1 cup olive oil
8 to 15 cloves garlic

3 to 6 shallots
2 teaspoons salt
  Freshly ground, coarse black pepper,
  to taste

1. Preheat the oven to 425 degrees.
2. Bring a large pot of water to a boil and add the potatoes. Reduce the heat to medium and cook for 10–15 minutes until barely tender.
3. Meanwhile, cook the yams in the microwave for about 15 minutes on medium to high power, until just barely tender.
4. When the potatoes and yams are cool enough to handle, remove the skin from the yams and leave the skin on the potatoes. Cut them into a medium dice.
5. Place the potatoes and yams in a large baking pan and toss with the olive oil mixture.
6. Bake in the preheated oven for 30–60 minutes, depending on how crisp you want them.

FAST: Can prepare up to Step 5 up to 2 days in advance and refrigerate.

FABULOUS: With fresh or dried rosemary and/or thyme added to the oil mixture.

Triple Sec Almond Chocolate Chunk Cake

Fast & fabulous!

Yield: 8 servings

Grated zest of 1 large orange
Grated zest of 2 lemons
¾ cup sugar
1 stick unsalted or half-fat butter
2 jumbo eggs or egg substitute
2 teaspoons vanilla extract
½ cup Triple Sec or any orange-flavored liqueur
½ cup buttermilk or low-fat or fat-free buttermilk

1 teaspoon baking soda
½ teaspoon salt
2 cups all-purpose flour or 1¾ cups flour and ¼ cup cornmeal
1 11-ounce package milk chocolate chips
1 cup toasted, sliced almonds

1. Combine the citrus zest with the sugar in a food processor fitted with the metal blade.
2. Add the butter and process until a smooth mixture is formed.
3. Add the eggs or egg substitute, vanilla, Triple Sec, buttermilk, baking soda, and salt and process until fully combined. Process in the flour. Mix in the chocolate chips and almonds.
4. Butter a nonstick 9¼ × 5¼ × 2¾-inch loaf pan and preheat the oven to 350 degrees.
5. Bake for 50 minutes, until a cake tester inserted into the middle comes out clean.

FAST: Can prepare up to 3 days in advance and store at room temperature, or freeze for up to 3 months.

FLASHY: Serve à la mode.

FABULOUS: With toasted walnuts instead of almonds.

Risotto Cake Lunch

This is another party with a Mediterranean spirit. It pays reverence to fall and its beautiful produce. Despite the long list of ingredients and steps, the dishes in this menu are extremely simple and straightforward. As you will notice, I try to break my recipes into short, logical steps.

This luncheon begins with an extremely interesting citrus salad packed full of Mediterranean goodness. The menu's star is a Risotto Cake. In case you have not had any close encounters with risotto, let me elaborate. This is an Italian rice dish classically prepared with arborio rice, but you can substitute short grain or pearl rice. Risotto differs from pilaf in that the liquid is stirred into the rice slowly, in stages. The end result is a creamy, soft, almost-a-bit-saucy rice dish. For this recipe, the risotto is chilled and then when firm, formed into patties coated with cornmeal and baked in a hot oven. Risotto cakes are to Italians what fried rice is to Chinese—simply a creative way to use leftover rice. It is scrumptious, especially served with an Italian vegetable mixture. For the finale, another simple loaf cake is elevated to new heights.

For the centerpiece, a terra cotta bowl filled with beautiful oranges is perfect. If you like, add rosemary cuttings and place them in the spaces between the oranges. Scatter unshelled walnuts directly on the table and use simple but colorful placemats.

Menu

Mediterranean Citrus Salad
Risotto Cakes with Italian Vegetable Sauté
Chocolate Buttermilk Loaf

Faster & Flashier Menu

Risotto Cakes with Italian Vegetable Sauté
Chocolate Buttermilk Loaf

Sauvignon Blanc
Coffee

☨   TIMETABLE   ☨

Up to 3 days in advance	Chocolate Buttermilk Loaf
Up to 2 days in advance	Mediterranean Citrus Salad. Risotto Cakes through Step 8. Italian Vegetable Sauté through Step 2.
Up to 1 day in advance	Set the table. Chill the wines.
Party day!	Bake the risotto. Finish the vegetables.

Mediterranean Citrus Salad

Refreshing and delicious.

Yield: 8 servings

2 large grapefruits, peeled, with pith cut away
2 large oranges, peeled, with pith cut away
4 green onions, minced
¼ to ½ cup extra virgin olive oil
2 to 4 tablespoons balsamic vinegar
½ cup toasted walnuts, chopped

½ cup pitted calamata olives, or more
8 or more pepperoncini, stemmed and thinly sliced
¼ to ½ cup crumbled bleu cheese, or more, to taste
Salt and freshly ground, coarse black pepper

1. Slice the citrus into thin rounds and then cut each round in half. Place them on a platter.
2. Sprinkle all the ingredients over the citrus and let sit for at least 1 hour before serving.

FAST: Can prepare up to 2 days in advance and refrigerate.

FABULOUS: With canned green chiles instead of pepperoncini. Seasoned with fresh basil, cilantro, or rosemary. With feta or Parmesan cheese instead of bleu cheese.

Risotto Cakes with Italian Vegetable Sauté

Yield: 8+ servings

2 tablespoons extra virgin olive oil
1 large yellow onion, coarsely chopped
⅓ pound pancetta,* cut up finely
1½ cups arborio rice*
1 cup dry vermouth
2 bay leaves
Grated zest of 2 lemons
4½ cups chicken broth, homemade or canned

4 to 6 tablespoons minced Italian parsley
Juice of ½ to 1 lemon
½ cup freshly grated Parmesan cheese
Salt and white pepper, to taste
1 extra-large egg or egg substitute, plus 2 tablespoons water, lightly beaten
½ cup cornmeal
½ cup sesame seeds, toasted
Italian Vegetable Sauté (recipe follows)

1. Sauté the onions in 2 tablespoons of olive oil over medium-low heat until tender.
2. Meanwhile, put the pancetta on a plate and microwave until crisp, about 6–10 minutes, or place in an ovenproof pan and bake in a 375 degree oven for 20–30 minutes, until crisp.
3. Drain the rendered fat off and add the pancetta to the onions, along with the dry vermouth, bay leaves, and lemon zest. Stirring from time to time, cook over medium-low heat until it is absorbed.
4. Stir in half of the broth and bring it to a boil over high heat. Reduce the heat to medium-low until the broth is absorbed, stirring from time to time.
5. Repeat this with the remaining chicken broth.
6. Stir in the lemon juice, parsley, and Parmesan cheese. Taste and adjust the seasonings.
7. Transfer to a 9 × 13-inch oiled glass pan and cool to room temperature, then refrigerate for at least 2 hours.
8. Form the risotto into patties or cut into squares. Combine the cornmeal and sesame seeds on a plate. Dip each risotto cake in the egg mixture and then into the cornmeal mixture. Place on an oiled cookie sheet. Cover with plastic wrap and refrigerate for at least 1 hour or up to 2 days.
9. Bake in a preheated 425 degree oven until hot, about 15 minutes.

FAST: Can prepare through Step 8 up to 2 days in advance and refrigerate. Bake right before serving.

FLASHY: Serve with any saucy entrée.

FABULOUS: Seasoned with almost any fresh or dried herb. With bacon, ham, or sausage instead of pancetta.

Italian Vegetable Sauté

This dish was inspired by a trip to the farmers market in Monterey. The vegetables were so wonderful that I couldn't wait to create something with them.

Yield: 8+ servings

¼ cup extra virgin olive oil
4 leeks, white and tender green parts, minced or thinly sliced
10 to 20 dried shiitake mushrooms, rehydrated, stemmed and sliced
2 pounds domestic mushrooms, thinly sliced
½ cup dry vermouth
½ cup chicken broth, homemade or canned

2 bunches chard, cut up (including the stems)
¼ to ½ cup fresh dill, minced
Salt, white pepper, and fresh lemon juice, to taste
2 to 4 ounces chèvre cheese
2 tablespoons unsalted butter (optional)

1. Sauté the leeks, shiitake mushrooms, and domestic mushrooms in the olive oil over medium heat, until the liquid that the domestic mushrooms release cooks away, about 10–15 minutes.
2. Increase the heat to high and add the wine, chicken broth, chard, and dill. Cook until the liquid is reduced to almost a glaze.
3. Season to taste and stir in the chèvre and butter (optional).

FAST: Can prepare through Step 2 up to 2 days in advance and refrigerate. Bring to room temperature and finish cooking before serving.

FLASHY: Serve hot over Risotto Cakes, polenta, rice, and/or pasta.

FABULOUS: Seasoned with fresh or dried tarragon instead of dill. With sautéed seafood mixed in.

FURTHER: Toss leftovers into hot pasta.

Chocolate Buttermilk Loaf

A quick chocolate fix!   **Yield: 1 loaf**

1½ cups all-purpose white flour or
    1 cup flour and ½ cup cornmeal
1½ to 1¾ cups sugar
   Grated zest of 2 to 3 oranges
 1 cup unsweetened cocoa
11 ounces semisweet chocolate chips
 1 teaspoon baking soda

¼ teaspoon salt
 8 tablespoons unsalted butter, melted
 2 teaspoons vanilla
 1 cup buttermilk or low-fat or fat-free
    buttermilk
¼ cup Kahlua

1. Combine the first 8 ingredients in a food processor fitted with the metal blade or in a mixing bowl using an electric mixer.
2. Add the remaining ingredients and process until just combined.
3. Transfer to a buttered loaf pan and bake in a preheated 350 degree oven for about 30 minutes or until a toothpick inserted into the center comes out clean.

FAST: Can prepare up to 3 days in advance and refrigerate, or freeze for up to 3 months.

FLASHY: Serve with a scoop of vanilla ice cream or frozen yogurt, sliced bananas, toasted chopped nuts, and maybe even a drizzle of hot chocolate sauce or a liqueur.

Pumpkin Soup & Turkey Salad Lunch

*T*here's nothing better than a bowl of warm soup on a cool, crisp fall day. What could be more appropriate than Pumpkin, Leek & Mushroom Soup during this season? Even though it is full of interesting ingredients and rich flavors, it is quick enough to be prepared at the drop of a hat. Hat droppers, you are in luck! A hearty and satisfying hors d'oeuvre consisting of a puree of white beans and spinach, seasoned with chèvre and toasted pumpkin seeds for textural contrast, is the prelude to this lunch. A turkey salad, using leftover turkey from Thanksgiving, rounds out the menu. It is so delicious that you might be tempted to cook a turkey just so you can make this salad. Not to worry; you can just buy cooked turkey. For the grand conclusion, we have Apricot Oatmeal Nuggets.

I used woven, earth-tone placemats with large beige napkins for the table. Instead of flowers, a big basket of beautiful persimmons and baby pumpkins with walnuts in their shells was in the center of the table.

This simple lunch could easily be served as a light but delicious dinner.

Menu

Warm White Beans Florentine with Chèvre & Walnuts
Pumpkin, Leek & Mushroom Soup
Tossed Salad with Turkey & Cambozola Vinaigrette
French Bread & Butter
Apricot Oatmeal Nuggets

Faster & Flashier Menu

Pumpkin, Leek & Mushroom Soup
Tossed Salad with Turkey & Cambozola Vinaigrette
French Bread & Butter
Dessert (purchased)

Dry White Wine or Light Red Wine and Coffee

❧ TIMETABLE ❧

Up to 2 weeks in advance and refrigerated	Cambozola Vinaigrette. Apricot Oatmeal Nuggets (store at room temperature in a glass jar or plastic bag).
Up to 4 days in advance and refrigerated	Pumpkin, Leek & Mushroom Soup
Up to 3 days in advance and refrigerated, or freeze for up to 6 months	Warm White Beans Florentine with Chèvre & Walnuts
Up to 1 day in advance, or freeze for up to 3 months	Set the table. Chill the wines.
Party day!	Heat the beans.
Up to 4 hours in advance and refrigerated	Assemble the salad without dressing; toss right before serving. Warm the soup.

Warm White Beans Florentine with Chèvre & Walnuts

This is a wonderfully rustic hors d'oeuvre.

Yield: About 4 cups

4 ounces chèvre cheese*
2 cups cooked and drained white beans,
    or 1 15-ounce can
1 10-ounce package frozen spinach,
    thawed and squeezed to remove
    the excess moisture

2 to 4 green onions, minced
1 cup pumpkin seeds, toasted*
    Salt and white pepper, to taste

1. Combine the first 4 ingredients in a food processor fitted with the metal blade.
2. Add the remaining ingredients and process in, using several quick on-and-off motions so as not to destroy the texture.
3. Heat in a 350 degree oven for about 10 minutes.

FAST: Can prepare up to 3 days in advance and refrigerate or freeze for up to 3 months.

FLASHY: Serve with Garlic Crostini (page 66), sliced baguettes, and/or Pita Chips (page 112).

FABULOUS: With 1 6-ounce jar marinated artichokes added at Step 2. Seasoned with fresh or dried thyme, dill, oregano, and/or rosemary. With walnuts instead of pumpkin seeds.

FURTHER: Add chicken broth to the leftovers to create a wonderful soup.

*Refer to Terms & Techniques.

Pumpkin, Leek & Mushroom Soup

This soup embodies the spirit of fall. You will be amazed at how quick it is to prepare.

Yield: 8 or more servings

2 to 4 tablespoons unsalted or half-fat butter

3 to 6 leeks, trimmed, washed, and thinly sliced

1 to 2 ounces dried shiitake mushrooms, rehydrated, stemmed and minced, or thinly sliced

2 to 4 cloves garlic, minced

8 cups chicken broth, homemade or canned

½ cup dry vermouth

¼ to ½ cup cream sherry

Sage (fresh or dried), to taste

1 bay leaf

2 to 4 tablespoons minced Italian parsley

1-pound can pureed pumpkin

Salt and white pepper, to taste

1. Melt the butter in a large soup pot over medium heat.
2. Stir in the leeks, mushrooms, and garlic and cook, stirring frequently, until tender, about 10 minutes.
3. Stir in the remaining ingredients and bring it to a boil over high heat.
4. Reduce the heat to the lowest setting and simmer for about 15 minutes or until the flavors are pleasing.

FAST: Can prepare up to 4 days in advance and refrigerate, or freeze for up to 6 months.

FLASHY: Serve as a sauce for turkey, pork, or chicken.

FABULOUS: Seasoned with fresh or dried thyme and/or rosemary. With 1 cup sour cream mixed in right before serving.

Tossed Salad with Turkey

An excellent way to use leftover turkey!   **Yield: 8+ servings**

2 heads romaine lettuce, torn into
   bite-size pieces
1 to 2 avocados, sliced thinly and
   squirted with lemon juice to
   prevent darkening
 Turkey meat cut into small bite-size
   pieces, as much as you like
2 to 4 stalks of celery, sliced thinly

½ to 1 cup walnuts, toasted
 2 pears, cored, sliced thinly, and
   squirted with lemon juice to
   prevent discoloring
 Cambozola Vinaigrette (recipe
   follows)
 Salt and freshly ground black pepper,
   to taste

1. Combine the romaine, avocado, turkey, celery, walnuts, and pears in a
   salad bowl.
2. Toss with the desired amount of dressing. Taste and adjust the seasonings
   with salt and pepper.

FAST: Can combine all the ingredients in a salad bowl several hours in advance
and refrigerate. Toss before serving. To preserve the crispness of the lettuce,
put it on top of all the other ingredients.

FABULOUS: With any combination of greens, from spinach to endive. With
sliced fennel (sweet anise) instead of celery.

Cambozola Vinaigrette

To die for! Just as good as a sauce for steak, chicken,
or vegetables as for a salad.   **Yield: 1¾ cups**

¼ cup Cambozola cheese
 1 cup extra virgin olive oil
 2 tablespoons freshly grated Parmesan
   cheese

1 shallot
⅓ cup balsamic vinegar
   Salt, white pepper, and fresh lemon
   juice, to taste

1. Combine all the ingredients in a food processor fitted with the metal blade or in a blender. Taste and adjust the flavors.

FAST: Can prepare up to 2 weeks in advance and refrigerate.

FLASHY: Serve as a dunk! As a cold sauce or dressing for any kind of a salad, cooked vegetable, and/or grilled fish, beef, pork, or chicken.

FABULOUS: With bleu cheese instead of Cambozola cheese. To reduce the fat, replace half of the oil with low-fat or fat-free sour cream.

Apricot Oatmeal Nuggets

These flourless cookies are delightfully crisp, yet chewy and low-fat as well!

Yield: About 3 dozen

3 large eggs or egg substitute
1 cup packed brown sugar
2 tablespoons melted, unsalted butter
1 teaspoon vanilla extract
¼ teaspoon ground cinnamon, or more

¼ teaspoon salt
3 cups uncooked oatmeal
1 cup toasted walnuts
1 cup semisweet chocolate chips
1 cup chopped, dried apricots, packed

1. Combine all of the ingredients, except for the walnuts, chocolate, and apricots in a food processor fitted with the metal blade.
2. Add the remaining ingredients and process in, using several quick on-and-off motions so as not to destroy the texture.
3. Use a tablespoon to form balls and place them on an oiled cookie sheet. Bake in a preheated 350 degree oven for 15–20 minutes, until golden brown.

FAST: Can prepare up to 15 days in advance and store in airtight plastic bags or jars, or freeze for up to 3 months.

FABULOUS: With any kind of nuts or dried fruit.

Chicken Breast with Shiitake, Onion & Pear Sauce Dinner

This menu begins with a garlic lover's fantasy—an hors d'oeuvre with more garlic than most people can imagine. Surprisingly enough, it has a rich mellow flavor with a creamy texture.

Following the hors d'oeuvres is a delicious soup. This is the time of the year when we appreciate soups but often run out of interesting ideas. This California Chile Soup is far from ordinary. Contrary to what you might think, it is not extremely spicy. The Anaheim chiles are mild, with a slightly sweet flavor and just a hint of heat. The cilantro and chèvre lend a delightful herbal flavor to this rich, mellow soup.

As we all know, boneless, skinless chicken breasts have become quite the righteous entrée. You are placed high on the list of healthy eaters when you eat chicken breasts. This is not to say you are going to enjoy the experience. Too often the sanctimonious chicken breast is poorly prepared, dry, and anything but tasty. I would rather starve than eat such a bird, and that is not the case with this menu. I have discovered that buttermilk performs magic when chicken breasts marinate in it. After marinating, they are briefly sautéed and then sauced with seasonal ingredients. Couscous with Carrots complements the chicken. Both of these dishes have subtle Southwestern influences. Chocolate Cheesecake Mousse Chee Wow Wa is a memorable finish.

As for the table, I used Southwestern woven placemats in earth tones with dark green napkins. Two old copper pots held a mixture of leather ferns and purple statice. Here's another idea for a centerpiece: just fill a glass bowl with beautiful fall leaves and pears. White pillar candles on tall wrought iron candlesticks completed the look.

Menu

Roasted Garlic Decadence from Heaven

Roasted Garlic Decadence from Hell

Garlic Rosemary Crostini

California Chile Soup

*Marinated Chicken Breast with Shiitake Mushrooms,
Onion & Pear Sauce*

Couscous with Carrots

Chocolate Cheesecake Mousse Chee Wow Wa

Faster & Flashier Menu

Warm Black Bean Dip (using canned beans)

Tossed Salad

Chicken Fillets with Shiitake, Shallot & Pear Sauce

Couscous

Dessert (purchased)

Sauvignon Blanc, Pinot Noir, and/or Chardonnay

Coffee

✄ TIMETABLE ✄

Up to 3 months in advance and frozen	Roasted Garlic Decadence from Heaven and Hell. Garlic Rosemary Crostini.
Up to 4 days in advance	California Chile Soup
Up to 3 days in advance	Marinate the chicken.
Up to 2 days in advance	Couscous with Carrots.
Up to 1 day in advance	Set the table. Chocolate Cheesecake Mousse. Chill the wines.
Party day!	Heat beans and soup. Bake the chicken.

Roasted Garlic Decadence from Heaven

Guaranteed to keep vampires away.

Yield: About 1½ cups; 12 or more servings

3 heads garlic, or about 1½ to 2 cups
    prepeeled garlic
  Olive oil
2 to 4 tablespoons cream sherry

8 ounces chèvre cheese, or 4 ounces
    chèvre and 1 stick unsalted or
    half-fat butter
Salt and ground white pepper, to taste

1. Preheat the oven to 250–325 degrees. Cut one-third of the garlic off from top of bulb to expose all the cloves.
2. Place the bulbs or the peeled garlic cloves in a baking dish or heavy skillet and coat with olive oil to prevent burning. Cover with a lid or aluminum foil. Bake until the cloves are soft and buttery, about 2 hours.
3. Transfer the cloves of garlic into a food processor fitted with the metal blade and add the remaining ingredients. Process until smooth.
4. Pack into an oiled, plastic-wrap-lined bowl or mold. Chill until firm, about 2 hours.

FAST: Can prepare up to 5 days in advance and refrigerate, or freeze for up to 3 months.

FLASHY: Unmold and top with toasted pine nuts (page 13) and/or roasted garlic cloves. Serve with thinly sliced baguettes, crackers, or Garlic Rosemary Crostini (recipe follows).

FABULOUS: With ½ cup toasted and chopped pecans or blanched or unblanched almonds. On grilled poultry, meats, or cooked vegetables. With cream and/or 2 cups chicken broth added and heated to create a marvelous entrée sauce. Add ¼ to ½ cup of cream sherry to the garlic before roasting it.

FURTHER: Toss leftovers into hot pasta or rice.

Roasted Garlic Decadence from Hell

A garlic-lover's fantasy with an X rating.

Yield: About 1½ cups; 12 or more servings

3 or more heads garlic, or about 1½ to
    2 cups prepeeled garlic
    Olive oil
4 ounces feta cheese
¼ pound (1 stick) unsalted or half-fat
    butter
3 to 6 dried pasilla chiles, rehydrated,*
    stemmed and seeded

¼ cup minced, softened sun-dried
    tomatoes*
    Fresh or dried rosemary, to taste
2 to 4 tablespoons cream sherry
    Salt and ground white pepper,
    to taste

1. Preheat the oven to 250–325 degrees. Cut one-third of the garlic off from the top of the bulb to expose all of the cloves.
2. Place the bulbs or the peeled garlic cloves in a baking dish or a heavy skillet and coat with olive oil to prevent burning. Cover with a lid. Bake until the cloves are soft and buttery, about 2 hours.
3. Squeeze the garlic cloves out of their wrappers or transfer the cloves into a food processor fitted with the metal blade and add the remaining ingredients. Process until smooth.
4. Pack into an oiled, plastic-wrap-lined bowl or mold. Chill until firm, about 2 hours.

FAST: Can prepare up to 5 days in advance and refrigerate, or freeze for up to 3 months.

FLASHY: Unmold and top with toasted pine nuts (page 13), pink peppercorns, and/or roasted garlic cloves. Serve with thinly sliced baguettes, crackers, or Garlic Rosemary Crostini (recipe follows).

FABULOUS: With ½ cup toasted and chopped pecans or blanched or unblanched almonds. On grilled poultry, meats, or cooked vegetables. With 2 cups chicken broth added and heated to create a marvelous entrée sauce. Add ¼ to ½ cup of cream sherry to the garlic before roasting.

FURTHER: Toss leftovers into hot pasta or rice.

*Refer to Terms & Techniques.

Garlic Rosemary Crostini

A delicious and cholesterol-free way to prepare garlic bread.
The seasoned oil is something you may want to keep on hand
in your refrigerator as a cooking oil for almost anything.   **Yield: About 70 crostini**

1 sourdough or French baguette, thinly
    sliced
2 to 4 cloves garlic, minced, or to taste
1 cup extra virgin olive oil

⅓ cup red wine vinegar
    Salt and fresh or dried rosemary,
    to taste

1. Place the baguette slices on a cookie sheet and preheat the oven to 350 degrees.
2. Combine the garlic, oil, vinegar, and seasonings in a food processor fitted with the metal blade or in a blender. Taste and adjust the seasonings.
3. Brush the slices of bread with the seasoned oil and bake until crisp, about 15 minutes.

FAST: Can prepare oil up to 5 days in advance and store in a jar or plastic bags. Can prepare through step 3 up to 2 days in advance and refrigerate covered with foil or plastic wrap.

FLASHY: Serve at room temperature, or warm in a napkin-lined basket or on a plate.

FABULOUS: With any herb. With butter or a combination of butter and oil. Top with grated Parmesan, Romano, and/or mizithera cheese.

California Chile Soup

Simply divine and brimming with enticing
Southwestern flavors—and a snap to make.

Yield: 8 to 10 servings,
about 8 cups

1½ cups canned mild green chiles,
    deveined and seeded
2 to 3 tablespoons unsalted butter,
    peanut oil, or cooking spray
1 large white, red, or yellow onion,
    minced
½ cup cilantro, minced, or more
3 to 6 cloves garlic
2 tablespoons all-purpose flour

½ cup dry white wine
6 cups chicken broth, canned or
    homemade
¼ to ½ cup heavy cream or low-fat or
    fat-free sour cream
½ cup chèvre or grated Jack cheese, or
    more
    Salt, white pepper, and ground
    cumin, to taste

1. Purée the chiles in a food processor or blender.
2. In a saucepan, melt butter or heat up the peanut oil and sauté the onion
   and garlic until tender.
3. Stir in the flour and cook over low heat for 2 minutes.
4. Stir in the puréed chiles, wine, and broth. Bring to a boil, reduce heat, and
   simmer for 10 minutes. Season to taste.
5. Stir in the cream or sour cream, cheese, and cilantro. Cook until the cheese
   melts over medium-low heat.

FAST: Can be prepared up to 4 days in advance, or frozen for up to 3 months.

FLASHY: Serve with minced cilantro, green onions, and/or any nontoxic flower
topping the soup.

FABULOUS: As a sauce for pasta or rice. With fresh, raw, shelled shrimp, crab,
and/or scallops added along with the cheese. Seasoned with dried oregano,
chipotle chiles, and/or pasilla chiles.

Marinated Chicken Breast with Shiitake Mushrooms, Onion & Pear Sauce

This dish has a rich and delicate Southwestern influence. You will be amazed at how moist and flavorful the chicken is.

Yield: 8+ servings

8 to 16 chicken breast halves, boned, skinned, and pounded to a thickness of about ¼ inch

The Marinade:
2 cups buttermilk or low-fat or fat-free buttermilk
4 to 6 cloves minced garlic
1 teaspoon ground cumin, or more

Peanut oil, as needed
1 cup all-purpose flour
4 tablespoons unsalted butter, peanut oil, or cooking spray
3 ounces dried shiitake mushrooms, rehydrated, stemmed, and thinly sliced (reserve the soaking liquid)

1 large red onion, chopped
2 to 3 firm pears, halved, cored, and thinly sliced or chopped
1 cup cream sherry
1 cup chicken broth, homemade or canned
1 cup beef broth, homemade or canned
1 teaspoon ground cumin, or more
Juice and grated zest of 1 to 2 limes
2 teaspoons green peppercorns
Salt and white pepper, to taste
2 tablespoons cornstarch dissolved in 2 tablespoons water

1. Place the chicken in a glass, ceramic, or plastic pan and top with all the ingredients for the marinade. Cover with plastic wrap and marinate in the refrigerator for a minimum of 4 hours or a maximum of 24 hours.
2. Preheat the oven to 350 degrees.
3. Melt 2 tablespoons of the butter or heat the peanut oil in a large skillet.
4. Dredge the chicken in the flour and sauté it in the butter or oil. Add more butter or oil as needed. Do this in several batches. Do not overcrowd the chicken or it will not brown well. Sauté for several minutes on each side on medium to medium-high heat, until golden and firm. Transfer the chicken to an ovenproof pan and set aside.
5. Meanwhile, melt the other 2 tablespoons of butter or heat the peanut oil in another skillet, and sauté the red onions and shiitake mushrooms until the onions are translucent.

6. Stir in the reserved, strained soaking liquid from the shiitake mushrooms and cumin, and bring the mixture to a boil, while whisking periodically. Cook until the mixture reduces by half, about 6–10 minutes.

7. Add the pears, sherry, chicken, and beef broth to the skillet. Return it to a boil, and season to taste with cumin, green peppercorns, lime juice, zest, salt, and pepper. Continue boiling and stir in the dissolved cornstarch mixture.

8. Pour the sauce over the chicken and bake for about 20 minutes in the preheated oven.

FAST: Can assemble up to 2 days in advance and refrigerate. Bake before serving. Can prepare the sauce up to 4 days in advance, and refrigerate or freeze for up to 6 months.

FLASHY: Serve with rice, white or black beans, or polenta. Use this sauce on anything from pork to pasta.

FABULOUS: Seasoned with dried oregano, and/or fresh or dried rosemary or thyme.

Couscous with Carrots

This dish will break you out of the rice doldrums.   **Yield: 6 to 8 servings**

2 to 4 tablespoons peanut oil
2 to 4 shallots, minced
4 cups baby carrots, halved or quartered
   lengthwise
1 to 2 dried pasilla chiles, rehydrated,
   stemmed, seeded, and minced

2 cups uncooked couscous
2 cups chicken broth, homemade or
   canned
¼ cup sherry wine (medium or cream)
¼ cup parsley and/or cilantro, minced
   Salt and white pepper, to taste

1. Heat oil in a saucepan and sauté the shallots and carrots until the carrots are tender.
2. Stir in the pasilla chiles and couscous. Cook over medium heat, stirring until the couscous is well coated.
3. Stir in the chicken broth and sherry. Bring to a boil and stir.
4. Cover with a lid and remove pan from the burner. Let sit for 10–15 minutes and stir in the parsley and/or cilantro. Season with salt and pepper to taste.

FAST: Can prepare up to 2 days in advance and refrigerate. Reheat over double boiler or in the microwave.

FLASHY: Serve in a large bowl or platter, garnished with sprigs of parsley and/or whole raw chiles.

FABULOUS: Season with any herb and add sautéed mushrooms, sun-dried tomatoes, and/or skinned, seeded, and minced fresh tomatoes.

FURTHER: Use leftovers as a salad enlivened with fresh lemon or lime juice or add to soups.

Chocolate Cheesecake Mousse Chee Wow Wa

A rich and opulent dessert with a light texture that can even be made fat-free.

Yield: 8 to 12 servings

4 large egg yolks or egg substitute
½ cup sugar
¼ cup Triple Sec
¼ cup coffee-flavored liqueur
8 ounces bittersweet chocolate, broken up into small pieces
Grated orange zest from 2 to 3 oranges

Ground cinnamon, to taste
1 teaspoon vanilla extract
½ cup plain yogurt or low-fat or fat-free plain yogurt
2 cups sour cream or low-fat or fat-free sour cream
Sliced almonds, assorted fresh berries for garnishing

1. Combine egg yolks or egg substitute and sugar in top of double boiler over barely simmering water. Whisk until thick and lemon colored, or use a hand-held electric mixer or blender on a stick.
2. Blend in the chocolate, cocoa, liqueur, zest, cinnamon, and vanilla for several minutes until the chocolate melts.
3. Transfer the mixture to a metal bowl. Stir yogurt and sour cream into the mixture and place in freezer to chill for 15–30 minutes, or chill in the refrigerator for at least 1 hour.

FAST: Can prepare up to 2 days in advance and refrigerate, or freeze for up to 3 months.

FLASHY: Serve with sprinkling of almonds and fresh berries in stemmed glasses with butter cookies. Garnish with fresh mint leaves and/or any nontoxic flowers.

FABULOUS: With any liqueur instead of Triple Sec or coffee-flavored liqueur.

Fall Rigatoni Dinner

Our party begins with a delicious seasonal hors d'oeuvre, Leek Croustades. Leeks at one time were known as the "Poor Man's Asparagus." Now they are no longer a bargain. If you aren't familiar with this vegetable, I think you are going to enjoy it. Leeks are a member of the onion family, but their flavor is richer and rounder. Croustades are sourdough toast cups that can be filled with anything.

The Tossed Fall Salad is a tasty salute to fall incorporating lots of the season's produce. It is a nice prelude to our gutsy pasta. This is a big, robust, cold-weather dish that is designed to knock your socks off, not to be soft-spoken. An Apple Apricot Crisp à la Mode brings this dinner to an end with yet another tribute to the season. It is not only full of flavor but also abundant with texture. This crisp will be equally well received for brunches, lunches, or dinners.

A pumpkin-colored tablecloth was my starting point for creating the look of this dinner party. A grand old copper kettle filled with rust-colored mums, along with mint cuttings, lent charm and a touch of nostalgia. The mint was added for two reasons, both color and aroma. Mums often do not have a very pleasant fragrance. I hope you agree that I made that claim with all the finesse of a politician. Substantial red wine goblets held earth-tone kitchen towels in place of napkins. White pillar candles in terra cotta saucers along with whole, raw yellow onions and walnuts in their shells were scattered down the center of the table. All of these elements came together to create an exciting and warm ambience.

Menu

Leek Croustades

Tossed Fall Salad with Tarragon Vinaigrette

Rigatoni with Mushrooms,
Sun-Dried Tomatoes & Italian Sausage Sauce

Apple Apricot Crisp à la Mode

Faster & Flashier Menu

Hors D'Oeuvres (purchased)

Tossed Fall Salad with Tarragon Vinaigrette

Rigatoni with Mushrooms,
Sun-Dried Tomatoes & Italian Sausage Sauce

Dessert (purchased)

Sparkling Wine and/or Sauvignon Blanc

Zinfandel or Pinot Noir and Coffee

TIMETABLE

Up to 3 months in advance and frozen, or up to 3 days in advance and refrigerated	Italian Sausage Sauce. Leek Croustade Filling.
Up to 5 days in advance	Tarragon Vinaigrette
Up to 2 days in advance	Set the table. Chill the wine.
Up to 1 day in advance	Marinate the salad. Cook the rigatoni. Assemble Apple Apricot Crisp. Assemble Brie & Walnut Triangles.
Party day!	Assemble and heat Leek Croustades. Toss salad. Heat the pasta and sauce. Bake the Apple Apricot Crisp.

Leek Croustades

Delicious and seasonal, leeks are too often overlooked!

Yield: About 60 croustades

2 to 3 tablespoons unsalted or half-fat butter

4 medium-size leeks (the white and tender green parts),* trimmed, halved lengthwise, rinsed, and cut crosswise into thin pieces

3 cloves garlic, minced

1 tablespoon all-purpose flour

½ cup chicken broth, homemade or canned

4 tablespoons medium-dry sherry

½ cup heavy cream or low-fat or fat-free sour cream

2 tablespoons minced fresh parsley

Salt, ground white pepper, fresh lemon juice, and grated nutmeg, to taste

About 60 croustades (page 107)

2 tablespoons grated Pecorino Romano

¼ cup grated Muenster, jack, or Gruyère cheese

1. Preheat the oven to 350 degrees. Melt the butter in a skillet over medium heat. When it begins to foam, add the leeks and garlic. Cook, stirring, until tender.
2. Stir in the flour; blend well and cook for 1 minute.
3. Stir in the broth and sherry and simmer while stirring, until thickened. Remove from the heat and whisk in the cream or sour cream.
4. Add the parsley and seasonings; taste and adjust them. Return to the burner and cook over low to medium heat if using sour cream. Cook until thickened.
5. Fill the croustades, place on an ungreased cookie sheet, and top with the cheeses. Place in a 350 degree oven until the cheese melts, about 5–10 minutes.

FAST: Can assemble up to 3 hours in advance, leave at room temperature, and bake at 350 degrees for 10–15 minutes; serve immediately. Can prepare the filling up to 3 days in advance and refrigerate, or freeze for up to 3 months.

FLASHY: Serve hot on a platter and garnish with a leek blossom and/or any nontoxic flower or leaves.

FABULOUS: With blanched broccoli or cauliflower, or sautéed onions instead of the leeks.

*Refer to Terms & Techniques.

Tossed Fall Salad

A salute to fall produce.

3 red peppers, roasted,* peeled, and seeded

3 golden peppers, roasted, peeled, and seeded

30 to 50 baby Brussels sprouts, blanched and refreshed

1 cup celery root, peeled, cut into matchstick pieces, and squirted with lemon juice to retain the color

½ cup pumpkin seeds, toasted

Assorted baby salad greens

Tarragon Vinaigrette (page 278)

1. Combine the roasted peppers and Brussels sprouts in a large salad bowl with the desired amount of dressing and let marinate for at least 1 hour or up to 24 hours refrigerated.

2. Add the remaining ingredients and more dressing (if needed) and toss.

FAST: Can prepare up to 2 days in advance through Step 1 and refrigerate. Finish before serving.

FLASHY: Serve in individual salad bowls.

FABULOUS: With fresh, minced basil leaves and/or sliced pears. With purple cabbage or fennel instead of lettuce. As a composed salad on a large platter instead of tossing it.

*Refer to Terms & Techniques.

Rigatoni with Mushrooms, Sun-Dried Tomatoes & Italian Sausage Sauce

A bold, cold-weather entrée.

Yield: 8 servings

6 to 8 Italian sausages, hot, mild, or a combo (or low-fat Italian turkey sausages)
2 onions, thinly sliced
4 to 8 cloves garlic, minced
¼ cup olive oil
1 cup minced Italian parsley
1 tablespoon fennel seeds, or more
2 cups thinly sliced crimini or cultivated mushrooms
½ cup sun-dried tomatoes, minced, or more

½ cup dry vermouth
1½ cups chicken broth, homemade or canned
1 cup heavy cream or low-fat or fat-free sour cream
Salt and freshly ground, coarse black pepper
Crumbled feta cheese and/or freshly grated Parmesan, to taste
2 pounds rigatoni cooked al dente and tossed with a few tablespoons of olive oil

1. Remove sausages from casings and fry in a large sauté pan until fully cooked. Break up sausage while cooking. Remove to a bowl or plate lined with paper towels to drain off the fat.
2. Pour off all but 2 tablespoons of the fat from the pan and add 2 tablespoons olive oil. Sauté the onions and garlic until tender.
3. Add the fennel seeds and mushrooms. Sauté until the mushrooms are cooked. Add the sun-dried tomatoes, dry vermouth, broth, and sausages. Bring to a boil and reduce by about one-third.
4. Add the cream and bring to a boil. Cook for about 5 minutes, or until the flavors are pleasing. If using sour cream, do not boil or it will curdle. Stir in the cheeses.
5. Toss the rigatoni into the hot sauce and cook until the pasta is hot.

FAST: Can prepare the sauce up to 3 days in advance and refrigerate, or freeze for up to 3 months. Can cook the rigatoni up to 2 days in advance and refrigerate. Before serving, heat the sauce and toss in the pasta.

FABULOUS: As a sauce for lasagna. With eggplant cubes mixed in.

Apple Apricot Crisp
A full-flavored and well-textured homey dessert!

Yield: 8 servings

1½ cups quick-cooking oats
½ cup toasted, chopped walnuts
½ cup packed brown sugar
1 teaspoon ground cinnamon
¼ cup unsalted or half-fat butter, melted
8 cups sliced, cored apples

1 cup dried apricots
3 tablespoons all-purpose flour
¼ cup brandy or bourbon
2 tablespoons fresh lemon juice
Extra unsalted or half-fat butter, cut into small pieces

1. Toss together the oats, walnuts, ¼ cup of the brown sugar, and ½ teaspoon of the cinnamon.
2. Work the butter in thoroughly, using a fork.
3. In another bowl, toss the apples and apricots with the rest of the brown sugar, cinnamon, brandy, and lemon juice.
4. Butter a 10-inch-square baking dish and put the apple mixture in evenly.
5. Sprinkle the oat topping mixture over the apples. Scatter extra butter over the top. Bake in a preheated 350 degree oven for 30 minutes, or until the apples are tender and the topping is golden.

FAST: Can assemble up to 1 day in advance and refrigerate, or freeze for up to 3 months. Bake before serving.

FLASHY: Serve with a scoop of French vanilla ice cream or frozen yogurt.

FABULOUS: With almost any fruit! Try peaches in the summer.

Roast Pork Loin Dinner

*H*ere's an important dinner party menu for special occasions that works especially well as a holiday dinner. It is what I call a dinner with dignity. To reflect this spirit, I used a black tablecloth and gold napkins with a green-and-gold-brocade table runner. Pomegranates, gourds, and dried Indian corn sprayed gold were strewn down the table. A large glass bowl filled with persimmons decorated the center of this grand table.

The party begins with an hors d'oeuvre of warm Brie smothered with a heavenly mushroom mixture. Then we proceed to a refreshing, crisp salad that is embellished with pears and walnuts. Pork loin is the starring entrée at this party. Believe me, it is no ordinary "just-thrown-in-the-oven pork roast." First, it is marinated to perfection and infused with balsamic vinegar, Dijon mustard, and herbs. After it is cooked, it gets sauced with a deep brown Orange Port Sauce. To gild the lily, there are also condiments for the pork. You can either prepare all of them or just pick one. I think it is very festive to do it all, which is always my approach to cooking. An unusual potato spinach dish and Roasted Carrots complete the entrée. A Pumpkin Mousse with a Caramel Walnut Sauce serves as the grand finale.

Menu

Brie with Italian Mushroom Caviar

Tossed Greens with Walnuts & Pears

Pork Loin with Condiments: Onion & Pancetta Confit,
Orange Port Sauce, Sherried Plums (optional)

Roasted Carrots (optional)

Red Potatoes & Spinach

Pumpkin Mousse with Caramel Walnut Sauce

Faster & Flashier Menu

Brie with Crackers

Tossed Greens with Walnuts & Pears

Pork Loin with Orange Port Sauce

Roasted Carrots

Dessert (purchased)

Chardonnay, Pinot Noir, Coffee, and/or Sparkling Wine

TIMETABLE

Up to 5 days in advance	Herbed Walnut Vinaigrette. Onion & Pancetta Confit with Port. Sherried Plums, Orange Port Sauce.
Up to 3 days in advance	Brie with Italian Mushroom Caviar. Marinate the pork. Caramel Pumpkin Mousse with Caramel Walnut Sauce.
Up to 2 days in advance	Set the table. Chill the wines.
Up to 1 day in advance	Prep salad greens. Bake the pork. Potato Torta through Step 4.
Party day!	Roast the pork and broccoli. Finish the potatoes.

Brie with Italian Mushroom Caviar

A religious experience and definitely a splurge!   **Yield: 8+ servings**

4 tablespoons extra virgin olive oil
1 onion, minced
4 ounces prosciutto trimmings, chopped
1 pound mushrooms, chopped
¼ cup dry red wine

Salt and freshly ground, coarse black pepper, to taste
½ cup toasted pine nuts, coarsely chopped
1-pound wheel or wedge of Brie

1. Heat the olive oil in a large skillet and add the onion and prosciutto. Cook over medium heat until the onions are golden.
2. Add the mushrooms and red wine. Continue cooking over medium heat until the mushrooms release their liquid and it cooks away, about 30–45 minutes. Stir in the pine nuts and season to taste.
3. Place the Brie on an ovenproof serving plate surrounded with the mushroom caviar. Serve at room temperature or bake in a 350 degree oven for about 25 minutes.

FAST: Can prepare up to 3 days in advance and refrigerate, or freeze for up to 3 months.

FLASHY: Serve with Garlic Rosemary Crostini (page 192)

FABULOUS: Tossed on hot pasta!

Tossed Greens with Walnuts & Pears

Yield: 8 servings

1 head romaine leaves
1 bunch spinach leaves, stemmed
2 heads butter lettuce
1 cup walnut halves, toasted (page 13)

4 bosc pears, sliced and squirted with lemon juice to prevent discoloring
Herbed Walnut Vinaigrette (recipe follows)

1. Combine all the ingredients in a large salad bowl and toss with the desired amount of dressing. Use only as much lettuce as you want.

FAST: Can prep and mix together the greens and walnuts up to 1 day in advance and refrigerate. Add the pears and dress before serving.

FABULOUS: With cooked shrimp or crab or sliced avocado or fennel bulb tossed in. With pecans, almonds, pine nuts, or pumpkin seeds instead of the walnuts. With thinly sliced prosciutto and a red bell pepper.

Herbed Walnut Vinaigrette   *Yield: About 1¼ cups*

¼ cup chopped walnuts, toasted (page 13)
1 cup extra virgin olive oil
⅓ cup sherry wine vinegar
2 to 4 tablespoons minced shallots
¼ cup minced fresh parsley

2 tablespoons capers, drained, rinsed, and minced
1 to 2 tablespoons fresh thyme leaves, minced
Salt and ground white pepper, to taste

1. Combine all the ingredients in a food processor fitted with the metal blade or in a blender and process, or whisk together in a bowl. Taste and adjust the seasonings.
2. Store in a tightly covered jar in the refrigerator. Shake or stir before using.

FAST: Can prepare up to 5 days in advance and refrigerate, or freeze for up to 3 months.

FLASHY: On any combination of tossed greens.

FABULOUS: As a marinade or sauce for vegetables, seafood, beef, lamb, poultry, or park. On any salad. With almonds or pine nuts instead of walnuts. To reduce the fat, replace half of the oil with low-fat or fat-free sour cream.

Pork Loin with Condiments

This pork is so good it can stand alone, but all the side dishes just make it more special.

Yield: 8 servings

1 6- to 8-pound boneless pork loin
Several cloves garlic, cut into slivers

The Marinade:
1 cup balsamic vinegar
1 cup olive oil or low-fat or fat-free
   plain yogurt
¼ cup Dijon mustard
Fresh or dried sage, thyme, and
   rosemary, to taste
2 tablespoons fennel seeds
20 cloves garlic

2 onions, sliced thinly
Salt and freshly ground black pepper,
   to taste

¼ to ½ cup brandy
8 thin slices pancetta
Sprigs of fresh parsley, watercress,
   and/or rosemary
Orange Port Sauce (recipe follows)
Onion & Pancetta Confit with Port
   (recipe follows)
Sherried Plums (recipe follows)

1. Cut several slashes in the pork using a sharp knife; insert the garlic slivers.
2. Combine the ingredients for the marinade.
3. Place the pork in a glass or ceramic pan and pour the marinade over it. Cover with plastic wrap and allow it to marinate in the refrigerator for at least 24 hours. Turn the roast over at least once during that time.
4. Bring it to room temperature before cooking. Remove it from the marinade, and blot dry with paper towels. Place thinly sliced onions in the bottom of the baking pan. Set the pork on top, season with salt and pepper and drape with the thin slices of pancetta. Bake in a 325 degree oven until it reaches an internal temperature of 160 degrees, about 20–25 minutes per pound.
5. Transfer the pork to another pan or platter, and tent with aluminum foil to keep warm.
6. To deglaze the pan, discard all of the remaining fat in the pan and stir in the brandy, using a wooden spoon or a wire whisk. Cook over high heat, stirring or whisking vigorously to dissolve the brown bits that cling to the bottom of the pan, until the liquid has cooked down into a rich, almost syrupy liquid, about 4–5 minutes. Strain the juices through a fine mesh strainer into the Orange Port Sauce.
7. Slice the pork and drizzle some of the sauce over the pork. Serve the remaining sauce on the side, separately.

FAST: Can marinate for up to 3 days in advance and refrigerate. Cook before serving.

FLASHY: Serve on a platter with a mound of Onion & Pancetta Confit and garnish with sprigs of parsley, watercress, and/or rosemary. Serve the Sherried Plums separately in a bowl.

FURTHER: Make a sauce or use leftover sauce, if you are lucky enough to have any, and heat up leftover pork in it along with sautéed mushrooms and the apples, onions, and pancetta.

Orange Port Sauce

A magnificent, dark, rich sauce that is very low in fat!   **Yield: About 3 cups**

⅓ cup sugar
2 cups chicken or beef broth, homemade or canned
½ cup port
¼ cup orange marmalade
2 to 3 tablespoons Dijon mustard

2 tablespoons cornstarch dissolved in 2 tablespoons water
Salt and white pepper, to taste (optional)
2 tablespoons unsalted butter at room temperature

1. Place the sugar in a heavy saucepan and caramelize the sugar.*
2. Remove the saucepan from the burner and add the broth carefully, because it will probably splatter.
3. Return the pan to the heat and dissolve the caramel over high heat.
4. Add the port, marmalade, and mustard. Bring this to a boil over high heat and simmer for about 5 minutes, until the flavors are pleasing.
5. Bring the sauce back to a boil and stir in as much of the dissolved cornstarch mixture as required to reach the desired thickness.
6. Before serving, swirl in the butter for added richness.

FAST: Can prepare up to 5 days in advance and refrigerate, or freeze for up to 6 months.

FLASHY: On anything from duck to pork.

FABULOUS: With any kind of broth (fish, seafood, ham, pork). With the deglazing and/or pan juices of whatever it is being served with added to the sauce.

*Refer to Terms & Techniques.

Onion & Pancetta Confit with Port

Yield: About 3 cups

2 to 4 tablespoons olive oil
½ to 1 pound pancetta or smoked ham,
    chopped
4 to 6 large onions, sliced or chopped

Salt and freshly ground, coarse black
    pepper
¼ to ½ cup port
½ cup toasted walnuts, or more

1. Combine all the ingredients except for the walnuts in a heavy baking pan.
2. Place in a 300–325 degree oven for 2–3 hours, until the onions are golden and very soft.
3. Transfer the mixture to a food processor fitted with the metal blade. Puree or chop finely, then process in the walnuts, using several quick on-and-off motions so as not to destroy the texture of the walnuts.

FAST: Can prepare up to 5 days in advance and refrigerate, or freeze for up to 3 months.

FLASHY: Serve at room temperature or warm with Garlic Crostini (page 66), bagels, or Pita Chips (page 112).

FABULOUS: Seasoned with fresh or dried thyme, sage, and/or rosemary. With crumbled feta, chèvre, or grated Parmesan. Add cranberries and use this for the holidays.

Sherried Plums (Drunken Plums)

Great with turkey!   **Yield: About 3 cups**

1 to 1½ cup plums, pitted
½ cup brown sugar
2 cups cream sherry
1 to 2 teaspoons salt

¼ cup pickled ginger
1 to 2 tablespoons toasted fennel and
    mustard seeds
1 tablespoon Szechuan peppercorns*

1. Place all the ingredients in a saucepan and bring it to a boil. Reduce the
    heat to medium and simmer for about 30 minutes, until the flavor and
    texture are pleasing.

FAST: Can prepare up to 7 days in advance and refrigerate, or freeze for up to
6 months.

FLASHY: Serve with roasted meat or poultry.

FABULOUS: Made with any fruit.

*Refer to Terms & Techniques.

Roasted Carrots

A simple method that produces rich, earthy results.   ***Yield: 8 servings***

1½ to 2 pounds baby carrots
   2 to 4 tablespoons olive oil
   1 bunch green onions, cut into 1½- to
     2-inch lengths

2 to 4 tablespoons fresh rosemary,
   cut up
  Salt, white pepper, and freshly grated
   nutmeg, to taste

1. Preheat oven to 375 degrees.
2. Put the carrots in a mixing bowl and toss with all of the ingredients.
3. Transfer the broccoli to a baking dish and roast for 10 minutes.

FAST: Can assemble up to 3 days in advance and refrigerate. Bring to room temperature before roasting.

FABULOUS: With sesame oil instead of olive oil. With broccoli, celery, green beans, cauliflower, eggplant, and zucchini instead of carrots.

Red Potatoes & Spinach

*Don't let this long list of ingredients frighten you from preparing this
dish. It is a snap! It will also serve you well as a vegetarian entrée.*   **Yield: 8+ servings**

1½ quarts chicken broth, homemade or
    canned
1½ quarts beef broth, homemade or
    canned
1 cup dry white wine
2 teaspoons dried tarragon, or to taste
2 bay leaves
½ cup minced parsley
8 cloves garlic
    Salt and white pepper, to taste
3 pounds red potatoes, thinly sliced
1 stick unsalted or half-fat butter

4 10-ounce packages frozen spinach,
    thawed and squeezed to remove
    the excess moisture
¾ cup sour cream or low-fat or fat-free
    sour cream
1 cup freshly grated Parmesan cheese
4 to 8 green onions, minced
½ to 1 cup minced fresh dill
3 to 4 tablespoons pureed calamata
    olives (optional)
2 large eggs or egg substitute
    Grated nutmeg to taste

1. Preheat the oven to 325–350 degrees. Oil a large baking dish or paella pan.
2. Put the broth and wine in a large pot and bring it to a boil along with the
   next 4 ingredients.
3. Put the potatoes in the boiling broth and simmer for 5–10 minutes until the
   potatoes are almost tender, still slightly crunchy.
4. Remove the potatoes, using a slotted spoon, and transfer them to a mixing
   bowl. Gently toss them with about 4 tablespoons of the butter. Season
   with salt and pepper.
5. Place a generous layer of the potatoes in the bottom of the oiled dish or
   pan.
6. Combine the spinach, sour cream, ⅓ cup of the Parmesan cheese, green
   onions, fresh dill, calamata olives, and eggs in a food processor fitted with
   the metal blade. Season with salt, white pepper, and nutmeg.
7. Place the spinach on top of the potatoes, then top with the remaining
   potatoes. Ladle 2 cups of the broth over the potatoes. Sprinkle a generous
   amount of Parmesan cheese over the potatoes and dot with butter.
8. Bake in preheated oven for 1–1½ hours.

FAST: Can prepare up to 3 days in advance and refrigerate. Bring to room
temperature before baking.

FLASHY: With chicken or vegetable broth instead of beef broth. As an entrée
for a meatless menu.

Pumpkin Mousse with Caramel Walnut Sauce

Rich autumn flavors.

Yield: 8+ servings

4 large egg yolks or egg substitute
¾ cup packed brown sugar
¼ cup bourbon
   Grated zest of 1 large orange
1 tablespoon unflavored gelatin
      softened in 2 tablespoons of
      bourbon
1¼ cups canned pumpkin puree

   Pumpkin pie spice to taste
1¾ cups milk or nonfat milk
2 teaspoons vanilla
   Caramel Walnut Sauce (recipe
      follows)
1 cup heavy cream or low-fat or
      fat-free sour cream

1. Combine the egg yolks and sugar in the food processor fitted with the metal blade until thick and creamy.
2. Process in the bourbon, orange zest, softened gelatin, pumpkin, and pumpkin pie spice.
3. Meanwhile, place the milk in a saucepan and scald it.
4. Transfer the pumpkin mixture to the saucepan and cook over medium-low heat, stirring until the mixture begins to thicken. Do not allow this to boil.
5. Chill the pumpkin mixture in the refrigerator or freezer.
6. Meanwhile, whip the cream until it holds peaks in the food processor fitted with the metal blade or with an electric mixer.
7. Fold the whipped cream or the sour cream into the chilled pumpkin mixture, place in an oiled and plastic-wrap-lined soufflé dish, and refrigerate until set, at least 4 hours.

FAST: Can prepare up to 3 days in advance and refrigerate, or freeze for up to 3 months.

FLASHY: Serve unmolded on a platter and spoon the Caramel Walnut Sauce around the mousse.

FABULOUS: With bananas, papayas, or mangos instead of pumpkin.

Caramel Walnut Sauce

This makes a lovely gift.   **Yield: About 3 cups**

1 cup sugar
3 tablespoons bourbon
1 cup hot water
  Grated zest of 1 large orange

1 cup toasted walnuts
½ cup heavy cream or low-fat or
  fat-free sour cream
1 teaspoon vanilla

1. Place the sugar and bourbon in a heavy saucepan and caramelize the sugar.*
2. Remove the pan from the heat and add all of the remaining ingredients, except for the cream or sour cream and vanilla. Be careful; it will splatter.
3. Return the pan to the burner and cook over medium heat to dissolve the caramel. Stir in the cream or sour cream and vanilla.

FAST: Can prepare up to 5 days in advance and refrigerate.

FLASHY: Serve Pumpkin Mousse at room temperature.

FABULOUS: As a sauce on ice cream, cakes, and crepes.

*Refer to Terms & Techniques.

Pasilla Chile & Pork Ragout Dinner

*L*ight a fire or turn on a football game and prepare to kick back and have fun. The recommended attire is anything uninhibited, such as warm-ups. Dress your table with the same spirit. For the centerpiece, create a seasonal still life using nuts in the shell and a variety of dried or fresh chiles, then intersperse bulky candle pillars. As an alternative to nuts, use a variety of dried beans or simply use a basket of onions and votive candles. The impact of these tablescapes comes from the use of items not normally considered decorative. This provides an element of surprise and creates an energy otherwise known as atmosphere.

The menu itself offers the cook maximum convenience while at the same time providing a maximum amount of robust flavor. The evening begins with an hors d'oeuvre that could not be any more uninhibited in spirit. The fall salad is a swan song to summer, utilizing items that are in season now but are on their way out. The entrée, Pasilla Chile and Pork Ragout, is a marvelous earthy stew. Southwestern Bulgur is designed not only to complement and contrast the ragout but, more importantly, to catch the sauce. The menu concludes with an interesting adult version of an ice cream sundae, which soothes the palate and comforts the soul.

Menu

Guacamole with Chips & Belgium Endive
Escarole Salad with Mango, Papaya & Black Beans
Pasilla Chile & Pork Ragout
Tex Mex Cracked Wheat with Corn
Brandied Apple Pear Sundae

Faster & Flashier Menu

Guacamole with Chips (purchased)
Escarole Salad with Mango, Papaya & Black Beans
Pasilla Chile & Pork Ragout
Cracked Wheat on Rice
Vanilla Ice Cream with Tuaca

Margaritas, Sparkling Wine, Zinfandel, and/or Beer
Coffee

✄ TIMETABLE ✄

Up to 3 months in advance and frozen	Guacamole
Up to 4 days in advance	Sautéed Brandied Apples & Pears
Up to 2 days in advance	Pasilla Chile & Pork Ragout through Step 6. Tex Mex Cracked Wheat & Corn through Step 2.
Up to 1 day in advance	Set the table. Chill the wine and/or beer.
Party day!	Up to 6 hours in advance, assemble salad greens. Toss right before serving. Heat the ragout and finish it. Assemble the dessert.

Guacamole

Mexican nirvana!   ***Yield: About 1½ cups***

2 large, ripe avocados, peeled, pitted,
  and chopped
  Canned chopped green chiles,
    to taste
2 to 4 cloves garlic, minced, or to taste
¼ cup minced cilantro (fresh coriander)
  and green onions, or to taste

1 to 2 teaspoons ground cumin
  Salt, hot pepper sauce, and fresh
    lemon or lime juice, to taste
¼ to 1 fresh red jalapeño pepper,
  seeded, deveined, and minced
  (optional)

1. Combine all the ingredients in a food processor fitted with the metal blade
   or in a blender, or mix together in a mixing bowl. The texture can be
   smooth or chunky. Taste and adjust the seasonings.

FAST: Can prepare up to 3 days in advance and refrigerate, or freeze for up to
3 months.

FLASHY: As a dunk for Tortilla Chips, Belgium endive leaves, jicama sticks,
poultry, lamb, pork, beef, fish, or seafood. Garnished with minced cilantro,
green onions, and/or any nontoxic flower.

FABULOUS: As a dressing for rice or black bean salads or use as a sauce for
poultry, pork, seafood, or fish. As an entrée sauce for beef, pork, poultry,
seafood, pasta, or rice. With about ½ cup chopped tomatillos thrown in.

Escarole Salad with Mango, Papaya & Black Beans

Great colors and flavors!

Yield: 8 servings

1 pound tender escarole leaves, washed and dried
1 15-ounce can black beans, drained
2 bunches watercress leaves
2 mangos, pitted, peeled, and sliced
1 large papaya, peeled, seeded, and sliced

½ pound jicama, or to taste, peeled and cut into thin matchstick pieces or cubed
4 to 8 green onions, minced
1 cup pitted calamata olives
    Cilantro Vinaigrette (page 130)

1. Place all salad ingredients in a large bowl and toss with desired amount of Cilantro Vinaigrette.

FAST: Can assemble up to 6 hours in advance and refrigerate. Dress and toss right before serving. To prepare in advance, put avocados in bottom of bowl and liberally squirt with lemon juice. Top with mangos, papayas, and black beans, then jicama, green onions, and olives. Add escarole leaves and cover with a few paper towels placed over the top.

FLASHY: Toss avocados, mangos, papayas, and jicama separately with dressing. Toss escarole, olives, and onions together with dressing and arrange on salad plates. Surround with individually tossed ingredients in decorative manner.

FABULOUS: With matchstick strips of celery root instead of jicama, and thinly sliced mushrooms. Substitute romaine, spinach, or endive for escarole.

Pasilla Chile & Pork Ragout

This Southwestern stew abounds with earthy, lusty flavors.   **Yield: 6 to 8 servings**

6 tablespoons peanut oil, or more as
   needed
3 large onions, sliced thinly
1 pound mushrooms, halved or
   quartered
4 to 8 cloves garlic, minced
3 tablespoons flour
4 pounds pork shoulder (boneless), cut
   into ½-inch cubes
3 ounces dried pasilla chile pods,
   rehydrated,* stemmed, and seeded
2 cups tomatillos, husked*
¾ cup sherry wine

5 cups chicken or pork broth,
   homemade or canned
   Dried oregano, to taste
1 teaspoon ground cumin, or more
2 yams, peeled and sliced thinly
1 cup sour cream or low-fat or fat-free
   sour cream
½ cup packed, fresh basil leaves
2 bunches of cilantro
   Salt, white pepper, and oregano,
   to taste
   Black olives, radishes, green onions,
   and/or thin strips of tortilla, fried
   until crisp

1. Heat 3–4 tablespoons of oil in a large skillet and slowly sauté onions, mushrooms, and garlic until mushrooms are tender and onions are golden. Stir from time to time. This can also be done in a 350 degree oven.
2. Place flour in a plastic bag with pork, and shake to coat well.
3. Heat 2–4 tablespoons of oil in a large soup pot or casserole and add pork. Increase heat, season with salt and pepper, and brown. Do this in batches so the pork will brown.
4. When chiles are softened, pull out stems and shake out seed.
5. Cut chiles into pieces and place in a food processor fitted with the metal blade. Add tomatillos and purée.
6. Stir purée into pork along with sherry, cumin, broth, and browned onion mixture. Add yams.
7. Bring to a boil. Reduce heat to low and simmer for about 1 hour or until tender, or bake in a 325 degree oven.
8. Combine sour cream, basil, and cilantro in a food processor fitted with the metal blade.
9. Skim off any fat that rises to the top and stir in sour cream mixture. Taste and adjust seasonings.

FAST: Can prepare through Step 7 up to 2 days in advance and refrigerate, or freeze for up to 3 months.

*Refer to Terms & Techniques.

FLASHY: Garnish with black olives, thinly sliced radishes, green onions, and/or crisp-fried thin strips of tortillas. Serve on a bed of couscous in large soup bowls.

FABULOUS: Add nopales, diced eggplant, or sliced okra. With beef, chicken, or monk fish instead of pork.

FURTHER: Add chicken, beef, or pork broth, a touch of wine, and possibly cream to create a soup, Pasilla Chile and Yam Bisque. Add cooked white, red, or black beans or hominy and serve over a crisped tortilla with grated cheese and guacamole to create a tostada. Wrap in a flour tortilla and top with cheese and sour cream for a burrito.

*Refer to Terms and Techniques.

Tex Mex Cracked Wheat with Corn

Bulgar's earthiness complements the entrée, while mint and other flavors provide a fresh contrast.

Yield: 8 servings

3 cups chicken broth, homemade or canned	1 10-ounce package thawed frozen corn
Grated zest of 2 oranges	¼ cup green onions, minced
1 teaspoon ground cumin, or more	¼ cup cilantro, minced
½ cup sherry wine	2 to 4 tablespoons fresh mint leaves, minced
2 cups cracked wheat	Salt and white pepper, to taste

1. Bring chicken broth, orange zest, cumin, and sherry to a boil.
2. Stir in bulgar and reduce heat to medium. Cover and cook for about 10 minutes or until water is absorbed and bulgar is tender.
3. Stir in green onions, cilantro, and mint. Season with salt and pepper.

FAST: Can prepare through Step 2 up to 2 days in advance and refrigerate. Bring to room temperature and add a bit more chicken broth to keep moist. Reheat in microwave or in oven.

FABULOUS: With orzo or couscous instead of bulgar.

FURTHER: Cold as a salad with vinaigrette, olives, sliced fennel, and avocado.

Brandied Apple & Pear Sundae

Unspeakably delicious!

Sautéed Brandied Apples & Pears
  (recipe follows)

French vanilla ice cream or vanilla fat-
  free frozen yogurt
Toasted pecans

1. Prepare the Sautéed Brandied Apples & Pears as directed.
2. Scoop the ice cream or frozen yogurt and spoon the Sautéed Brandied
   Apples & Pears on top.

FAST: Can prepare the Sautéed Brandied Apples & Pears up to 4 days in
advance and refrigerate, or freeze for up to 6 months.

FLASHY: Garnish with a sprinkling of toasted pecans.

FABULOUS: On top of apple spice or pound cake.

Sautéed Brandied Apples & Pears

Yield: 8 servings

4 Granny Smith or Pippin apples,
    quartered, cored, and thinly sliced
4 firm pears, quartered, cored, and
    thinly sliced
2 tablespoons unsalted butter
  Fresh lemon juice, to taste

2 to 4 tablespoons orange marmalade
2 to 4 tablespoons apricot preserves
¼ to ½ cup brandy
  Nutmeg, freshly grated, to taste
  Ground cinnamon, to taste

1. Squirt the apple and pear slices with the lemon juice to prevent discoloring.
2. Heat butter in a large skillet over medium heat.
3. Add marmalade, preserves, and fruit and sauté until tender, stirring frequently, for about 15 minutes.
4. Add brandy and season with nutmeg and cinnamon. Cook until brandy evaporates.

FAST: Can prepare up to 4 days in advance and refrigerate, or freeze for up to 6 months. Reheat in microwave for about 10 minutes or in preheated 300 degree oven for 15–30 minutes.

FLASHY: On ice cream or in crepes. Serve warm or cold.

FABULOUS: Seasoned with apple pie or pumpkin pie spice seasonings instead of cinnamon. With minced or sliced onions and garlic sautéed with the apples and seasoned with thyme and rosemary, as a condiment to serve with chicken, pork, or apples.

Eggplant & Lamb Shank Antipasto

If you are familiar with antipasto, you know it is an appetizer. The name itself means "before pasta." I decided to turn it into an entrée. Because of its wonderful peasant-like quality, I thought it would make a perfect match for lamb shanks. The entrée is served with a selection of starches. You can choose any or all of the rice, pasta, lentil, polenta, couscous, or bean dishes to complement the eggplant and lamb. Offering choices is always a good way to break the ice at parties.

This menu is a snap to prepare and, as a bonus, is also very healthy. I know this sounds too good to be true, but just wait until you taste it.

Our party opens with a fun, flavorful, and fabulous Sun-Dried Tomato Pesto, served with Garlic Crostini. Again, the preparation couldn't be simpler, or the flavors better. From this taste fantasy, we move on to an Escarole Salad with a Sesame-Mustard Vinaigrette. Escarole is one of my very favorite salad greens, but if you can't find it, or don't care for it, use your favorite green. Spinach is a good substitute. The dressing is so delicious that you will find all sorts of uses for it.

When it is time for the entrée, serve it buffet-style in a Spanish earthen-ware cazula or a wok—something primitive. As for the side dishes, they too should be rustic. Use pottery, blue-and-white spatterware enamel, or cast-iron skillets. Use a textured cotton bedspread in a festive color. I used lavender. Tie colorfully striped napkins with rope. The centerpieces for the buffet and table can be a combination of natural baskets and terra cotta pots you have sprayed black. Arrange stale breadsticks, baguettes, rolls, and round loaves with statice and bamboo cuttings. For an added touch, spray some or all of the bread with glossy black paint or an accent color of your choice. It sounds bizarre, but it's visually dramatic!

Menu
Sun-Dried Tomato & Roasted Garlic Pesto

Garlic Crostini

Watercress, Escarole & Persimmon Salad
with Sesame-Mustard Vinaigrette

French Bread

Warm Eggplant & Lamb Shank Antipasto with Side Dishes

Caramel Mousse with Vanilla Nutmeg Sauce

Faster & Flashier Menu
Tossed Salad with Sesame-Mustard Vinaigrette

Warm Eggplant & Lamb Antipasto with Pasta

Dessert (purchased)

TIMETABLE

Up to 5 days in advance	Garlic Crostini. Sun-Dried Tomato & Roasted Garlic Pesto.
Up to 3 days in advance	Warm Eggplant & Lamb Antipasto. Sesame-Mustard Vinaigrette. Vanilla-Nutmeg Sauce.
Up to 2 days in advance	Prepare side dishes. Caramel Mousse.
Up to 1 day in advance	Prep the salad ingredients. Set the table. Chill the wines.
Party day!	Assemble the salad and refrigerate. Warm the lamb and side dishes.

Sun-Dried Tomato & Roasted Garlic Pesto

A guaranteed hit!

Yield: About 3 cups

½ to 1 cup sun-dried tomatoes,
softened and minced
3 to 4 cups peeled garlic cloves,
roasted*
3 to 6 pasilla chiles, rehydrated,*
stemmed, seeded, and minced
4 green onions, minced
½ cup Italian parsley, minced

½ cup pine nuts, toasted
½ to 1 cup extra virgin olive oil
¾ cup feta cheese, crumbled, or more
Rosemary, fresh or dried, to taste
Freshly ground, coarse black pepper,
to taste
Hot pepper sauce and fresh lemon or
lime juice, to taste

1. Combine all ingredients in a bowl or in a food processor fitted with the metal blade using quick on-and-off motions so as not to destroy the texture.
2. Taste and adjust seasonings.

FAST: Can prepare up to 5 days in advance and refrigerate, or freeze up to 6 months.

FLASHY: Serve with Garlic Crostini (page 66).

FABULOUS: With calamata olives. On beans or pasta. As a pizza topping. On grilled fish, lamb, or beef. As an omelette filling.

*Refer to Terms and Techniques.

Watercress, Escarole & Persimmon Salad with Sesame-Mustard Vinaigrette

Yield: 8 servings

1 head escarole, washed, dried, and torn

2 bunches watercress, washed and stemmed

½ cup sesame seeds, toasted

2 to 4 Japanese persimmons,* peeled and sliced

Sesame-Mustard Vinaigrette (recipe follows)

1. Combine watercress, escarole, and sesame seeds in a large bowl.
2. Toss with persimmons and desired amount of dressing.

FAST: Can prep the ingredients up to 1 day in advance. Toss right before serving.

FABULOUS: With prosciutto or crisp, crumbled bacon or pancetta mixed in.

*Refer to Terms & Techniques.

Sesame-Mustard Vinaigrette

Yield: 1½ cups

¼ cup Chinese sesame oil
¾ cup olive or peanut oil
⅓ cup raspberry wine vinegar, or more
2 tablespoons Dijon mustard

2 to 3 cloves garlic
1 teaspoon salt
  White pepper, to taste

1. Combine ingredients in a food processor fitted with the metal blade. Taste
    and adjust seasonings.

FAST: Can prepare dressing up to 5 days in advance and refrigerate. Can
assemble salad (without persimmons) up to 6 hours in advance, then cover
with a damp paper towel. Add persimmon and toss before serving.

FABULOUS: With crumbled feta. With pickled ginger mixed in. As a marinade
and/or sauce for asparagus, chicken, pork, or fish.

Warm Eggplant & Lamb Shank Antipasto

Rich and full of gusto! A great cold weather choice.   **Yield: 8+ servings**

2 eggplants, cut into ½-inch-wide strips
  Olive oil
8 to 16 lamb shanks (depending
    whether you want to serve 1 or 2
    apiece)
4 to 10 cloves garlic, minced
2 large onions, thinly sliced
1 bunch celery, cut into 1-inch lengths,
    including the leaves
1 cup Italian parsley, minced
2 6-ounce jars marinated or water-
    packed artichoke hearts, drained
1 cup Greek or Italian olives, pitted
2 teaspoons fennel and mustard seeds
2 bay leaves
4 tablespoons brown sugar
  6 ounces tomato paste

1½ cups sherry wine vinegar
  2 cups chicken broth, homemade
    or canned
    Salt, white pepper, and freshly
      ground, coarse black pepper
    Fresh or dried rosemary, oregano,
      marjoram, thyme, and/or basil,
      to taste

Side Dishes:
Rice, cracked wheat, lentils,
polenta, couscous, beans, and/or
pasta (tossed with olive oil to
prevent sticking)
Feta cheese, crumbled
Parmesean cheese, freshly grated

1. Place eggplant in a colander in sink. Toss with salt and allow to sit for at least 1 hour to draw off bitter juices.
2. Meanwhile, blot lamb dry using paper towels. Brown in a skillet with some olive oil. Do this in several batches—do not crowd. Remove to large casserole or earthenware baking dish.
3. Add garlic and onions to skillet and sauté until tender and golden.
4. Stir in all remaining ingredients, except reserved artichoke marinade, eggplant, side dishes, and cheese. Bring to a boil.
5. Return lamb to skillet and simmer until lamb is tender.
6. Meanwhile, rinse eggplant and blot with paper towels.
7. Place eggplant in a bowl and toss along with enough olive oil to coat eggplant. Season with salt and pepper.
8. Transfer to a baking dish and bake in a 350–400 degree oven until cooked.
9. Add eggplant to lamb mixture. Simmer for several minutes and serve.

FAST: Can fully prepare up to 3 days in advance and refrigerate, or freeze for up to 6 months. Can prepare side dishes up to 2 days in advance and reheat in microwave.

FLASHY: Serve buffet-style, surrounded by bowls of any or all of the suggested side dishes, and with feta and/or Parmesan.

FABULOUS: With short ribs or chicken instead of lamb.

FURTHER: Add tomato juice to leftovers and you have a soup to die for!

Caramel Mousse

What flavor! What texture! A perfect conclusion to a big meal.   **Yield: Up to 12 servings**

10 large eggs, separated, at room
   temperature, or equivalent egg
   substitute
Pinch of cream of tartar
3⅓ cups heavy cream or low-fat or
   fat-free sour cream

2 teaspoons vanilla extract
2 cups sugar
1 cup dark rum
2 envelopes unflavored gelatin
½ to 1 cup shaved bittersweet
   chocolate

1. Whip the egg whites with the cream of tartar, using an electric mixer or a food processor fitted with a metal blade, until they hold stiff peaks. Transfer to a large bowl and place in the freezer.

2. Whip the cream with the vanilla until it holds soft peaks. If using sour cream, just combine the sour cream with the vanilla. Transfer this to the bowl containing the egg whites and fold it in, then return it to the freezer.

3. Combine the sugar plus half of the rum in a heavy saucepan. Cook over medium-low heat until the sugar dissolves while holding the pan by the handle and swirling it frequently. Increase the heat to medium-high and cover with a tight-fitting lid for 1–2 minutes, until the mixture boils and has thick bubbles, then uncover and cook until it turns a light golden caramel color, swirling the pan frequently. Remove the pan from the heat and continue to swirl until the syrup turns a rich, deep caramel color. Place the pan over a pan of cold water until it cools slightly, to prevent it from turning too dark. Do not let it harden. At this point, if necessary, the pan can be placed over very low heat to maintain a liquid consistency. As a word of caution, never let your skin come in contact with hot caramel. It burns you instantly.

4. Place the egg yolks or egg substitute in a food processor fitted with a metal blade and process until light and lemon-colored, or beat with an electric mixer.

5. Next, process in the caramel while the machine or mixer is running. Transfer the mixture to a large, heavy saucepan and place over medium-low heat until it thickens a bit more, whisking constantly, about 10 minutes.

6. Place the gelatin and remaining rum in a small bowl. Mix well and dissolve over a larger bowl of hot water or in the microwave for about 30 seconds on low power.

7. Slowly process in the dissolved gelatin through the feed tube while the machine is running.
8. Transfer the mixture to a large bowl and place in the freezer to chill for about 10 minutes. Thoroughly fold in a third of the egg whites, then fold in the rest.
9. Refrigerate at least 2 hours, until set.

FAST: Can prepare up to 2 days in advance and refrigerate, or freeze for up to 3 months. Thaw in the refrigerator for 2 days.

FLASHY: Serve in stemmed goblets and garnish with a sprinkling of shaved chocolate and with a piece of Lemon Sesame Shortbread (page 281).

FABULOUS: With slices of cooked or raw apple or pear.

Vanilla Nutmeg Sauce

You can make all sorts of plain-Jane desserts glamorous with this sauce!

Yield: About 2 cups

½ vanilla bean, cut lengthwise
4 tablespoons brown sugar
½ cup brandy

Nutmeg, freshly grated, to taste
1¾ cups heavy cream or low-fat or fat-free sour cream

1. Place vanilla bean, brown sugar, and brandy in saucepan. Bring to boil and grate in nutmeg. Cook until reduced by half.
2. Stir in cream and continue to cook over high heat until flavor and consistency are pleasing. If using sour cream, remove the saucepan from the burner and stir in the sour cream.

FAST: Can prepare up to 3 days in advance and refrigerate, or freeze for up to 6 months.

FLASHY: On crepes, fresh fruit, or pound cake. Serve hot or cold.

FABULOUS: With rum, bourbon, or tequila instead of brandy.

Winter

Winter South-of-the-Border Brunch

*B*old, daring, and festive flavors abound in this menu. It is a great way to brighten up spirits and shake off the doldrums that often accompany winter. This menu is extremely rich, which makes it perfectly suited for a New Year's Day Brunch. Needless to say, as with all Fast & Fabulous parties, it can be completely prepared in advance. This makes it especially convenient for those times when you have house guests. Prepare this menu before they arrive, and when you throw this spectacular party, you will become their hero.

We start off with Chile Polenta Squares with Avocado Dipping Sauce. This sauce is a smoother and more complex version of guacamole. Burritos Rancheros, the party's stars, are luscious brunch burritos that combine well-seasoned black beans with cheese and scrambled eggs, wrapped in a flour tortilla and deliciously sauced. For a variation, this can be assembled as a Tex Mex Lasagna using tortillas instead of noodles. The side dish, Papas Pancho Villa, is a superb melange of potatoes, Canadian bacon, and red chard. This is seasoned with a green chile sauce and could be a meal in itself. For the finale, a rich and positively wicked Pumpkin Pecan Crème Brûlée.

To create the ambiance, focus on bright colors such as yellow, orange, and purple. Dried red chile strands, ceramic pitchers filled with jubilant flowers, and Mexican serapes or shawls are all great props to create a fabulous tablescape. Instead of a tablecloth, you might opt for covering the table with white freezer paper and use bright Mexican shawls as table runners. For an alternative to standard vases, place jars holding flowers in lunch bags. Tie several pieces of bright yarn or rafia around the top. This is a menu for all-out fun!

Menu

Chile Polenta Squares with Avocado Dipping Sauce
Burritos Rancheros
Papas Pancho Villa
Pumpkin Pecan Crème Brûlée

Faster & Flashier Menu

Guacamole & Chips
Burritos Rancheros
Papas Pancho Villa
Dessert (purchased)

Beer, Margaritas, and/or Sparkling Wine
Coffee and Kahlua

TIMETABLE	
Up to 5 days in advance	Salsa
Up to 3 days in advance	Papas Pancho Villa
Up to 2 days in advance	Burritos Rancheros. Pumpkin Pecan Crème Brûlée. Avocado Dipping Sauce.
Up to 1 day in advance	Chile Polenta (or freeze for up to 3 months). Set the table. Chill the beverages.
Party day!	Bring Chile Polenta Squares to room temperature. Heat up Papas Pancho Villa. Burritos Rancheros.

Chile Polenta Squares

Here's an assertive mouthful!   ***Yield: 8 servings***

1 stick unsalted or half-fat butter, cut into small pieces
1 to 2 pasilla chiles, rehydrated, stemmed, and seeded
1 cup sour cream or low-fat or fat-free sour cream
2 cloves garlic, or more, to taste
¾ cup polenta
1¼ cups all-purpose flour
1 teaspoon baking powder

2 teaspoons cumin
½ teaspoon salt
2 large eggs or egg substitute
¼ cup dry white wine
7 ounces whole green chiles (canned), seeded, deveined, and minced
1 teaspoon dried oregano
¼ cup minced cilantro, or more, to taste
2 to 4 green onions, minced
1 cup crumbled feta cheese

1. Preheat oven to 375 degrees.
2. Combine the butter, pasilla chiles, sour cream, and garlic in a food processor fitted with the metal blade.
3. Add all the dry ingredients and process until combined.
4. While the machine is running, add the eggs and wine through the feed tube. Process until well blended. Process in the green onions, cilantro, chiles, and oregano using several quick on-and-off motions so as not to destroy the texture.
5. Butter a glass baking pan 13½ inches × 9½ inches. Pour in the batter and tilt the pan to distribute the batter evenly. Sprinkle with feta cheese and bake for about 30 minutes, or until the cheese melts and the mixture is firm and a tester inserted into the middle comes out clean.
6. Cut into the desired size squares and serve warm or at room temperature.

FAST: Can assemble through Step 5 and refrigerate up to 1 day in advance, or freeze for up to 3 months. Allow it to come to room temperature before baking. If frozen, thaw before baking.

FABULOUS: With chopped or sliced black or green olives and/or any kind of chile added to the batter instead of pasilla and green chiles.

Avocado Dipping Sauce

If you think guacamole is good, wait until you taste this!   **Yield: About 1½ cups**

2 ripe avocados
2 large tomatillos, or more
2 to 6 green onions, minced
½ to 1 cup salsa (recipe follows) or your
    favorite brand
1 bunch cilantro, chopped

½ cup sour cream or low-fat or fat-free
    sour cream
2 cloves of garlic
1 tablespoon ground cumin
    Salt, white pepper, and fresh lime
    juice, to taste

1. Combine all ingredients, except the garnish, in a food processor fitted with
   the metal blade. Taste and adjust seasoning.

FAST: Can prepare up to 2 days in advance and refrigerate.

FLASHY: With tortilla chips, cold cooked shrimp, and/or spears of jicama.
Garnish with sprigs of cilantro and a marigold.

FABULOUS: As a dressing for pasta, couscous, potato, rice, or bulgar salad.

Salsa

Jars of red salsa will never please you after this.   **Yield: About 2 cups**

3 large ripe tomatoes, cut up
½ cup red or white onions, cut up
½ cup chopped cilantro
2 to 4 green chiles (canned), seeded
    and deveined
2 to 4 tomatillos, husked and cut up

2 cloves garlic, or more
    Fresh red jalapeño, as big a piece as
    you can handle, seeded and
    deveined
    Salt, white pepper, fresh lime juice,
    dried oregano, and sugar, to taste

1. Combine all ingredients in a food processor fitted with the metal blade,
   using quick on-and-off motions so as not to destroy the texture. Taste and
   adjust the seasonings.

FAST: Can prepare up to 5 days in advance and refrigerate, or freeze for up to
1 year.

FABULOUS: To season anything or to use in place of rich sauces.

Burritos Rancheros

A good choice for New Year's Day.   **Yield: 8 servings**

The Ranchero Sauce:

2 to 4 tablespoons olive oil
2 to 4 cloves garlic, minced
2 medium-size onions, minced
1 large green pepper, minced
½ cup minced green onions
4 to 8 green chiles (canned), deveined
    and seeded
4 to 6 dried pasilla chiles, rehydrated,
    stemmed, seeded and chopped

2 cups peeled tomatoes, fresh or canned
Salt
Pinch of sugar
1 teaspoon chile powder
1 teaspoon dried oregano
1 bunch cilantro, minced
½ teaspoon ground cumin, or more
2 tablespoons apple cider vinegar
¼ to ½ cup beer

1. In a skillet add the oil and heat. Sauté the onions, garlic, and green pepper until tender.
2. Add the green onions, cilantro, tomatoes, chiles, vinegar, beer, and seasonings. Let this simmer for 5 minutes and correct the seasonings. Keep warm until ready to use.

The Beans:

1 pound cooked black beans, canned or
    homemade
1 cup grated jack cheese
1 cup grated sharp cheddar cheese

½ teaspoon ground cumin, or more
½ teaspoon chile powder, or more
½ cup minced green onions

1. Combine all of the above ingredients in a food processor fitted with the metal blade. Taste and adjust the seasonings.

The Eggs (optional):

About 16 to 20 jumbo eggs or egg substitute, lightly scrambled

Flour tortillas

To Assemble:

1. Place some of the bean mixture and scrambled eggs (optional) in the center of a tortilla. Fold up burrito-style (like an envelope) and place in an oiled baking/serving pan. Instead of preparing this burrito-style, it can be layered lasagna-style. Repeat until all of the filling is used up.

2. Top with the Ranchero Sauce and bake in a preheated 350 degree oven until hot, about 30 minutes.

FAST: Can prepare up to 2 days in advance and refrigerate, or freeze for up to 3 months.

FLASHY: Garnish each burrito with a dollop of sour cream and a sprinkling of minced green onions, cilantro, and/or radishes.

FABULOUS: With cooked ham, sausages, chicken, pork, beef, and/or turkey mixed into the beans.

Papas Pancho Villa

Also known as Potatoes with Chard in a Green Chile Sauce, these
potatoes will serve you well, whether it's for a brunch or a dinner party.   ***Yield: 8+ servings***

¼ cup olive oil
2 onions, minced
4 cloves garlic, minced
1½ pounds Canadian bacon or ham,
    cubed
1 bunch chard, cut up or chopped
    (including the stems)
½ cup sherry

3 to 6 green onions, minced
1-pound can Green Chile Sauce
3 pounds potatoes, sliced, and cooked
    until tender
Salt and pepper, to taste
Grated Parmesan and jack cheese
    (optional)

1. Heat olive oil in a large skillet or wok and sauté the onions until tender.
2. Add the garlic, Canadian bacon, or ham along with the chard. Cook,
   stirring, until the chard wilts.
3. Add the sherry, green onions, and the can of sauce. Bring to a boil, then
   reduce heat, and simmer for about 5 minutes until the flavors develop.
4. Place the cooked, drained potatoes in a baking/serving pan. Top with the
   mixture in the skillet and add a layer of grated cheeses (optional).
5. Bake in a preheated 350 degree oven for about 30 minutes, until hot.

FAST: Can prepare up to 3 days in advance and refrigerate, or freeze for up to
6 months.

FABULOUS: With beans, pasta, or rice instead of potatoes.

Pumpkin Pecan Crème Brûlée

Pure ambrosia! **Yield: 8 to 10 servings**

1 cup sugar
¼ cup bourbon
3 cups low-fat milk or half and half
1 cup heavy cream or low-fat or
   nonfat milk
12 large egg yolks or egg substitute
2 cups pumpkin puree, canned
½ cup cream cheese or low-fat or
   fat-free cream cheese

¾ to 1 cup brown sugar, packed well
1 teaspoon pumpkin pie spice, or
   to taste
   Nutmeg, freshly grated, to taste
1 cup pecans, toasted
   Grated zest of 2 oranges
2 teaspoons vanilla extract
   Brown sugar

1. Preheat oven to 350 degrees.
2. Heat sugar with bourbon in a saucepan over low heat until melted.
3. Increase heat to medium-high and cook until sugar turns nutty brown. Remove it from the heat. Do not stir!
4. Stir the milk and cream into the saucepan. Be careful; it will splatter.
5. Return it to the burner, and cook over low heat until the caramel dissolves, stirring from time to time.
6. Beat the yolks with the pumpkin, brown sugar, pumpkin pie spice, and nutmeg in a food processor fitted with the metal blade or by hand with a whisk.
7. Process the milk mixture into the yolks. Add vanilla and orange zest.
8. Place the pecans in a buttered soufflé dish or in custard cups. Gently pour the custard in the soufflé dish or cups. Place in a baking pan with hot water that reaches halfway up sides of custard.
9. Bake for 1 hour or more, until tester inserted into the middle comes out clean. Do not overbake. Cool to room temperature, then chill in refrigerator.
10. Top custard with a layer of brown sugar. Place the custard in baking pan filled with ice and put under the hot broiler until the sugar melts and browns. Serve warm or cold.

FAST: Can assemble up to 1 month in advance and freeze. Can prepare up to 2 days in advance and refrigerate.

FABULOUS: Create a coconut crème brûlée by adding 8 ounces of unsweetened coconut to the custards and omit the pumpkin and pumpkin pie spice.

Winter Mediterranean Brunch

rom calamata olives to red wine biscotti, this is a brazen brunch, perfect for a lazy winter Sunday. I use pumpkin-colored woven placemats. For the centerpiece, fill a basket with firm heads of cabbage. To avoid having to purchase a zillion heads, simply stuff the basket with crumpled newspapers or paper bags, then top it with the cabbages. Stick sprigs of fresh rosemary in the spaces between the cabbages and voila!

You will find that every dish in this menu is something that you will get a great deal of use out of. Starting with the hors d'oeuvres, the Grecian Bliss is extremely versatile, not to mention delicious. I love to use it on pasta. The Celery Root & Rutabaga Salad is no ordinary salad. It is equally wonderful at a picnic as at a dinner party. Unlike its bland distant cousin, the oh-so-ordinary iceberg salad with bottled dressing, this salad is packed with flavor, texture, and nutrition. The Florentine Polenta with Marinara Pronto is a marvelous light entrée that can gracefully leap out of the brunch arena into a lunch or dinner menu. It is very light, flavored with basil, and, to my taste, better than a soufflé. Besides which, you can whip it up in minutes, or make it in advance. This brunch culminates with another version of a biscotti, which, I should warn you, could be addictive.

Menu

Grecian Bliss with Crostini

Florentine Polenta Timbale with Marinara Pronto

Celery Root & Rutabaga Salad

Grilled Sausages (optional)

Italian Bread with Butter and/or Olive Oil

Red Wine & Fennel Biscotti

Fresh Fruit

Faster & Flashier Menu

Grecian Bliss with Sliced Baguettes

Florentine Polenta Timbale with Marinara Sauce (purchased)

Italian Bread with Butter and/or Olive Oil

Biscotti (purchased)

Fresh Fruit

Sparkling Wine, Merlot, and/or Dry White Wine and Coffee

✄ TIMETABLE ✄

Up to 14 days in advance	Red Wine & Fennel Biscotti
Up to 5 days in advance and frozen for up to 6 months	Marinara Pronto. Grecian Bliss (or frozen for up to 3 months). Crostini (or frozen for up to 3 months). Lemon Mustard Vinaigrette.
Up to 2 days in advance	Florentine Polenta Timbale (assemble)
Up to 1 day in advance	Set the table. Chill the wines.
Brunch day!	Grill or broil sausages (optional). Bake the timbale. Heat the marinara and bread.

Grecian Bliss

A luscious and robust full-flavored spread, also known as pâté.   **Yield: 8+ servings**

1 cup pitted calamata olives*
3 to 4 cloves garlic
1 to 3 pasilla chiles,* rehydrated,
    stemmed, and seeded
1 to 2 tablespoons minced fresh ginger

1 bunch Italian parsley
8 ounces unsalted or half-fat butter, cut
    up
6 to 8 ounces feta cheese, crumbled

1. Combine all the ingredients in a food processor fitted with the metal blade. Taste and adjust the flavors if necessary.
2. Oil a container and line it with plastic wrap. Transfer and pack the mixture into it. Chill in the refrigerator for several hours, or freeze for 1 hour until firm enough to unmold.

FAST: Can prepare up to 5 days in advance and refrigerate, or freeze for up to 3 months.

FLASHY: Serve with thinly sliced baguettes and/or crostini (page 66). Garnish with parsley and/or any nontoxic flower.

FABULOUS: With fresh basil and/or with pepperoncini instead of chiles. On pasta, chicken, lamb, or fish. To reduce the fat further, use low-fat or fat-free cream cheese instead of butter.

Celery Root & Rutabaga Salad

A unique combo with great flavors and textures.   **Yield: 8+ servings**

¼ to ½ cup vinegar
1 medium-size celery root*
2 rutabagas, peeled and grated*
    Fresh lemon juice

Lemon Mustard Vinaigrette (recipe
    follows)
¼ cup poppy seeds, or more
    Salt and white pepper, to taste

*Refer to Terms & Techniques.

1. Bring a large pot of salted water to a boil and add ¼ to ½ cup vinegar to it.
2. Cut away the peel from the celery root and grate it in a food processor fitted with the thick grating disc, or cut it into matchstick slices.3. Put the celery root in the boiling water for about 3 minutes. Remove it using a strainer, and shake off the excess water. Place the celery root in a salad or mixing bowl, along with the grated rutabagas. Sprinkle liberally with lemon juice and toss well.
4. Toss in the desired amount of vinaigrette and poppy seeds. Taste and adjust the seasonings.

FAST: Can prepare up to 2 days in advance and refrigerate.

FLASHY: Garnish with parsley, watercress, and/or any nontoxic flower.

FABULOUS: With toasted sesame seeds instead of poppy seeds. Seasoned with fresh dill and/or with baby shrimp or crab.

Lemon Mustard Vinaigrette

A fresh classic!   **Yield: About 2 cups**

Fresh lemon juice, to taste (about ⅔ cup)
2 cups extra virgin olive oil
1 tablespoon Dijon mustard, or to taste
1 tablespoon minced shallots
Salt and freshly ground white pepper, to taste

1. Combine all the ingredients in a food processor fitted with the metal blade or whisk together by hand. Taste and adjust the seasonings.

FAST: Can prepare up to 5 days in advance and refrigerate.

FABULOUS: With several cloves of garlic, minced fresh dill, oregano, or basil added. Use to marinate vegetables, poultry, fish, or seafood. To reduce the fat, replace half of the olive oil with low-fat or fat-free sour cream.

Florentine Polenta Timbale

This recipe is a real hybrid. I got my inspiration from baked egg
recipes and took a wild leap, using polenta instead of bread.

Yield: 8+ servings

2 to 4 tablespoons olive oil or
    butter
2 large yellow onions, chopped
4 to 8 cloves garlic, minced
3 to 4 10-ounce packages thawed
    frozen spinach, squeezed well to
    remove all the excess liquid
1 cup ricotta cheese or low-fat or fat-
    free ricotta cheese
1 cup sour cream or low-fat or fat-free
    sour cream
12 extra-large eggs or the equivalent
    amount of egg substitute
8 to 12 pepperoncini, stemmed,
    seeded, and minced (optional)

½ cup minced Italian parsley
2 to 3 teaspoons salt
    White pepper and ground nutmeg,
    to taste
1 to 2 cups packed, fresh basil leaves,
    or more
1 cup buttermilk or low-fat or fat-free
    buttermilk
1 cup instant polenta (page 14)
2 teaspoons baking powder
2 cups grated jack cheese
1 cup freshly grated Parmesan reggiano

1. Heat the olive oil or melt the butter in a skillet, and sauté the onion and garlic over medium heat until tender.
2. Meanwhile, combine all the remaining ingredients in an electric mixer or in a food processor fitted with the metal blade. It might be necessary to do this in several batches.
3. Mix in the onions.
4. Oil a large baking pan or casserole and turn the batter into it.
5. Bake in a preheated 350 degree oven until set, about 35–45 minutes, until a tester inserted into the middle comes out clean.

FAST: Can assemble and refrigerate for up to 2 days. Can fully prepare and refrigerate for up to 3 days, or freeze for up to 3 months. Thaw and reheat in a 400 degree oven for about 20 minutes.

FLASHY: Serve with Marinara Pronto.

Marinara Pronto

I love this sauce. It has a pure, fresh flavor and can be used on anything from pasta to veal. As a bonus, it is very low in fat.

Yield: About 3 cups

2 tablespoons olive oil
1 large yellow onion, minced
1 pound fresh peeled or canned Italian
    pear-shaped tomatoes
4 cloves garlic, or more

1 bunch Italian parsley
1 bay leaf
½ cup Madeira wine
    Salt, white pepper, and freshly grated
      nutmeg, to taste

1. Heat up the olive oil in a saucepan and sauté the onion until tender, about 5 minutes.
2. Meanwhile, puree the tomatoes, garlic, and parsley in a food processor fitted with the metal blade and add it to the onions. Add this and the bay leaf to the saucepan.
3. Add the wine and bring it to a boil over high heat. Reduce the heat to medium and simmer for about 20 minutes. Season to taste.

FAST: Can prepare up to 5 days in advance and refrigerate, or freeze for up to 6 months.

FABULOUS: Season with any fresh or dried herb. With ½ cup or more roasted garlic.

Red Wine & Fennel Biscotti

A version of the classic Italian cookie, designed to be dunked in coffee or red wine. It is baked twice to achieve a crisp texture. Great for breakfast or dessert!

Yield: About 70 biscotti

4 cups all-purpose flour
¾ cup granulated sugar
1 teaspoon baking powder
½ teaspoon salt
5½ tablespoons fennel seeds
2 jumbo eggs or egg substitute

½ cup full-bodied red wine, such as merlot or cabernet sauvignon
½ cup olive oil
Grated zest of 2 oranges
Freshly grated nutmeg, to taste

1. Preheat the oven to 350 degrees and oil a cookie sheet.
2. Combine the flour with the sugar, baking powder, salt, and fennel seeds in a food processor fitted with the metal blade or in a bowl.
3. While the machine is running, add the wine, olive oil, zest, and nutmeg through the feed tube, or add to the bowl and combine with an electric mixer.
4. Process until a soft dough forms.
5. Dust the work surface with flour, and lightly flour your hands. Divide the dough in thirds or fourths and form into 3 or 4 logs.
6. Place the logs on the cookie sheet and bake until a tester inserted in the middle of a log comes out clean, about 35–45 minutes.
7. Remove the logs from the oven, let cool slightly, and cut into slices about ¼ inch thick at an angle. Each slice can be cut in half lengthwise to make long, narrow cookies.
8. Return the cookie sheet to the oven, reduce the temperature to 300 degrees, and bake for 15–20 minutes more, until golden and crisp. Turn the oven off and leave the cookies in the oven with the door open for another 15 minutes.

FAST: Can prepare up to 14 days in advance and store in airtight jars or in plastic bags, or freeze for up to 6 months. Thaw at room temperature.

FLASHY: Serve with and dunk in red wine or coffee.

FABULOUS: With chopped, toasted almonds or walnuts mixed in. Roll in chopped, toasted nuts or sesame seeds before baking. Or dip half of each biscotti in melted milk or semisweet chocolate after baking, and coat with chopped nuts or sesame seeds. Add minced fresh rosemary and crushed green peppercorns to create an hors d'oeuvre.

Double Mushroom Marinara Soup Lunch

S oup, salad, and warm French bread with plenty of wine make a
wonderful lunch or casual dinner. On a cold winter day, it is perfect.

This simply divine menu begins with an extraordinary salad. It is based
on a refreshing mixture of romaine and radicchio leaves. This alone makes a
good salad, but we are going to travel beyond good into the realm of exciting.
Oranges, calamata olives, pine nuts, and dried cherries provide a riot of both
flavors and textures. This is a salad that you will want to use over and over.

A starring soup follows the salad. One taste of it and you would swear
that a short, Italian grandma slaved over it for hours. It is ambrosia in a bowl.
It can also be used as a pasta sauce or even as a base for simmered vegetables
and stews.

From our soup we move on to another glass of red wine with biscotti
and then a nap. What a Saturday!

In creating the tablescape for this leisurely afternoon affair, rough
textured placemats with paisley or plaid napkins work well. Small potted
white cyclamen create a beautiful centerpiece. Another choice might be a
basket of yellow onions, oranges, and red apples. A combination of the
onions and fruit along with potted flowers is also an option.

Menu

Romaine & Radicchio Salad

Double Mushroom Marinara Soup with Italian Sausage

Sourdough Bread

Chocolate Chip Oatmeal Biscotti

Faster & Flashier Menu

Romaine & Radicchio Salad

Double Mushroom & Marinara Soup with Italian Sausage
(using bottled marinara sauce)

Sourdough Bread

Biscotti (purchased)

Sauvignon Blanc

Merlot

Coffee

TIMETABLE

Up to 30 days in advance	Chocolate Chip Oatmeal Biscotti
Up to 2 weeks in advance	Balsamic Vinaigrette
Up to 4 days in advance	Double Mushroom Marinara Soup
Up to 1 day in advance	Set the table. Chill the wines.
Party day!	Toss the salad. Heat up the soup. Warm the bread.

Romaine & Radicchio Salad

A beautiful melding of flavors and textures.

Yield: 8 servings

2 heads romaine lettuce, torn into bite-size pieces

1 head radicchio leaves,* sliced or torn into bite-size pieces

2 oranges, peeled, membrane removed, and thinly sliced

¼ cup pine nuts, toasted (page 13), or to taste

½ cup pitted calamata olives*

¾ cups dried, pitted cherries*

Balsamic Vinaigrette (recipe follows)

Salt and freshly ground, coarse black pepper, to taste

1. Combine the greens, oranges, pine nuts, olives, and dried cherries in a large salad bowl.
2. Toss in the desired amount of dressing. Taste and season with salt and pepper.

FAST: Can prep ingredients up to 1 day in advance and refrigerate, storing the oranges and olives separately.

FABULOUS: With spinach instead of romaine.

*Refer to Terms & Techniques.

Balsamic Vinaigrette

Yield: About 3 cups

2 to 4 cloves garlic
2 to 4 teaspoons Dijon mustard
⅔ cup balsamic vinegar
¼ cup apple cider vinegar

2 cups extra virgin olive oil
1 teaspoon salt, or to taste
  Freshly ground white and black
    pepper, to taste

1. Combine all the ingredients in a food processor fitted with the metal blade or in a blender.
2. Taste and adjust the seasonings.

FAST: Can prepare up to 1 week in advance and refrigerate.

FLASHY: On anything!

FABULOUS: With about 2 tablespoons minced fresh ginger and/or green onions. To reduce the fat, replace half of the olive oil with low-fat or fat-free sour cream.

Double Mushroom Marinara Soup

This tastes as if someone's Italian grandma slaved away for hours.   **Yield: 8+ servings**

1 22-ounce can tomato sauce
1 pound Italian sausage or Italian
    turkey sausage, casings removed
    (sweet, hot, or a combo)
2 to 3 ounces shiitake mushrooms,*
    soaked in hot water until soft,
    stemmed, and thinly sliced (strain
    and save the soaking liquid)
½ to 1 pound cultivated mushrooms,
    thinly sliced
1 quart chicken broth, homemade or
    canned
½ cup dry sherry or Madeira

1 bunch Italian parsley, minced
1 large onion or 2 small onions,
    chopped
3 cloves of garlic, or more, minced
2 shallots, minced
1 teaspoon fennel seeds, or to taste
1 teaspoon dried oregano and
    marjoram, or to taste
2 bay leaves
¼ cup grated Parmesan cheese, or more
    Salt, freshly ground, coarse black
    pepper, and nutmeg, to taste

1. In a large skillet, cook the sausages until nicely browned, and break them up into smaller pieces while cooking.
2. Pour off all but 2 tablespoons of any oil that may have been given off from the sausages. If there is no remaining oil, use olive oil as needed.
3. Add the onion and shallots to the skillet and sauté until limp.
4. Add the mushrooms, parsley, and garlic and sauté until the liquid released by the mushrooms has cooked away.
5. Stir in all the liquid, including the soaking liquid from the shiitake mushrooms, and the seasonings, and cook gently for about 20 minutes or until the flavors develop to your liking. Stir in the Parmesan cheese.

FAST: Can prepare up to 4 days in advance and refrigerate, or freeze for up to 6 months.

FLASHY: Serve in soup bowls with extra cheese passed separately.

FABULOUS: With cooked beans, rice, potatoes, and cooked pasta, along with assorted vegetables.

*Refer to Terms & Techniques.

Chocolate Chip Oatmeal Biscotti

Great textures and flavors, yet low in fat. This sounds almost impossible!   ***Yield: About 70***

½ cup brown sugar, packed well
¾ cup granulated sugar
2 cups quick-cooking oatmeal
2 cups all-purpose flour
½ teaspoon salt
1 teaspoon baking soda

Ground nutmeg, to taste
4 large eggs or egg substitute
2 teaspoons vanilla extract
8 ounces semisweet chocolate chips
Grated zest of 2 oranges (optional)
1 cup walnuts, toasted

1. Preheat the oven to 375 degrees.
2. Combine the first 8 ingredients in a food processor fitted with the metal blade.
3. Process in the eggs and vanilla, then add the remaining ingredients and process in just until combined, so as not to destroy the texture (or place on a floured work surface and knead in the ingredients by hand).
4. Remove the dough from the food processor and dust with flour. Divide the dough into 4 equal pieces and form into long, narrow logs.
5. Place the logs on an ungreased cookie sheet and bake for 35–45 minutes until a tester inserted into the middle comes out clean.
6. Remove from the oven, cool slightly, and cut into thin slices. Reduce the oven temperature to 300 degrees.
7. Return the slices to the oven for about 15–20 minutes.

FAST: Can prepare up to 30 days in advance and store in airtight jars or in plastic bags, or freeze for up to 6 months. Thaw at room temperature for a few hours.

FABULOUS: With half of each cookie dipped in melted milk or semisweet chocolate after baking.

White Bean Soup &
Orzo Salad Lunch

This casual luncheon captures the warm comfortable feel of the Mediterranean. Calamata and Feta Melange is as close to nirvana as I care to get. It is also amazingly versatile. I must caution you not to use it on a chocolate mousse; other than that the possibilities are endless, whether it is used as an hors d'oeuvre with crostini, a bread spread, or a condiment with grilled meats or poultry. A white bean soup that requires about 10 minutes of your time but tastes as if someone has devoted hours of loving attention is the menu's star. It is accompanied by a Greek-Style Orzo Salad that could also stand alone as an entrée served either hot or cold. Naturally, French or sourdough bread is a must.

Now for the table to go with the menu. I wanted it to have a pronounced rustic Mediterranean feel. A cotton paisley bedspread from an import store in shades of green, purple, and cream with cream-colored napkins dressed the table. Purple stock and white mums were casually arranged in a ceramic pitcher.

Menu

White Bean & Lemon Soup
French Bread with Calamata & Feta Melange
Greek-Style Orzo Salad
Maple Pecan Bread

Faster & Flashier Menu

Calamata Olives
White Bean & Lemon Soup
French Bread with butter
Greek-Style Orzo Salad
Dessert (purchased)

Sauvignon Blanc
Coffee

✂ TIMETABLE ✂

Up to 5 days in advance	Calamata & Feta Melange. Maple Pecan Bread.
Up to 4 days in advance	Greek-Style Orzo Salad
Up to 3 days in advance	White Bean & Lemon Soup
Up to 1 day in advance	Set the table. Chill the wines.
Party day!	Heat the soup.

White Bean & Lemon Soup

Almost instant, but full of slow, old-world flavors!

Yield: 8 servings

2 to 4 tablespoons olive oil
1 huge white or yellow onion
⅛ pound prosciutto, chopped or cubed
6 or more cloves garlic
    Grated zest of 2 lemons and the juice
1 bay leaf
1 15-ounce can white beans (or
    cannellini beans), puréed

½ to 1 cup dry white wine
    Minced Italian parsley
    Dried oregano, salt, and white
      pepper, to taste
4 to 6 cups chicken broth, homemade
    or canned

1. In a medium-size soup pot, heat the olive oil and sauté the onion, garlic, and prosciutto until the onion is tender or golden (if you wish).
2. Add the lemon zest and bay leaf, and sauté over medium heat for several minutes.
3. Add the remaining ingredients and bring to a boil over high heat, stirring from time to time.

FAST: Can prepare up to 3 days in advance and refrigerate, or freeze for up to 3 months.

FABULOUS: With fresh rosemary instead of oregano. With ham instead of prosciutto.

Calamata & Feta Melange

A bread spread, hors d'oeuvre, and/or condiment.   **Yield: About 1½ cups**

8 ounces feta cheese
4 to 8 ounces plain yogurt or low-fat or
   fat-free yogurt
¼ cup pitted, minced calamata olives,*
   or more

Grated zest of 1 to 2 lemons
3 minced green onions
½ cup minced toasted almonds

1. Combine the feta and yogurt in a food processor fitted with the metal
   blade until fully blended. Taste and adjust the seasonings.
2. Add the remaining ingredients using several quick on-and-off motions so
   as not to destroy all the texture.

FAST: Can prepare up to 5 days in advance and refrigerate or freeze for up to 3
months.

FLASHY: Serve with bread, crackers, crostini (page 66), or Pasta Chips (page
112). Garnish with flowering kale or parsley.

FABULOUS: Tossed into hot pasta or as a seasoning for cooked vegetables. On
grilled meats, fish, or chicken instead of a rich sauce. As a seasoning pesto to
add to soups, dressings, vegetables, or pork.

*Refer to Terms & Techniques.

Greek-Style Orzo Salad

This is designed to end the pasta salad doldrums.

Yield: 8+ servings

1 package orzo (rice-shaped pasta)
8 ounces feta cheese, crumbled
¼ cup sesame seeds, toasted
¼ cup minced Italian parsley
1 tablespoon fresh mint leaves, minced, or more
1 to 2 red peppers, roasted, peeled, and seeded and cut into thin strips (or bottled)
¼ to ½ sweet red onion, cut into thin rings

½ pint pitted calamata olives, or to taste
½ cup cherry tomatoes, halved
4 to 8 anchovies, minced
½ cup extra virgin olive oil or low-fat or fat-free sour cream or plain yogurt
Lemon juice, to taste
Salt, white pepper, freshly ground black pepper, and dried oregano, to taste

1. Cook the orzo until al dente.
2. Drain and transfer to a large salad bowl. Toss orzo with the olive oil, lemon juice, and all the remaining ingredients, except for the feta and tomatoes. Taste and adjust the seasonings.
3. When the salad cooks to room temperature, toss in the feta and the tomatoes.

FAST: Can prepare up to 4 days in advance and refrigerate. Toss with extra dressing if dry.

FABULOUS: With artichoke hearts and pepperoncini.

Maple Pecan Bread

Great for breakfast, lunch, or dinner!   ***Yield: 1 loaf***

¾ cup dark brown sugar, packed
1 4-ounce stick unsalted butter, cut up
3 extra large eggs or egg substitute
¾ cup pure maple syrup
½ teaspoon baking soda

½ teaspoon baking powder
⅓ cup bourbon
2¼ cups cake flour
¾ to 1 cup pecan pieces, toasted

1. Preheat the oven to 350 degrees and oil a bread pan.
2. Combine the brown sugar and butter in a food processor fitted with the metal blade.
3. Process in the next 5 ingredients.
4. Add the flour and process in briefly.
5. Add the pecans and process in, using care not to destroy the texture of the nuts.
6. Transfer the batter to the prepared pan and bake for about 1 hour and 15 minutes until a tester inserted into the middle comes out clean.

FAST: Can prepare up to 5 days in advance and refrigerate, or freeze for up to 3 months.

FLASHY: With a scoop of vanilla ice cream on a slice of the bread, a drizzle of maple syrup, and a scattering of pecans.

Hors D'Oeuvres for a Holiday Cocktail Party

I have a pet peeve when it comes to the hors d'oeuvres. Everything should be easy to eat. How many times have you been at one of these parties and found almost nothing that you could eat without totally embarrassing yourself. For example, carved roast beef or ham with biscuits or bread. The meat is given to you in a hefty slab. You usually only have one free hand and no way to cut it. Hors d'oeuvres at stand-up parties should never require utensils to eat, and everything should be small enough to handle delicately.

With that said, let's get into the hors d'oeuvres. Hors d'oeuvres are designed to be fun and adventuresome. Cubes of cheese and deli platters are out. This challenge still causes panic attacks in many. After a quick glance at the Timetable, you can see what an easy task it is to stage a cocktail party. Everything is prepared far in advance, and most everything can be frozen. Even if you work, you can manage to throw the party with ease. I usually do crostini and bagel chips at night during the week. On weekends I do several hors d'oeuvres, and before you know it, the party is in the freezer.

It goes without saying that the look of this party should be festive and elegant. This is the official "glitz blitz" season. I like to cover my serving tables in gold and silver lamé cloths. If this sounds good to you but you do not feel like investing in these materials, I've got an alternative. Cover the tables in solid-color cloths such as black, red, or green, and buy pieces of lamé to use as runners or table throws. As a way of creating different elevations for your platters of hors d'oeuvres, try wrapping boxes in gold and silver paper. To further adorn the tables, use silver, gold, and/or black spray-painted artichokes and pinecones. Ribbons, tinsel, pine cuttings, and Christmas tree balls strewn everywhere on the table create a holiday mood. Have fun!

Menu

Spinach & Ham Chafing Dish with Garlic Rosemary Crostini
Shrimp & Feta Croustades
Chinese Sausage Potstickers with Dipping Sauces
Chèvre & Lox Torta with Bagel Chips
Prosciutto & Vegetables

Faster & Flashier Menu

Cold Shrimp with Dipping Sauce (purchased)
Spinach & Ham Chafing Dish with Sliced Baguette
Grilled Assorted Sausages with Dipping Sauces
Chèvre & Lox Torta with Bagel Chips (purchased)
Prosciutto & Vegetables
Pâté (purchased)

Sparkling Wine, Dry White Wine, and/or Mixed Drinks

✄ TIMETABLE ✄

Up to 6 months in advance and frozen	Garlic Rosemary Crostini. Croustades. Bagel Chips.
Up to 3 months in advance and frozen	Spinach & Ham Chafing Dish. Chinese Sausage Potstickers.
Up to 7 days in advance	Dipping sauces.
Up to 5 days in advance	Chèvre & Lox Torta
Up to 3 days in advance	Shrimp and Feta Croustades
Up to 1 day in advance	Prosciutto & Vegetables. Set the tables. Chill the wines.
Party day!	Garnish everything. Bake potstickers and croustades.

Spinach & Ham Chafing Dish

A luscious mixture.

Yield: About 3 cups; 24 or more servings; fills about 40 tartlets or croustades

4 tablespoons unsalted butter
2 to 3 cloves garlic, minced
1 onion, minced
4 tablespoons all-purpose flour
1 cup heavy cream or low-fat or fat-free milk
3 tablespoons brandy
2 10-ounce packages frozen chopped spinach, thawed and drained

½ cup chopped ham
1 to 2 teaspoons Dijon mustard
¼ cup minced fresh parsley
Grated nutmeg, to taste
Ground white pepper, to taste
½ cup grated Swiss or Gruyère cheese*

1. Melt the butter in a saucepan over medium heat. When it begins to foam, add the garlic and onions and cook, stirring, until tender.
2. Whisk in the flour and cook for 1 minute. Remove the pan from the burner and whisk in the cream and brandy. Return to the burner and cook, stirring, until thickened.
3. Stir in the remaining ingredients, except for the cheese. Stir until the flavors develop.
4. Stir in the cheese over low heat. Cook until it melts, and taste and adjust the seasonings.

FAST: Can prepare the filling up to 2 days in advance and refrigerate, or freeze for up to 3 months. Tartlets or croustades can be filled up to 3 hours in advance and left at room temperature. They can also be assembled completely and flash frozen for up to 3 months. Do not thaw before heating.

FLASHY: Serve in a chafing dish or fondue pot with crostini. Use as a filling for Croustades (page 267). Top with grated Parmesan, and place under a hot broiler for a few minutes until the Parmesan turns a golden color.

FABULOUS: For a faster version, spread the mixture on thinly sliced baguettes or pumpernickel squares. With minced Swiss chard, broccoli, bok choy, or asparagus instead of the spinach.

*Refer to Terms & Techniques.

Garlic Rosemary Crostini

A delicious and cholesterol-free way to prepare garlic bread. The seasoned oil is something you may want to keep on hand in your refrigerator as a cooking oil for almost anything.

Yield: About 70 crostini

1 sourdough French bread baguette
2 cloves of garlic, or more
1 cup olive oil

⅓ cup red wine vinegar
Salt and fresh or dried rosemary, to taste

1. Slice the baguette into thin slices and preheat oven to 350 degrees.
2. Combine all the remaining ingredients in a food processor fitted with the metal blade or in a blender. Taste and adjust the seasonings.
3. Line a cookie sheet with aluminum foil. Brush the slices of bread with seasoned oil and place on a baking sheet.
4. Bake until crisp, about 15 minutes.

FAST: Can prepare oil up to 5 days in advance and store in an airtight jar or plastic bag, or freeze for up to 6 months.

FLASHY: Serve at room temperature or warm in a napkin-lined basket or on a platter.

FABULOUS: With any herb. With butter or a combination of butter and oil. Top with grated Parmesan, Romano, and/or mizithera cheese.

Shrimp & Feta Croustades   *Yield: About 60 croustades*

About 60 croustades (recipe follows)
About 1 cup Roasted Red Pepper Sauce
  (page 121)
About 60 small- to medium-size raw
  shrimp, shelled and deveined

1 pound feta cheese, crumbled
6 to 8 green onions (scallions), white
  and green parts, minced
½ cup packed fresh basil leaves,
  minced, or more

1. Preheat the oven to 350 degrees. Place the croustades on several ungreased cookie sheets.
2. Fill each croustade with some of the pepper sauce. Add a raw shrimp or two to each croustade.
3. Combine the feta, green onions, and basil in a small bowl and top each croustade with some of the cheese mixture.
4. Bake until the shrimp is just cooked (opaque all the way through), about 15 minutes.

FAST: Can assemble up to 3 hours in advance, hold at room temperature, and bake just before serving. Can prepare filling up to 3 days in advance and refrigerate, or freeze for up to 3 months.

FLASHY: Serve hot on a platter and garnish with fresh basil and/or any nontoxic flower or leaves.

FABULOUS: With Brie, jack, Camembert, chèvre, or Saint André cheese substituted for the feta.

Croustades

This is a quick, low-cholesterol alternative to rich pastry tartlets.

Yield: About 35 croustades

1 cup extra virgin olive oil
2 to 4 cloves garlic, minced
½ teaspoon salt, or to taste

1 loaf sourdough bread (must be very fresh), sliced

1. Preheat the oven to 350 degrees.
2. Combine the olive oil with the garlic and salt in a food processor fitted with the metal blade, in a blender, or in a bowl.
3. Using a cookie cutter or wine glass, cut the bread into 2½-inch rounds.
4. Roll the bread rounds out with a rolling pin.
5. Brush mini-muffin tins with the garlic oil. Press the bread rounds into the cups and brush them with garlic oil.
6. Bake until completely crisp, about 15 minutes. Now they are ready to be filled.

FAST: Can store in airtight jars or plastic bags for up to 1 week, or freeze for up to 6 months. No thawing is needed.

FLASHY: Fill with anything.

FABULOUS: With fresh or dried herbs added to garlic oil. Made with any combination of peanut, canola, and/or olive oil. Can be made fat-free by using a nonstick mini-muffin tin and just baking the croustades plain.

Chinese Sausage Potstickers

Asian nirvana!

Yield: About 30 potstickers

¼ to ½ pound Chinese sausages,*
  minced or cut into thin slices
1 cup uncooked short-grain (Arborio)
  or pearl* rice
¼ cup minced pickled ginger, or to taste
4 large, dried shiitake mushrooms,*
  rehydrated, stemmed, and minced
  (reserve the soaking liquid)
1 tablespoon sweetened chile sauce* or
  Chinese plum sauce

4 green onions (scallions), white and
  green parts, minced
2 to 4 canned whole green chiles,
  seeded, deveined, and minced
1 cup dry white wine
  Salt and ground white pepper, to taste
1 package potsticker wrappers
  Chinese sesame oil for brushing

1. Cook the sausage in a saucepan over medium heat until some of the fat is rendered, about 5 minutes.
2. Add the rice, pickled ginger, mushrooms, chile sauce, green onions, and chiles, and reduce the heat to low. Stir and cook for a minute or two, without browning the rice.
3. Strain the reserved mushroom liquid through a double thickness of paper towels and add 1 cup of it, along with the wine, to the rice. Bring to a boil over high heat and cover. Reduce the heat to low and cook until all the water is absorbed, about 20 minutes. Taste and adjust the seasonings.
4. Transfer the rice mixture to a bowl and place in the freezer to chill for about 30 minutes.
5. Preheat the oven to 400 degrees.
6. Place a generous teaspoonful of the mixture in the center of each wrapper. Fold in half; slightly dampen the outer edges with cold water. Press the edges together to seal, using the tines of a fork or a potsticker mold.
7. Place on an oiled cookie sheet and brush the tops with sesame oil. Bake until crisp, about 15–20 minutes.

FAST: Can assemble up to 1 day in advance and refrigerate, or flash freeze* for up to 3 months. Do not thaw before baking; just add 5–10 minutes to the baking time.

*Refer to Terms & Techniques.

FLASHY: Serve hot on a platter and garnish with baby bok choy, cilantro, and/or any nontoxic flower or leaves. Serve with Cold Mustard Mint Sauce and Apricot Sesame Sauce (recipes follow).

FABULOUS: With Chinese barbecued pork substituted for the sausage. Cooked as a traditional potsticker. Use the filling as Chinese risotto.

Cold Mustard Mint Sauce

Great for fat watchers.   **Yield: About 1 cup**

2 tablespoons Dijon mustard
3 tablespoons port or dry sherry

⅔ cup balsamic vinegar
2 tablespoons minced fresh mint leaves

1. Combine all the ingredients in a food processor fitted with the metal blade or in a blender, and process, or whisk together in a bowl.
2. Shake or stir before using.

FAST: Can prepare up to 7 days in advance and refrigerate, or freeze for up to 6 months.

FLASHY: As a dunk for hot or cold grilled or roasted lamb, beef, pork, or chicken. Serve hot or cold. Garnish by floating fresh mint leaves and/or any nontoxic flower on top.

FABULOUS: With puréed roasted garlic* mixed in. With fresh rosemary and/or basil instead of or with the mint. Heated with ¼–½ cup heavy cream and served hot.

*Refer to Terms & Techniques.

Apricot Sesame Sauce

World class. Try it with ribs or chicken.   **Yield: About 1½ cups**

½ cup apricot preserves
¼ cup bourbon
1 tablespoon Dijon mustard
1 clove garlic, minced
2 to 4 tablespoons minced fresh
  ginger
¼ cup rice wine vinegar
¼ cup soy sauce
2 tablespoons sugar

1 to 3 tablespoons minced cilantro
  (fresh coriander)
1 tablespoon tahini
1 to 2 tablespoons sesame seeds,
  toasted
  Pinch of Chinese five-spice powder
  Salt and ground white pepper, to taste
1 tablespoon cornstarch, dissolved in 2
  tablespoons water (optional)

1. Combine all the ingredients, except for the cornstarch mixture, in a
   medium-size saucepan and bring to a boil over high heat.
2. Stir the cornstarch mixture into the boiling sauce. Cook until thickened,
   about 5 minutes, over medium heat, stirring continuously. Taste and adjust
   the seasonings.

FAST: Can prepare up to 7 days in advance and refrigerate, or freeze for up to
1 year.

FLASHY: Serve hot in a chafing dish, fondue pot, or over an alcohol burner or
at room temperature with any Asian-style hors d'oeuvre.

FABULOUS: As a seasoning sauce to enhance other sauces, marinades, vegetables, soups, and stir-fry dishes. As an entrée sauce for pasta, rice, seafood,
pork, or chicken.

Chèvre & Lox Torta

Sheer bliss! (also known as Jewish nirvana)

Yield: About 4 cups; serves 10 to 12

½ pound (2 sticks) unsalted or half-fat butter, cut into pieces
1 8-ounce package cream cheese or low-fat or fat-free cream cheese at room temperature
¾ pound chèvre or feta cheese
1 shallot, minced
2 to 4 tablespoons fresh lemon juice

Grated zest of 2 lemons
Ground white pepper, to taste
¾ pound lox (smoked salmon) or as much as your budget allows
1 cup green onions (scallions), white and green parts, minced
2 bunches fresh dill, stemmed and minced

1. Combine the first 7 ingredients in a food processor fitted with the metal blade and process until smooth, or combine in a bowl. Taste and adjust flavors.
2. Oil a 4- to 5-cup straight-sided mold, bowl, or pâté terrine. Line with plastic wrap (A large yogurt container works well).
3. Layer in all the ingredients. I usually start with the lox, then the green onion, the dill, and the cheese mixture. Repeat until container is full.
4. Fold the plastic wrap over the top, press gently to compress the layers, and chill until firm, at least 1 hour.
5. Invert onto a platter, remove the plastic wrap, and enjoy!

FAST: Can prepare up to 5 days in advance and refrigerate, or freeze for up to 3 months.

FLASHY: Serve on a platter with Bagel Chips (recipe follows), crackers, and/or breads. Garnish with minced lox, dill, lemon zest, green or red onions, and/or any nontoxic flower or leaves.

FABULOUS: With all the layered ingredients mixed into the cheese mixture and then molded. To further reduce the fat, replace some or all of the butter with cream cheese or feta cheese.

FURTHER: Use leftovers tossed into hot pasta or rice, or instead of a sauce on fish or poultry.

Bagel Chips

*You will love these and want to keep them on hand for nibbling.
I discovered them years before they were packaged commercially,
when I had a glut of bagels. These are much healthier than the
commercial variety.*

Yield: About 18 dozen

2 cups extra virgin olive oil, grapeseed
   oil, or peanut oil
6 to 8 cloves garlic, to taste
   Minced dill, fresh or dried, to taste

Salt, to taste
1 dozen bagels, cut into thin
   vertical slices

1. Preheat oven to 350 degrees.
2. Combine all the ingredients, except the bagels, in a food processor fitted
   with the metal blade or in a blender, and process until smooth. Taste and
   adjust the seasonings.
3. Place the bagel slices on an ungreased cookie sheet and brush with the
   flavored oil.
4. Bake until crisp, about 15 minutes. Watch carefully to prevent burning.

FAST: Can prepare up to 1 week in advance and store in airtight jars or plastic
bags, or freeze for up to 6 months. It just takes 15–20 minutes to thaw.

FLASHY: Serve at room temperature or warm in a napkin-lined basket or on a
platter.

FABULOUS: Seasoned with any herb, depending on what the chips are to be
served with. For a fat-free version, simply slice and bake. Keep the seasoned
oil on hand in the refrigerator to use as a sauté oil.

Prosciutto & Vegetables

A variation of the classic prosciutto with melon. There are no amounts; just have fun and create!

Thinly sliced prosciutto*
Avocado slices squirted with fresh
 lemon juice to prevent discoloration
Asparagus, blanched* until barely
 tender, 3–5 minutes
Raw zucchini spears

Baby corn, blanched until barely tender,
 3–5 minutes, or canned and drained
Cucumber spears
Jicama spears
Tiny red potatoes, blanched until barely
 tender, 5–8 minutes

1. Wrap a slice of prosciutto around each vegetable of your choice, and voila!

FAST: Can prepare up to 1 day in advance and refrigerate.

FLASHY: Serve chilled or at room temperature on a platter. Garnish with a nontoxic flower in the center of the platter. A camellia is perfect.

FABULOUS: With Westphalian ham, smoked salmon, and/or pastrami substituted for the prosciutto.

*Refer to Terms & Techniques.

Chicken & Leek Ragout Dinner

*T*his is a hearty, rustic menu full of deep, rich flavors. It exemplifies the true spirit of "Fast & Fabulous" in that the ragout must be prepared at least a day in advance. Besides improving the flavors, the excess fat rises to the top when refrigerated and can easily be lifted off and discarded.

The ragout, which is just French for "stew," is served with your choice of side dishes or possibly a selection of them. What makes this ragout special is the fact that the chicken is on the bone. For most of us, this is a rare experience. The difference between this and a dry chicken breast will amaze you. The salad can either be tossed or beautifully composed. You might want to serve it along with the ragout as it is a wonderful complement in terms of the flavors and textures. A Cranberry Champagne Sorbet and Lemon Sesame Shortbread conclude the menu.

The table for this party should reflect a rustic country feel. I used grape-leaf-patterned table runners instead of placemats. Tall iron candlesticks were placed down the center of the table, along with several loaves of country breads and a selection of all sorts of winter squashes.

Menu

Warm Pesto & Roasted Red Pepper Crostini

Mushroom, Endive & Pear Salad

Chicken & Leek Ragout

Assorted Country Breads and Butter

Orzo, Rice, Pasta, Polenta, and/or White Beans

Cranberry Champagne Sorbet and Lemon Sesame Shortbread

Faster & Flashier Menu

Brie with Pesto
(top Brie with prepared pesto and serve with sliced baguette)

Tossed Salad with Pears

Chicken & Leek Ragout

Orzo

Sherbert or Sorbet (purchased)

Shortbread (purchased)

Sauvignon Blanc or Sparkling Wine and Cabernet Sauvignon or Merlot
Sparkling Wine and Coffee

✄ TIMETABLE ✄

Up to 2 weeks in advance	Warm Pesto & Roasted Red Pepper Crostini (flash frozen)
Up to 7 days in advance	Tarragon Vinaigrette
Up to 5 days in advance	Lemon Sesame Shortbread
Up to 3 days in advance	Chicken & Leek Ragout
Up to 2 days in advance	Cranberry Champagne Sorbet. Set the table.
Up to 1 day in advance	Mushroom Endive & Pear Salad. Pasta or rice for the ragout. Chill the wines.
Party day!	Heat the crostini, ragout, bread, and pasta or rice.

Warm Pesto & Roasted Red Pepper Crostini

Mediterranean nirvana!

Yield: About 35 crostini

½ baguette, sliced thinly on the
  diagonal
½ cup pesto,* homemade or purchased
  (recipe follows)

½ pound Brie, cut up
4 red peppers, halved, seeded, roasted,
  skinned, and cut into small pieces

1. Place the baguette slices on a cookie sheet and toast in a 350 degree oven for about 15 minutes or until crisp.
2. Combine the Brie and pesto in a food processor fitted with the metal blade until smooth.
3. Spread each crostini (crisped baguette slices) with the pesto-Brie mixture and top with some pieces of the roasted red peppers.
4. Bake in a 350 degree oven for 7–10 minutes, until hot.

FAST: Can prepare the crostini up to 2 weeks in advance and store at room temperature in an air-tight container or plastic bags, or freeze for up to 6 months. Can assemble up to 4 hours in advance at room temperature, or flash freeze for up to 3 months. Do not thaw before heating.

FLASHY: Serve hot on a platter and garnish with a raw red bell pepper, basil leaves, and/or any nontoxic flower or leaves in the center of the platter.

FABULOUS: With Muenster or teleme cheese instead of Brie. Topped with toasted walnuts or pine nuts.

*Refer to Terms & Techniques.

Basil Pesto

Make extra, and store it in the freezer so you can enjoy it all year long.   **Yield: About 3 cups**

2 cups packed fresh basil leaves
⅓ cup packed, minced fresh parsley
2 to 4 cloves garlic
½ cup grated Romano, or to taste

½ cup extra virgin olive oil, or to taste
½ cup walnuts, toasted, or to taste
Salt and ground white pepper, to taste

1. Combine the first 5 ingredients in a food processor fitted with the metal blade or in a blender, and process until smooth.
2. Process in the walnuts, using quick on-and-off motions, so as not to destroy the texture.
3. Taste and adjust the seasonings.

FAST: Can prepare up to 4 days in advance and refrigerate, or freeze for up to 6 months.

Mushroom, Endive & Pear Salad with Tarragon Vinaigrette   **Yield: 8 servings**

2 to 4 Belgium endive, divided into leaves
2 to 3 pears, thinly sliced and squirted with lemon juice to prevent discoloring
¼ cup minced green onions

¼ to ½ cup walnuts, chopped and toasted
Tarragon Vinaigrette (recipe follows)
1 pound cultivated mushrooms, thinly sliced

1. Toss all the ingredients together, except for the endive, with the desired amount of Tarragon Vinaigrette. Taste and adjust the seasonings.

FAST: Can prepare up to 24 hours ahead and refrigerate.

FLASHY: On salad plates, arrange several endive leaves with pear-mushroom mixture. Top wth walnuts and enjoy.

FABULOUS: On a bed of spinach or baby greens instead of endive. With shrimp or crab.

Tarragon Vinaigrette

This is one of my favorite dressings to serve with a large, rich meal.
It is very digestive and refreshing.

Yield: About 2½ cups

⅔ cup tarragon wine vinegar
2 cups extra virgin olive oil
2 to 4 cloves garlic

Salt, freshly ground white or black
  pepper, and fresh lime juice to taste

1. Combine all ingredients in food processor fitted with the metal blade or in blender.
2. Taste and adjust the seasonings.

FAST: Can prepare up to 7 days in advance and refrigerate.

FABULOUS: On any salad, or as a sauce or marinade for poultry, fish/seafood, or vegetables. With Dijon mustard added. To reduce the fat, replace half of the oil with low-fat or fat-free sour cream.

Chicken & Leek Ragout

This is an uptown stew!

Yield: 8+ servings

½ pound pancetta, cut into small
  chunks
½ pound shallots, peeled and halved or
  quartered
4 tablespoons all-purpose flour
  Grated zest of 3 to 6 oranges
6 leeks,* the white and tender green
  parts, sliced thinly
3 to 4 chickens, cut into serving pieces
30 to 60 cloves garlic, whole
1 cup calamata olives, pitted
2 pounds peeled banana squash, cut
  into small chunks

10 cups chicken broth, homemade or
  canned
2 cups Merlot wine, or more
3 bay leaves
¼ cup fresh thyme or marjoram leaves,
  chopped
½ cup fresh Italian parsley, minced
4 to 6 dried pasilla chiles, rehydrated,
  stemmed, seeded, and chopped
¼ cup fresh rosemary leaves, chopped,
  or more
  Salt and white pepper, to taste

*Refer to Terms & Techniques.

1. Place the pancetta in a large, heavy skillet or baking dish along with the shallots, garlic, and leeks, and roast in a 350 degree oven until the pancetta is nicely browned.
2. Meanwhile, generously sprinkle them with salt and pepper and place them on another baking sheet. Bake the chicken pieces in a 375–400 degree oven until golden.
3. Transfer the pancetta mixture to a large saucepan or stockpot and stir in the flour. Cook, stirring, for about 3 minutes over medium heat.
4. Stir in the broth and wine and increase the heat to medium-high.
5. Add all the remaining ingredients.
6. Remove the browned chicken from the oven and place in the saucepan.
7. Bring it to a boil, then reduce the heat to low, and simmer for about 1 hour, covered. Skim off as much fat while cooking as possible. This dish is best if prepared at least 1 day in advance and refrigerated. Then all the excess fat congeals on the top and can easily be removed. Reheat before serving. Taste and adjust the seasonings.

FAST: Can fully prepare up to 3 days in advance and refrigerate, or freeze for up to 6 months.

FLASHY: Serve over wedges of baked or soft polenta, on pasta, wild rice, white beans, and such.

FABULOUS: With duck instead of chicken, or with one duck combined with chicken. With 2 pounds of any variety of mushrooms sautéed in butter or duck fat and added to the stew at Step 5.

Cranberry Champagne Sorbet

*A delightfully refreshing and fat-free sorbet that can be used as a
palate cleanser or dessert.*

Yield: 8+ servings

3 cups frozen cranberries
4 cups champagne or white wine
 Fresh lemon juice, to taste

1 to 1¼ cups sugar
2 large egg whites or ½ cup heavy
 cream, beaten until stiff peaks form

1. Rinse cranberries in a colander.
2. Combine cranberries with champagne or white wine, lemon juice, and sugar in a nonreactive saucepan. Bring this to a boil, then reduce the heat, and simmer for about 12 minutes, until berries are tender.
3. Transfer this mixture to the food processor fitted with the metal blade and puree. Then place in a plastic bowl and freeze until solid.
4. Reprocess in the food processor and fold in the egg whites or whipped cream. Return to the freezer for at least 2 hours.

FAST: Can prepare up to 1 month in advance and store in the freezer.

FLASHY: Serve in stemmed goblets and garnish with a mint leaf and/or johnny jump-ups. To gild the lily, drizzle chocolate sauce over the top. My Brandied Chocolate Sauce (page 75) is perfect for this! Serve with Lemon Sesame Shortbread.

FABULOUS: Prepared with almost any berry or fruit, fresh or frozen.

Lemon Sesame Shortbread

Shortbread is the ultimate buttery cookie and literally takes only a few minutes to prepare. It's almost too good to be true.

Yield: About 12 2-inch wedges

½ pound (2 sticks) unsalted butter, cut up
2 teaspoons vanilla extract
½ to 1 cup sugar, plus 2 tablespoons, depending on desired sweetness

2 cups all-purpose flour
½ cups sesame seeds, toasted*
Finely grated zest of 2 to 4 lemons, depending on desired tartness
Freshly grated nutmeg, to taste

1. Preheat the oven to 325 degrees.
2. Add the butter, vanilla, and sugar, minus the 2 tablespoons, to a food processor fitted with the metal blade, and process until well creamed, or beat together with an electric mixer until well creamed.
3. Process in the flour, sesame seeds, and zest until a ball forms, or beat in using an electric mixer until smooth. Then form dough into a ball.
4. Pat the dough into the bottom of two ungreased 8- or 9-inch square or round tart pans with removable bottoms. Sprinkle with the remaining sugar.
5. Use the tines of a fork to decorate the outer edge of the dough and a knife to score the dough into wedges or squares.
6. Bake until pale golden, about 25 minutes, then cut into wedges or squares along scored lines and cool in the pan. Remove the rim of the pan and use a spatula to remove the cookies.

FAST: Can prepare up to 5 days in advance and store in airtight jars, or freeze in plastic bags for up to 3 months. Thaw at room temperature for several hours.

FABULOUS: With poppy seeds or chopped nuts instead of the sesame seeds.

*See Terms & Techniques.

Osso Bucco Dinner

*H*ere is a menu that is definitely in sync with the current appreciation for country-style cooking and entertaining. Most of us remember when pretense and formality were the norm for parties. How refreshing that this has passed. This homey Italian dinner will serve you well for occasions such as Christmas eve and is great for crowds.

A contemporary, upbeat Italian feel was achieved for the party by covering the table with a black tablecloth with red, green, and/or checkered napkins. A casual mixture of flowers was arranged in colorful Italian cookie and coffee tins. Assorted shapes of pasta, along with heads of garlic, were scattered down the table.

As for the menu, it is simple Italian at its best. Garlic is no stranger and the flavors are far from timid. The hors d'oeuvre, Roasted Garlic & Balsamic Pesto, treats garlic with all the respect that it deserves. It is a marvelous mixture that can be used in countless ways, whether it is tossed into pasta or tops a perfectly grilled steak.

Osso Bucco is a country Italian stew based on veal shanks. It is complemented by the Saffron Barley & Brown Rice Risotto, which serves as a luxurious sponge for the delicious sauce.

For dessert, there is a very quick but delicious cake. It is a simple but sinful Almond Pear Cake. You may want to prepare two so that you can have one in reserve in the freezer.

Menu

Roasted Garlic & Balsamic Pesto with Sliced Baguettes

Escarole & Watercress Salad with Red Wine Vinaigrette

Osso Bucco

Saffron Barley & Brown Rice Risotto

Chard with Sweet Onions

Almond Pear Cake

Faster & Flashier Menu

Escarole & Watercress Salad with Red Wine Vinaigrette

Osso Bucco

Rice

Pears and Cheese

Sauvignon Blanc, Merlot, and Coffee

✁   TIMETABLE   ✁

Up to 3 months in advance and frozen	Almond Pear Cake
Up to 2 weeks in advance and refrigerated	Roasted Garlic Balsamic Pesto
Up to 5 days in advance and refrigerated	Red Wine Vinaigrette
Up to 3 days in advance and refrigerated	Osso Bucco (or freeze for up to 3 months). Saffron Barley & Brown Rice Risotto.
Up to 2 days in advance and refrigerated	Chard with Sweet Onions
Up to 1 day in advance and refrigerated	Set the table. Chill the wine.
Party day!	Up to 6 hours in advance, assemble the salad. Toss before serving.

Roasted Garlic & Balsamic Pesto

This is an extremely versatile, lusty, and earthy garlic spread.   **Yield: 2⅔ cups**

1½ cups roasted garlic cloves (recipe
　　follows)
　½ cup extra virgin olive oil
　⅓ cup balsamic vinegar*
　½ cup walnuts, toasted

Grated zest of 2 oranges
1 bunch Italian parsley
¼ cup chopped calamata olives*
　Salt, white pepper, and fresh lemon
　　juice, to taste

1. Combine all the ingredients in a food processor fitted with the metal blade,
   using several quick on-and-off motions so as not to destroy the texture, or
   in a blender. Taste and adjust the seasonings.

FAST: Can prepare up to 2 weeks in advance and refrigerate, or freeze for up
to 6 months.

FLASHY: Serve in a pottery bowl or crock and garnish with a sprig of fresh
herbs, nontoxic flowers, and/or a sprinkling of walnuts, with thinly sliced
baguettes, Pita Chips (page 112), or Bagel Chips (page 272).

FABULOUS: With almonds instead of walnuts, sour cream instead of olive oil,
and/or with 2 roasted red peppers (peeled and seeded) added. As a seasoning
for pasta, soups, sauces, and dressings. Spread on beef, lamb, pork, fish, or
poultry before grilling or broiling. To reduce the fat, replace all or half of the
olive oil with low-fat or fat-free sour cream.

*Refer to Terms & Techniques.

Escarole & Watercress Salad with Red Wine Vinaigrette

A simple and cleansing salad that will be equally appreciated at a casual lunch or at a more formal dinner.

Yield: 8 servings

1 large head escarole,* torn into bite-
   size pieces
2 to 4 Belgian endive, thinly sliced
1 bunch watercress leaves, stemmed
6 to 8 green onions, thinly sliced

Red Wine Vinaigrette (page 93)
Salt and freshly ground, coarse black
   pepper
Freshly grated Parmesan cheese,
   to taste

1. Place the escarole, endive, watercress, and onions in a large salad bowl and toss.
2. Add the desired amount of dressing, toss well, taste, and season with salt and pepper.

FAST: Can wash and prepare all salad greens up to 1 day in advance and refrigerate.

FLASHY: Serve on chilled salad plates.

FABULOUS: With crumbled bleu cheese, sliced pears (squirted with lemon juice to avoid discoloration), sliced tangerines, sliced fennel bulb, mushrooms, celery root, and/or toasted nuts mixed in.

*Refer to Terms & Techniques.

Osso Bucco

A country Italian veal shank stew.

Yield: 8 servings

8 large and meaty veal shank portions, or more
Flour for dusting the veal
Olive oil
½ pound pancetta, chopped coarsely
2 to 4 medium to large yellow onions, chopped
10 to 20 cloves garlic, minced
1 carrot, chopped
2 stalks celery, chopped
Fresh rosemary, chopped, to taste

3 cups dried porcini or shiitake mushrooms,* rehydrated (strain the soaking liquid to use in the sauce)
2 cups dry red wine
½ cup cream sherry
2 bay leaves
8 to 15 pepperoncini,* stemmed, seeded, and chopped, or more
2 pounds strained tomato puree
1 14½-ounce can peeled, cut tomatoes

1. Preheat the oven to 450–500 degrees. Dredge the veal shanks in flour and place in a baking pan. Season with salt and pepper and roast until nicely browned, about 30–45 minutes.
2. Meanwhile, heat the olive oil in a large saucepan. Add the pancetta and cook over medium heat until golden.
3. Add the onions and garlic and cook until tender and golden in color.
4. Stir in the carrot, celery, garlic, rosemary, and mushrooms. Raise the heat to medium-high and sauté until the vegetables are tender.
5. Stir in the remaining ingredients, along with the strained porcini liquid, and the browned veal. Bring it to a boil, then reduce the heat to medium-low and simmer covered for at least 1 hour or bake in a 350 degree oven until the flavors are pleasing and the veal is tender.

FAST: Can assemble up to 3 days in advance, or freeze for up to 3 months, and finish cooking right before serving.

FLASHY: Sprinkle minced Italian parsley and/or grated lemon zest over the top before serving.

FABULOUS: With lamb shanks instead of veal. With any variety of mushrooms.

FURTHER: Combine the leftover sauce with marinara sauce for pasta.

*Refer to Terms & Techniques.

Saffron Barley & Brown Rice Risotto

A delicious change of pace from plain rice.

Yield: 8 servings

¼ to ½ pound pancetta,* coarsely chopped (optional)
3 tablespoons unsalted butter or olive oil
2 tablespoons olive oil
2 yellow onions, chopped
1 cup barley

1 cup brown rice
1 cup dry white wine
5 cups chicken broth, homemade or canned
½ teaspoon saffron threads*
2 bay leaves
Salt and white pepper, to taste

1. Place the pancetta, butter, and olive oil in a saucepan and cook over medium-high heat until golden, stirring frequently.
2. Add the onions and cook until tender.
3. Stir in the barley, brown rice, and saffron. Continue cooking and stirring until the rice and barley is coated, about 2 minutes.
4. Stir in the wine and 1 cup of chicken broth. Cook over medium heat until the liquid is almost absorbed.
5. Add the remaining ingredients and reduce the heat to low. Cover with a lid and cook for 30 minutes, until just tender. Taste and adjust the seasonings.

FAST: Can prepare up to 3 days in advance and refrigerate. To reheat, place in a 350 degree oven, covered, for about 20 minutes, adding about 1 cup of hot chicken broth to keep it moist.

FLASHY: Garnish with a sprinkling of minced parsley.

FABULOUS: With 2 tablespoons of butter and ½ cup grated Parmesan or Romano cheese stirred in right before serving. With cultivated domestic, shiitake, porcini, or wild mushrooms added at Step 1.

FURTHER: Add chicken broth to the leftovers to create a soup.

*Refer to Terms & Techniques.

Chard with Sweet Onions

Just a fabulous dish!

Yield: 8 servings

4 regular-size bunches of chard* (about 2 pounds)
¼ to ½ cup extra virgin olive oil
2 large sweet onions (red, white, or yellow), coarsely chopped

½ cup chicken broth, homemade or canned
Salt, white pepper, fresh lemon juice, and ground nutmeg, to taste

1. Cut the chard stems into 1-inch pieces and cut up the leaves as desired.
2. Place the olive oil and onions in a sauté pan over medium heat. Cook gently for about 5–10 minutes until the oil is infused with the onion flavor.
3. Meanwhile, bring a large pot of salted water to a boil and blanch the chard very briefly.
4. Strain the excess liquid out of the chard.
5. Transfer the chard to a large, ovenproof casserole, add the onion-oil mixture and chicken broth, and season to taste.
6. Bake in a 350 degree oven for 15–20 minutes or microwave until hot.

FAST: Can prepare through Step 5 up to 2 days in advance and refrigerate. Bring to room temperature before heating it up in a 350 degree oven.

FLASHY: Serve hot or cold.

FABULOUS: With sun-dried tomatoes, cranberries, or cherries added. Seasoned with fresh rosemary or basil and/or with toasted pine nuts or walnuts.

*Refer to Terms & Techniques.

Almond Pear Cake

This recipe was inspired by Narsai David's Almond Cake. I fell
in love with it, and I think you'll understand why when you taste
it. It is unbelievably simple, yet rich and indulgent.

Yield: One 8-inch cake

7 ounces almond paste*
  Grated zest of 2 lemons
½ cup packed light or dark brown sugar
¼ pound (1 stick) unsalted butter, cut
  into 8 pieces
2 tablespoons kirsch*
  Grated nutmeg, to taste
3 large eggs or equivalent egg substitute

¼ teaspoon baking powder
¼ cup cake flour*
1 red bosc pear, cut into 8 slices and
  squirted with lemon juice to
  prevent discoloration
½ cup almonds, toasted (page 13) and
  chopped
  Brandied Chocolate Sauce (page 75)

1. Preheat the oven to 350 degrees. Butter and flour an 8-inch cake pan.
2. Combine the almond paste, zest, sugar, and butter in a food processor fitted with the metal blade, or cream together in a bowl with an electric mixer.
3. Process or beat in the kirsch, nutmeg, eggs, and baking powder.
4. Add the cake flour and process or beat in just until combined; do not over-process.
5. Line the cake pan with the pear slices arranged in a concentric circle.
6. Pour the cake batter on top of the pears.
7. Sprinkle the almonds over the top and bake for 40–50 minutes, or until a tester inserted in the center comes out clean.
8. Let cool, then invert onto a serving platter.

FAST: Can prepare up to 1 day in advance and refrigerate, or freeze for up to 3 months. Thaw in the refrigerator for 1 day or at room temperature for about 4 hours.

FLASHY: To serve, place some brandied chocolate sauce on each dessert plate and top with a slice of the cake. For an extra special touch, top each slice of cake with a dollop of kirsch-flavored whipped cream.

FABULOUS: Beyond a doubt.

*Refer to Terms & Techniques.

Pork Tenderloin with Shiitake Mushrooms & Shallots

*H*ere is a party menu with an uptown, luxurious feel. To reflect this look, I dressed the table in a black cloth with thin stripes in bright colors, and black napkins. A can of gloss black spray paint proved invaluable in preparing the rest of the tablescape. Terra cotta flower pots sprayed black were used as vases for baby's breath and camellias. My favorite prop—dried artichokes—was also sprayed (need I say with what) and scattered down the table. Then I interspersed brass candlesticks with black candles. This created a table that was bold and beautiful.

You will love the ease with which this "dinner with dignity" can be assembled. The Seafood Mousse is a beautiful way to begin the evening, besides which it can be prepared well in advance and pulled out of your freezer. From seafood to salad, this dish is another simple composition full of luxurious flavors and textures. If you haven't used pumpkin seeds before, you are in for a treat. A health food store is your best bet for finding them.

The entrée, Pork Tenderloin, can be likened to that timeless black dress hanging in your closet. It's perfect for almost any special occasion. The Orzo is not only a delicious side dish, it also represents two dishes in one. What I mean is that it combines the starch and vegetables into one dish. For a fabulous grand finale there is an Apple Bread Pudding with a Brandy Sauce. It is a snap to make, and delightfully naughty. All of this is accomplished without any culinary sacrifice.

Menu

Seafood Mousse

Tossed Salad with Pears & Mustard Thyme Vinaigrette

Pork Tenderloin with Shiitake Mushrooms & Shallots
in a Madeira Sauce

Roasted Garlic & Parmesan Orzo with Chard

Apple Bread Pudding with Brandy Sauce

Faster & Flashier Menu

Tossed Salad with Pears & Mustard Thyme Vinaigrette

Pork Tenderloin with Shiitake Mushrooms & Shallots
in a Madeira Sauce

Orzo (with frozen spinach and Parmesan cheese)

Dessert (purchased)

Chardonnay and/or Sparkling Wine

Merlot

Coffee

✄   TIMETABLE   ✄

Up to 5 days in advance	Mustard Thyme Vinaigrette
Up to 3 days in advance	Seafood Mousse. Brandy Sauce.
Up to 2 days in advance	Pork Tenderloin (through Step 8). Roasted Garlic & Parmesan Orzo.
Up to 1 day in advance	Apple Bread Pudding. Chill the wines. Set the table.
Party day!	Prep the salad. Toss the salad. Heat and finish cooking the pork. Heat up the orzo.

Seafood Mousse

An elegant beginning!

**Yield: About 5 cups;
40 or more servings**

½ cup medium-dry or dry sherry
1 cup chicken broth, homemade or
   canned, or bottled clam juice or
   shrimp stock
2 envelopes unflavored gelatin
1 cup sour cream or low-fat or fat-
   free sour cream
¼ to ½ cup chèvre cheese*
1½ pounds cooked shrimp, peeled and
   deveined, or crabmeat, picked over
   for cartilage

1 cup mayonnaise, homemade or
   purchased, or low-fat or fat-free
   sour cream or plain yogurt
1 teaspoon prepared horseradish, or
   to taste
2 tablespoons capers,* drained and
   rinsed, or to taste
3 tablespoons shallots,* minced
   Salt, ground white pepper, fresh
   lemon juice, and dried tarragon,
   to taste

1. Oil a 6-cup mold or several smaller ones.
2. Combine the sherry, broth, and gelatin in a saucepan and heat until the gelatin dissolves.
3. Stir the sour cream into the gelatin mixture.
4. Combine the seafood, mayonnaise, horseradish, capers, shallots, seasonings, and dissolved gelatin in the food processor and process until smooth. Taste and adjust the seasonings.
5. Pour the mousse into the prepared molds. Refrigerate until firm, about 4 hours. For faster results, chill in the freezer. Invert onto a platter and remove the plastic wrap.

FAST: Prepare up to 3 days in advance and refrigerate, or freeze for up to 3 months.

FLASHY: Serve with Bagel Chips (page 372), Pita Chips (page 112), thinly sliced baguettes, squares of pumpernickel, and/or crackers. Garnish with capers, minced fresh or dill parsley, watercress leaves, thinly sliced cucumbers, grated lemon zest, and/or any nontoxic flower or leaves.

FABULOUS: With cooked chicken, chicken livers, lobster, or salmon substituted for the shrimp or crab.

*Refer to Terms & Techniques.

Tossed Salad with Pears & Mustard Thyme Vinaigrette

Sweet pears and astringent watercress are a magnificent match.   **Yield: 8 servings**

2 heads butter and/or romaine lettuce
½ to 1 cup pumpkin seeds,* toasted, or
    to taste
2 cups packed watercress leaves

3 pears, cored and sliced
    Mustard Thyme Vinaigrette (recipe
    follows)

1. Combine all the ingredients in a large salad bowl.
2. Add the desired amount of dressing and toss.

FAST: Can prepare through Step 1 up to 8 hours in advance and refrigerate. Toss before serving.

FABULOUS: With any toasted nut or seed instead of the pumpkin seeds. With sliced apples or pieces of tangerine added. With a piece of chèvre or bleu cheese on top of each salad.

*Refer to Terms & Techniques.

Mustard Thyme Vinaigrette
Yield: About 3 cups

2 cups peanut oil
⅔ cup red wine vinegar
2 teaspoons Dijon mustard, or to taste
1 teaspoon dried thyme, or to taste

2 shallots
2 cloves garlic
Salt and freshly ground white pepper, to taste

1. Combine all the ingredients together in a food processor fitted with the metal blade or in a blender.
2. Taste and adjust the seasonings.

FAST: Can prepare up to 14 days in advance and refrigerate.

FABULOUS: With any kind of oil, vinegar, and/or herb. As a marinade or sauce for poultry, seafood, lamb, or pork. To reduce the fat, replace half of the olive oil with low-fat or fat-free sour cream.

Pork Tenderloin with Shiitake Mushrooms & Shallots in Madeira Sauce

Yes, this dish contains cream, but 1 cup divided into 8 servings is not a death sentence.

Yield: 8 servings

4 to 8 cloves garlic, minced
½ cup extra virgin olive oil
½ cup Italian parsley, minced
Fresh or dried thyme and/or rosemary, minced, to taste
4 to 6 pounds pork tenderloin cut into ¾- to 1-inch-thick slices
3 tablespoons unsalted butter
1 to 2 cups shallots, peeled

2 to 3 ounces shiitake mushrooms, rehydrated, stemmed, and cut into thin strips (reserve soaking liquid)
2 cups chicken or beef broth, homemade or canned
½ cup Madeira wine
1 cup heavy cream (optional)
Salt and white pepper, to taste
Freshly ground black pepper, to taste

1. Combine the garlic, olive oil, ¼ cup parsley, and herbs in a food processor fitted with the metal blade.
2. Place the pork in a ceramic or glass pan with the above mixture and some black pepper. Cover with plastic wrap and marinate for up to 48 hours, refrigerated.
3. Melt 3 tablespoons of butter in a skillet and gently sauté the shallots and mushrooms until they are golden and tender.
4. Meanwhile, heat up a heavy cast iron skillet. Blot the pork dry, using paper towels. Brown the pork on both sides (about 6 minutes) until just pink on the inside. Remove to a warm platter and tent with foil. Do this in small batches or it will not brown properly.
5. Strain the reserved soaking liquid and add it to the skillet that the pork was cooked in. Reduce it to about ½ cup.
6. Add the broth and wine to the shallots, along with the herbs. Cook until it reduces by half.
7. Stir the reduced mushroom liquid into the skillet. Cook over high heat until the flavors are pleasing, about 5 minutes.
8. Stir the heavy cream (if you are using it) and parsley into the skillet and cook until it reduces to the desired thickness. Taste and adjust the seasonings. To speed up the thickening process, you can use 1 tablespoon of cornstarch dissolved in 2 tablespoons of Madeira.
9. Return the pork and any released juices to the skillet and cook over low heat for about 3 minutes. Transfer to a warm platter. Do not overcook it, or it will be very dry.

FAST: Can prepare through Step 8 up to 2 days in advance and refrigerate. Bring the pork and sauce to room temperature. Heat the sauce and add the pork to it to reheat.

FLASHY: Garnish with sprigs of fresh herbs, parsley, and/or watercress.

FABULOUS: Substitute veal, beef, or even chicken breasts for the pork. Add Dijon mustard and capers to the sauce. Instead of reducing the sauce for so long, thicken it with some cornstarch dissolved in water.

Roasted Garlic & Parmesan Orzo with Chard

A unique and earthy pasta dish.

Yield: 8 to 10 servings

2 bunches chard,* cut coarsely
2 pounds cooked orzo
½ cup roasted garlic, or more
½ cup freshly grated Parmesan cheese,
   or to taste

Salt, white pepper, and freshly grated
   nutmeg, to taste
½ cup extra virgin olive oil

1. Bring a large pot of water to a boil over high heat. Add the chard and cook until wilted, about 3 minutes.
2. Transfer the chard to a colander placed in the sink under cold running water until the chard is cool. Squeeze out all the excess moisture from the chard by hand or by placing it in a clean kitchen towel and squeezing. Chop it finely.
3. Return the chard to the pot or an ovenproof pan. Mix in all the remaining ingredients. Taste and adjust the seasonings.
4. Reheat on top of the stove for about 10 minutes, stirring frequently over medium heat, or in a 350 degree oven, covered, for about 20 minutes.

FAST: Can prepare through Step 4 up to 2 days in advance and refrigerate, or freeze for up to 3 months.

FABULOUS: With ¼ cup minced parsley and/or 1 pound frozen, thawed, and squeezed spinach.

FURTHER: Use leftovers in sauces, salads, and/or fillings.

*Refer to Terms & Techniques.

Apple Bread Pudding with Brandy Sauce

A satisfying, homey dessert that is making a comeback after being forgotten for a long time.

Yield: 8+ servings

3 large eggs or egg substitute
½ cup packed light or dark brown
    sugar, plus extra
1 cup sour cream or low-fat or fat-free
    sour cream
2 cups milk or buttermilk or nonfat
    milk or buttermilk
¼ cup brandy
    Ground cinnamon and freshly grated
    nutmeg, to taste
2 teaspoons vanilla extract

3 to 4 cups crustless sourdough or egg
    bread cubes
2 large Pippin or Granny Smith apples,
    cored, peeled, thinly sliced, and
    squirted with lemon juice
½ cup chopped dried apricots
½ cup walnuts, toasted and chopped
4 tablespoons unsalted butter, cut into
    small pieces
    Brandy Sauce (recipe follows)

1. Preheat the oven to 350 degrees.
2. Combine the eggs, sugar, sour cream, milk, brandy, cinnamon, nutmeg, and vanilla in a large bowl.
3. Add the bread cubes, apples, apricots, and walnuts. Let sit for about 15 minutes.
4. Butter a 6- or 8-cup casserole, baking dish, or soufflé dish. You can also use individual soufflé or custard cups or large muffin tins.
5. Pour the mixture into the buttered casserole, and top with the cut-up butter and extra brown sugar if desired.
6. Place the pudding in a larger pan, with hot water reaching halfway up the sides of the casserole. Bake until a tester inserted into the middle comes out clean, about 1 hour.

FAST: Can assemble up to 1 day in advance and refrigerate. Bring to room temperature and bake before serving, or bake for half the time up to 1 day in advance and refrigerate. Bring to room temperature and finish baking.

FLASHY: Serve Brandy Sauce over the pudding and an optional scoop of vanilla ice cream or a dollop of whipped cream.

FABULOUS: With almonds or pecans instead of walnuts, dates instead of dried apricots, or pears instead of apples.

Brandy Sauce

A delicious splurge!

Yield: About 3 cups

1 cup sugar
½ pound (2 sticks) unsalted butter,
    cut up
½ to ¾ cup brandy

2 large eggs or egg substitute
    Freshly grated nutmeg and ground
    cinnamon, to taste

1. Dissolve the sugar in a large, heavy saucepan over medium-low heat. Do not stir; rather, hold the pan by the handle and swirl throughout the process. Raise the heat to medium and cook until the sugar turns golden brown, about 3–5 minutes.
2. Remove the pan from the heat and stir in the butter, then the brandy.
3. Meanwhile, in a food processor fitted with a metal blade process the eggs until light and lemon-colored, or beat with a mixer in a large bowl.
4. Slowly add the sugar mixture through the feed tube while the machine is running, or stir into the bowl.
5. Return the mixture to the pan and cook, stirring, for several minutes over low heat. Season with the nutmeg and cinnamon.

FAST: Can prepare up to 3 days in advance and refrigerate, or freeze for up to 6 months. Thaw in the refrigerator for 2 days or at room temperature for about 4–8 hours. Reheat over barely simmering water in a double boiler, stirring until warm.

FLASHY: Over anything from poundcake to bananas.

FABULOUS: With Scotch, bourbon, or any liqueur instead of the brandy.

Bouillabaisse Dinner

"Bouillabaisse." Just saying the word conjures up excitement and anticipation. This party is close to a religious experience for seafood lovers. My table was dressed in a goldish yellow cotton bedspread (from an import store), and I used kitchen towels in a green-and-gold plaid for napkins. Fish-netting was used as a table runner with shells, baby's breath, and purple statice interspersed. Terra cotta saucers filled with sand held votive candles.

The party starts off with a delicious pâté-like mixture. Potted Pork Degan is simple and versatile. From there we move on to a tossed salad. The fennel in it provides a refreshing quality as well as a nice crunch. Toasted pecans add another dimension, as does the sensational dressing! Next, the main event. Bouillabaisse is a simple Mediterranean fish stew. Preparation is a no-brainer, and the results are exquisite. I like serving it with Grilled Polenta and/or orzo to sap up all those precious juices. It is perfectly kosher to just serve lots of good French bread for sopping. This is definitely a party that requires heavy sopping. Even the dessert, Orange Almond Biscotti, is designed for more sopping, because the biscotti are dunked in coffee or wine.

The Bleu Cheese with Madeira serves as an excellent excuse to enjoy one more glass of red wine.

Menu

Potted Pork Degan

Tossed Greens with Fennel

Bouillabaisse

Grilled Polenta and/or Orzo (optional)

French Bread

Pears, Grapes & Walnuts with Bleu Cheese & Madeira Spread

Orange Almond Biscotti

Faster & Flashier Menu

Pâté with Crackers (purchased)

Tossed Greens with Fennel

Bouillabaisse

French bread

Pears & Walnuts with Biscotti (purchased) & Gorgonzola

Sparkling Wine and/or Sauvignon Blanc

Zinfandel, Pinot Noir, or Merlot

✂ TIMETABLE ✂

Up to 3 months in advance	Orange Almond Biscotti
Up to 5 days in advance	Fennel Parmesan Vinaigrette. Cheese & Madeira Spread.
Up to 3 days in advance	Bouillabaisse through Step 3. Potted Pork Degan.
Up to 2 days in advance	Polenta through Step 4 (optional)
Up to 1 day in advance	Assemble the salad. Assemble the cheese and fruit platter. Set the table. Chill the wines.
Party day!	Grill the polenta and/or boil orzo (optional). Finish the bouillabaisse. Toss the salad.

Potted Pork Degan

This pâté-like spread is rustic in feeling, great for picnics, holiday gatherings, and gifts.

Yield: About 6 cups; 48 or more servings

3 pounds boneless pork roast
¼ cup minced fresh Italian parsley
1 medium-size onion, coarsely chopped
1 medium-size carrot, coarsely chopped
2 cups dry white wine
8 cups chicken broth, or more, homemade or canned

Salt, black peppercorns, garlic cloves, bay leaves, and fresh or dried thyme and rosemary, to taste
1 pound unsalted or half-fat butter or low-fat or fat-free cream cheese, at room temperature
White pepper, Dijon mustard, and fresh rosemary, to taste
Port or Madeira wine

1. Place the first 7 ingredients in a large pot and cover with water. Bring to a boil and let boil for about 5 minutes.
2. Reduce the heat to low and simmer until the pork is tender, about 2 hours.
3. Cool to room temperature and chill, covered, overnight. Skim off the fat and drain the meat, reserving the liquid. Discard the bay leaves. Shred the meat by hand or in a food processor fitted with the metal blade.
4. In the meantime, reduce the defatted cooking liquid until the flavors are rich or until the liquid is cooked down to about ¼ of what it was.
5. Combine the shreds with the butter and some of the reduced cooking liquid and wine in a food processor fitted with the metal blade or in a mixing bowl. Season with salt, Dijon mustard, white pepper, fresh rosemary, and Port or Madeira wine, to taste.
6. Pack the mixture into crocks, jars, or small serving containers.

FAST: Can prepare up to 3 days in advance and refrigerate, or freeze for up to 4 months.

FLASHY: Serve at room temperature with Dijon mustard, cornichons, and baguette slices.

FABULOUS: With low-fat cream cheese or just using the cooking liquid instead of butter. Seasoned with pickled onions; lemon or orange zest; caraway seeds; minced fresh dill; chopped, roasted red or green peppers; chopped green chiles; capers; fresh thyme; green peppercorns; or your favorite seasoning.

Tossed Greens with Fennel

Simply marvelous!   **Yield: 8 servings**

1 head romaine lettuce
1 pound baby greens
½ to 1 cup pecan halves, toasted
    (page 13)

1 medium-size bulb of fennel,*
    trimmed and thinly sliced
Fennel Parmesan Vinaigrette (recipe
    follows)

1. Combine all the ingredients in a large salad bowl and toss with the desired amount of dressing.

FAST: Can prep and mix together the greens and pecans up to 1 day in advance and refrigerate. Dress before serving.

FABULOUS: With watercress leaves, cooked shrimp, crab and/or sliced avocado tossed in. With walnuts, almonds, pine nuts, or pumpkin seeds instead of the pecans. With a medium-size shredded celery root tossed in.

Fennel Parmesan Vinaigrette

A very distinctive dressing.   **Yield: About 2⅔ cups**

2 to 4 tablespoons fennel seeds
4½ teaspoons anchovy paste
4 to 6 cloves garlic
2 cups extra virgin olive oil

⅔ cup balsamic vinegar
2 teaspoons Szechuan peppercorns*
½ cup freshly grated Parmesan cheese

1. Combine all the ingredients in a food processor fitted with the metal blade or in a blender.
2. Taste and adjust the seasonings.

FAST: Can prepare up to 5 days in advance and refrigerate.

FABULOUS: With sherry wine vinegar instead of balsamic. With minced fresh rosemary or cilantro instead of fennel seeds. To reduce the fat, replace half of the olive oil with low-fat or fat-free sour cream.

*Refer to Terms & Techniques.

Bouillabaisse

Don't let this long list of ingredients scare you off. This delicious seafood stew is as easy to make as spaghetti. If you have access to seafood shells, make a broth instead of using clam sauce.

Yield: 8+ servings

4 tablespoons olive oil
3 pounds leeks,* white and tender green parts, thinly sliced
4 to 6 stalks celery, including the leaves, thinly sliced
1½ pounds cultivated mushrooms, quartered
10 cloves of garlic, minced, or more
2 1-pound cans strained tomatoes
12 cups bottled clam juice or homemade fish stock, or more

3 cups dry vermouth
Freshly ground, coarse black pepper, to taste
2 to 4 bay leaves
3 tablespoons fennel seeds
1 teaspoon saffron threads, or to taste
1 bunch Italian parsley, minced
2 pounds sea bass, cut into 1-inch pieces
2 pounds prawns, shelled and deveined
3 pounds mussels, scrubbed
2 pounds clams, scrubbed

1. Heat up the olive oil in a large pot and sauté the leeks and celery over medium heat until tender.
2. Add the cultivated mushrooms and garlic and continue cooking over medium heat for about 5 minutes, stirring from time to time.
3. Add the strained tomatoes, clam juice or fish stock, water, wine, saffron threads, and Italian parsley. Bring this to a boil over high heat. Reduce the heat to medium and simmer covered for 30–60 minutes until the flavors develop. Add more wine or broth according to your taste.
4. Stir in the seafood and cook for about 5 minutes until the clam and mussel shells open up and the fish is cooked.

FAST: Can prepare through Step 3 up to 3 days in advance and refrigerate, or freeze for up to 6 months. Finish right before serving.

FLASHY: Serve in a large soup terrine or in large individual soup bowls. Serve with freshly grated Parmesan cheese and a slice of polenta in the bowl.

FABULOUS: With 1 cup fresh, minced basil and fresh or dried thyme, to taste. With any variety of shellfish and/or any firm, textured fish.

*Refer to Terms & Techniques.

Grilled Polenta

Italian soul food.

Yield: 8 servings

8 cups chicken broth, homemade or
   canned
1 cup dry white wine
2 cloves garlic, or more, minced
¼ cup green onions, or more, minced

¼ cup Italian parsley, or more, minced
   Fresh rosemary sprigs or dried
   rosemary, to taste
3 cups instant polenta*
¼ cup olive oil

1. Add all ingredients, except the olive oil, to a large pot, and bring to a boil.
2. Slowly stir the polenta into boiling liquid. Lower heat and cook, stirring frequently, until polenta comes away cleanly from sides of the pan when stirred, about 30–50 minutes.
3. Transfer the polenta onto an oiled cookie sheet. Cool to room temperature, then chill in the refrigerator.
4. When firm, cut polenta into desired-size squares, circles, or triangles.
5. Oil the barbecue grill or a cookie sheet and brush squares of polenta with oil. Grill until hot, or bake in the oven.

FAST: Can prepare through Step 4 up to 3 days in advance and refrigerate.

FLASHY: Serve the polenta in the bottom of each bowl of bouillabaisse, or pass it around after all the seafood has been eaten. The remaining sauce can be sopped up with the polenta.

FABULOUS: With fresh, minced basil rather than rosemary. Can also use regular polenta.

*Refer to Terms & Techniques.

Pears, Grapes & Walnuts with Bleu Cheese & Madeira Spread

This is a refreshing and satisfying end or prelude to any meal. As you can see, no amounts are given—it's up to you.

Assorted clusters of grapes (green, purple, black)
Walnut halves, toasted
Bleu Cheese & Madeira Spread (recipe follows)

Water crackers or a sliced baguette
Grape leaves, fresh mint sprigs, and/or marigolds for garnishing

Present this on a large wooden or ceramic platter. Place cheese spread in the middle on several grape leaves, surrounded with crackers. Place walnut halves attractively, then the grapes. Remember, grapes should be chilled. Make sure to put several small spreading knives on the platter for the cheese.

Bleu Cheese & Madeira Spread

A delicious hors d'oeuvre or dessert!   **Yield: About 1½ cups**

½ pound (8 ounces) bleu cheese or
    Gorgonzola at room temperature
4 ounces unsalted or half-fat butter at
    room temperature

3 tablespoons Madeira wine
    Salt and white pepper, to taste
1 teaspoon green peppercorns, or more

1. Cream all ingredients, except the peppercorns, in a food processor fitted with the metal blade.
2. Add the peppercorns with several quick on-and-off motions, using care not to destroy the texture.
3. Pack the cheese mixture into an oiled, plastic-wrap-lined mold. Refrigerate until firm, about 4 hours.

FAST: Can prepare up to 5 days in advance and refrigerate, or freeze for up to 3 months.

FLASHY: To serve, invert mold onto platter. Garnish with grapes and/or any sliced fruit. Serve with crackers, French bread, and/or apple slices.

FABULOUS: Add nuts and/or herbs.

Orange Almond Biscotti

One of my favorites!

Yield: About 7 dozen

4½ cups all-purpose flour
¾ to 1 cup granulated flour
½ to 1 teaspoon nutmeg
½ teaspoon salt
1 teaspoon baking soda

4 extra-large eggs or 1 cup egg
   substitute
1 teaspoon vanilla extract
¼ to ½ cup orange-flavored liqueur
1½ cup almonds, toasted
Grated zest of two oranges

1. Preheat oven to 375 degrees.
2. Combine 4 cups of the flour with the sugar, nutmeg, salt, and baking soda in a food processor fitted with the metal blade.
3. Process in the butter, eggs, vanilla, and liqueur until a soft dough is formed. Add some water or more liqueur if the dough is too crumbly to hold together.
4. Add almonds and orange zest. Process with several on-and-off motions so as not to destroy the texture.
5. Dust the work surface with the remaining flour and lightly flour your hands. Divide the dough into thirds or fourths and form each into log shapes.
6. Place the logs on an oiled cookie sheet and bake until a tester inserted in the middle comes out clean, about 35–45 minutes.
7. Remove logs from the oven and cool slightly. Cut the logs into ½-inch slices. You can cut each slice in half lengthwise for long narrow slices.
8. Return the slices to the cookie sheet, reduce the temperature to 300 degrees and bake until crisp, about 15–25 minutes more. Turn the oven off and leave the cookies in the oven with the door ajar for another 15 minutes.

FAST: Can prepare up to 14 days in advance. Store in airtight jars or plastic bags, or freeze for up to 6 months. Thaw at room temperature for a few minutes.

FABULOUS: With walnuts, pecans, or pine nuts instead of almonds. With half of each cookie dipped in chocolate.

Index